THE JOHN WAYNE SCRAPBOOK

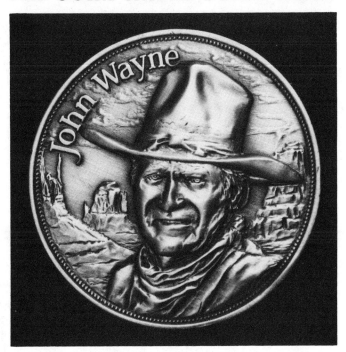

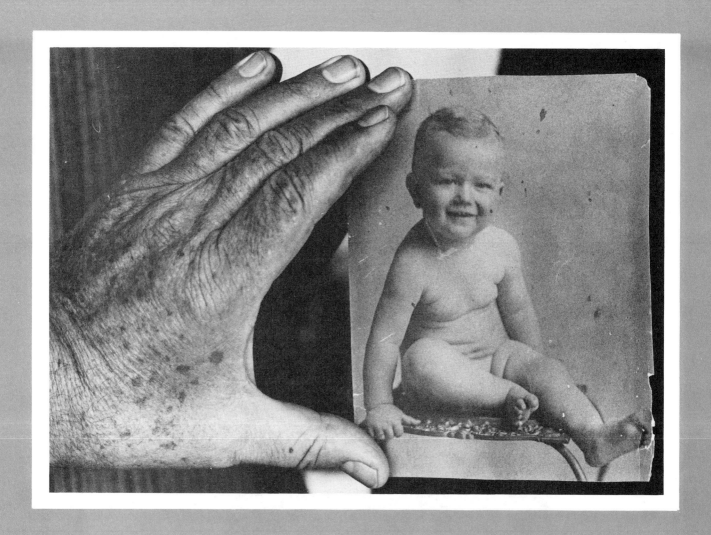

The JOHN WAYNE Scrapbook

REVISED AND UPDATED

by Lee Pfeiffer

CITADEL PRESS
KENSINGTON PUBLISHING CORP.
www.kensingtonbooks.com

CITADEL PRESS books are published by

Kensington Publishing Corp.
850 Third Avenue
New York, NY 10022

All Kensington titles, imprints, and distributed lines are available at special quantity discounts for bulk purchases for sales promotions, premiums, fund raising, educational, or institutional use. Special book excerpts or customized printings can also be created to fit specific needs. For details, write or phone the office of the Kensington special sales manager: Kensington Publishing Corp., 850 Third Avenue, New York, NY 10022, attn: Special Sales Department, phone 1-800-221-2647.

Design by Paul Chevannes

First Kensington printing: August 2001

10 9 8 7 6 5 4 3 2 1

Printed in the United States of America

Library of Congress Control Number: 2001092619

ISBN 0-8065-2230-5

FOR MY FATHER HAROLD AND
MY FATHER-IN-LAW TONY PLAZA

"'lest we forget"
(from *She Wore a Yellow Ribbon*, 1949)

ACKNOWLEDGMENTS

There are many people who helped make this book possible. Top of the list is my old friend Walter Brinkman, whose superb photographic abilities are responsible for most of the reproductions of rare collectibles found herein. In addition to being a skilled photographer, Walt is the only other living person I know who will admit to classifying "The Ghost and Mr. Chicken" as a comic masterpiece. Others I am indebted to include: Ron Plesniarski, Steve Balash, Bill Chemerka, Dustin Doctor, Duke Trombley, Rusty Pollard, Tim Lilley, Roger Nash (the U.K.'s foremost Wayne buff), Ashley Ward, and Leon Matuszak.

The aforementioned individuals are collectors of Wayne memorabilia, which they graciously shared with me. Thanks also to Mike Boldt for sharing his collectibles and expertise on "The Alamo." The John Wayne Birthplace was also cooperative, and I encourage readers to donate to this non-profit cause. The address is listed in the "Collectibles" chapter. Thanks also to my former secretary Tina Owens who has earned the title of "Miss Photocopy," and Richard Vogt and Howard Hughes (not the same perpetrator of *The Conqueror*) for their technical assistance.

Photo acknowledgements are: Warner Bros., MGM/UA, 20th Century-Fox, Paramount, Universal, CBS, NBC, ABC, Ron Zalkind of Zadoc Marketing, Werner Lehman, Jerry Ohlinger's Movie Memorabilia Store, Film Favorites, Custom Quality Studio, and my good friends Phil and Maryann Lisa and Sylvia Elsabry. Special thanks to Allan Wilson, the editor of this book, for the creative control he has allotted me, and Pilar Wayne for her encouragement. Last, I'd like to thank my wife Janet for finally buying me a decent enough typewriter to get me motivated and my daughter Nicole for reminding me of everything wonderful in the world.

CONTENTS

INTRODUCTION

When I mentioned to a fellow author that I was preparing a book about John Wayne, he cynically replied, "Great! Just what we need—some more 'startling revelations' about the Duke." His criticism was justified. Over the past couple of decades, it appears that everyone and his brother has written a book about "the real John Wayne." Hopefully, this one will be entirely unique in that I state categorically that I never knew or even met John Wayne. I have no desire to "expose" any secrets or dig up any dirt. My goal is simple: honor a man whose films I have enjoyed for most of my life.

This book is designed to be fun. Hopefully, you can open to any page and be entertained. If you are looking for scandal, search elsewhere. If you require a scholarly research work, you will not find it here. This is meant not to enlighten, but to entertain. You may learn nothing in reading these pages, but, hopefully, you will find a great deal of enjoyment in not expanding your horizons while purusing the book.

I would hope that the legions of John Wayne fanatics and collectors are pleased with this effort. I tried to design the book from a fan's point of view. I suppose the book should have been dedicated to every other collector of Wayne memorabilia. You know who you are. Like me, you're probably in possession of anything bearing Wayne's likeness, even if you know there is no practical reason for having such material. Somewhere, we all have tucked away that tacky

blanket upon which is a depiction of the Duke bearing the same artistic merit as those velvet paintings sold in Florida gas stations.

I have been a lifelong fan of Wayne's, and I guess I owe my mother some thanks for not discarding my memorabilia when I was much younger. (See, Mom, I told you collecting this stuff would pay off someday!) Wayne's films were a central part of my childhood as they were with so many other people's. The memories they evoke are bittersweet. On cold winter nights and hot summer days, my father would take my brother Ray and me to see the Duke's latest extravaganza. These were pleasant times, when theatres still served real butter on popcorn, and you could count on a double feature (occasionally two Wayne films for the price of one).

The first John Wayne film I can remember seeing was *The Horse Soldiers* in Union City, New Jersey, in 1959. Even at age three, I recall recognizing the Duke, thereby indicating I must have been exposed to his movies even before that early part of my life. As I grew older, other priorities began to encroach on the blissful innocence of youth. And yet, I never lost my interest in Wayne or his films. Fathers would take their sons to see him onscreen, sometimes accompanied by their moms. This did not occur too often, as mothers seemed to realize that for the men of the house, seeing a Wayne film together was the most basic act of "male bonding." As kids we all felt that as long as our fathers and John Wayne stood tall the world would hold no peril for us.

My father has long since gone, and so has John Wayne. The world we live in is becoming a far more frightening place than perhaps they would have cared to see. And yet, on cold winter nights and hot summer days, I sometimes reflect back on those innocent times when the world—and we—were somehow more carefree, and the only worry I had was getting to the next Wayne movie on time with my dad. The naiveté of youth is permanently lost, but I hope my recollections of those times stay with me forever. Maybe they will. Thanks for the memories, Duke.

Lee Pfeiffer
Piscataway, N.J.
April 1989

10

THE BEST OF JOHN WAYNE

In the following pages, we will take a look at the features which, in my totally subjective opinion, represent the greatest screen work of John Wayne. You may agree or disagree, but hopefully, the chapter will encourage people to review the films in question once more. One of the most common complaints about John Wayne is that he couldn't act. I defy anyone reading this book to propagate that opinion after watching any of the films described here, particularly *The Searchers*, *Red River*, *The Shootist* and *She Wore a Yellow Ribbon*. People are entitled to their opinions, but

I've found that most of Wayne's most short-sighted critics will agree sheepishly that they cannot recall having seen a Wayne film in many years. For so long, Duke was one of the most unfairly maligned actors of his time. Happily, he lived to see his work accepted and praised. To the few remaining critics who maintain there is no difference between John Wayne films or performances, then I advise them to sit in front of their "Masterpiece Theatre" presentations and pretend they are not bored. As for me, I'll take Rooster Cogburn any day of the week.

11

THE BIG TRAIL (1930)

Cast: John Wayne, Marguerite Churchill, El Brendel, Tully Marshall, Tyrone Power, Sr., David Rollins, Ian Keith. *Director:* Raoul Walsh. *Screenplay:* Jack Peabody, Marie Boyle and Florence Postal. *From a Story by* Hal G. Evarts. *Music:* Arthur Kay. *Released by* Fox. *Running Time:* 125 Minutes.

Although *Stagecoach* is widely credited as being the film which delivered John Wayne from the largely indistinguishable "B" Westerns in which

he had starred since his acting debut some ten years previously, it was actually *The Big Trail* which afforded the aspiring young actor his first opportunity for stardom. One-time actor Raoul Walsh had already made a name for himself in Hollywood by the time sound had taken the movie capital by storm. It was not Walsh's acting skills, however, that endeared him to the studio chieftains, but, rather, his late-found abilities as director.

It was Walsh's dream to create a Western epic

WITH MARGUERITE CHURCHILL

that would top the silent classic *The Covered Wagon*, which had been released to great acclaim some years before. He managed to get $3 million allocated from Fox Films to finance the movie—a staggering sum at that time. With production costs so high, however, there was little money left with which to attract major stars. Originally Walsh envisioned either Gary Cooper or Tom Mix in the lead role of a young trailblazer who encounters both romance and danger while tracking two killers who have signed on with a wagon train traveling into Indian territory. When budget and contractual obligations precluded either man from accepting the role, Walsh found himself desperately in need of a star.

There are conflicting tales as to just how Wayne eventually landed the lead role. The generally accepted version had been related by Wayne himself. The Duke recalled some years later that while moving furniture around as a prop man on the Fox lot, he was spotted by one of Walsh's assistants and promised a screen test. When Wayne arrived for the big moment, he was understandably nervous. Although he was not given a copy of the script to read, he was asked to rehearse a scene with actor Ian Keith, who not only had the script memorized, but understood more about Wayne's character than did the Duke himself.

Under the watchful eye of Walsh and the crew, the screen test began. Wayne quickly became frustrated as he found himself unable to answer Keith's consistent questions about the specifics of the wagon train's journey. Wayne let his temper

ARMING HIS FELLOW TRAVELERS FOR THE BIG TRAIL AHEAD

flare and he spontaneously responded with a barrage of unrehearsed inquiries of his own, leaving Keith looking quite the fool. Wayne later recalled that he felt his cockiness would have resulted in his termination. Instead, Walsh was so impressed by his aggressiveness that he not only gave Wayne the lead, but used the screen test sequence in the finished film.

By all counts, *The Big Trail* should have been considered a classic. Its huge budget masked an unremarkable storyline which found Wayne trailing two of his friend's murderers to a wagon train. Wayne signs on presumably to add protection for the riders, when in actuality he seeks brutal justice for the killers. The film evolves into a cat-and-mouse game as both Wayne and his adversaries attempt to do away with each other. Thrown in for good measure is a subplot in which Wayne romances Marguerite Churchill, who is quite slow to respond to his advances.

Despite the huge production values and state-of-the-art technology, *The Big Trail* was destined to become the *Heaven's Gate* of its day. Walsh insisted on using location shooting instead of the usual backlot sets. This resulted in increased production costs, technical problems, and a demoralized cast which had to endure the relentless heat of the Arizona desert. Tempers rose while spirits dropped. Wayne became violently ill with "Montezuma's Revenge" and was unable to work for the first several weeks. Upon his emergence from his sick bed, his first scene required him to feign drinking some "rotgut" whiskey with some fellow actors. Little did he know that actual whiskey was in the bottle. After taking a big gulp, Duke almost passed out, leaving the crew amused at his predictable reaction.

Complicating matters was the fact that the film was being shot in a new process called Fox Grandeur, a 70mm forerunner of CinemaScope. Although technically outstanding, few theatres were willing to invest in 70mm projection equipment at a time when the Depression was ravaging the land. Foreseeing this problem, the studio had the film shot in a 35mm version as well. Additionally, a German language production was being shot simultaneously with different leads! Without question, Raoul Walsh earned his salary for *The Big Trail*, even though it was considerably more than Wayne's pay.

In terms of performances, one is not overwhelmed today if judging the theatrics. However, considering the unrestrained overacting that was synonymous with the silent films which immediately preceded *The Big Trail*, many of the cast could be accused of underplaying their roles. In fact, the only truly "hammy" performance is that of Tyrone Power, Sr., whose one-note characterization of the evil wagon train leader left little room for subtleties.

The rest of the cast comes across admirably, with Churchill, Tully Marshall and El Brendel standouts. (The last portrays an inept immigrant thrown in for comic effect, although Brendel was also doubling as the lead in the German version of the film.) As for Wayne, one can only give him a great deal of credit for overcoming inexperience and the many obstacles which befell *The Big Trail*. He is undeniably impressive, even when one watches the film today. Wayne should also be praised for having the common sense and spunk to fight the studio's original plans for making him a matinee idol. The initial plan, which mandated that Wayne become proficient at riding, roping and knife-throwing, made sense and can be credited for Wayne's naturalness in performing these functions. However, the studio also made him take lessons in dialogue delivery from a British voice teacher who excelled at Shakespeare. One can imagine Duk's uneasiness at being transformed into the John Barrymore of the West, and he refused to continue. The studio backed down, which was fortunate. Had the plan succeeded, it could have changed our entire view of the Old West, and may have eventually made it possible for John Houseman to have landed the role of Rooster Cogburn!

As the premiere date grew nearer, the studio insisted on Wayne touring the nation in a series of public appearances in which he was to prove he was an actual cowboy. This was to be accomplished by dressing him up in a preposterous western outfit, complete with a white ten gallon hat. This act may have played in Peoria, but when Wayne arrived in New York, audiences laughed at his appearance. He again went against

REACTING TO A MOMENT OF CRISIS — WAYNE AND FRIENDS BATTLE THE INDIANS

the studio bosses, and told a press conference that he felt as foolish as he looked, and would stop the publicity tour immediately.

It is doubtful Wayne's appearances—or anything else—could have helped *The Big Trail*. Soon after it opened, it became apparent that despite good if not enthusiastic reviews, audiences were staying away in droves. The film took a loss at the box-office, and Wayne would find himself reverting back to "quickie" bottom grade Westerns for almost another decade until *Stagecoach* would revive his career.

The pity of this is that *The Big Trail* has always been woefully neglected by cinema students. Like it's modern day counterpart, *Heaven's Gate*, it was faulted more for its wastefulness than for its many attributes. Wayne fans should be encouraged to give *The Big Trail* several viewings. There are scenes that are literally breathtaking, made all the more impressive by the knowledge of how

primitive working conditions were at that period in time. Indeed, the river crossings and the lowering of the wagons down sheer embankments are as impressive as any sequence any other spectacle might provide. Likewise, the hardships endured by the settlers on the wagon train are presented in a realistic manner which makes us genuinely feel for the losses of these brave pioneers.

Fortunately, *The Big Trail* was restored with some missing footage several years ago, and given a new "premiere" that included extensive coverage by the press. The film can now be seen on video, although several minutes of indecipherable dialogue have been enhanced by the addition of sub-titles. Several awkward cuts make it apparent that the full footage has yet to be found. Hopefully, in time the entire version of this masterful and wrongfully ignored epic can be seen and appreciated by modern audiences.

STAGECOACH (1939)

Cast: John Wayne, Claire Trevor, Andy Devine, Thomas Mitchell, John Carradine, George Bancroft, Louise Platt, Berton Churchill, Tim Holt, Donald Meek. *Director:* John Ford. *Screenplay:* Dudley Nichols. *From the Story* "Stage to Lordsburg" by Ernest Haycox. *Music:* Richard Hageman, W. Franke Harling, John Leipold, Leo Shuken, Louis Gruenberg, Walter Wanger. *Released by* United Artists. *Running Time:* 97 Minutes.

The year 1939 almost certainly encompassed the most auspicious 365 days in the history of film. Consider just some of the classics released that year: *Gone With the Wind, Wuthering Heights,*

Ninotchka, Goodbye Mr. Chips, Gunga Din, The Wizard of Oz . . . The list goes on. One of the films which always appears prominently on any list of the masterpieces released that during that time frame is John Ford's epic Western *Stagecoach*. This was no ordinary "horse opera." In fact, it was a movie which not only elevated the Western genre, but also helped John Wayne achieve the stardom which had eluded him after the fiasco of *The Big Trail*.

For all its merits, however, *Stagecoach* was very nearly dismissed by every studio John Ford had initially approached. At the time, Hollywood had taken great pride in the progress films had made since the inception of the sound era. The

industry was maturing at a rapid pace, and the exaggerated and overacted melodramas and "B" Westerns which helped establish films as a popular entertainment had now become embarrassments. The Western, in effect, was considered to be yesterday's news.

Ford had seen a short story by Ernest Haycox titled *Stage to Lordsburg*. Immediately smelling box-office gold, Ford bought the rights for $2500. An established and respected name in the business by 1938, Ford felt he would have little difficulty selling the premise of the tale to the studio chiefs. To his astonishment, he was turned down. He finally convinced independent producer Walter Wanger to finance the film as part of a deal in which it would be distributed through United Artists. Wanger had only one demand: the key part of the Ringo Kid must be played by rising idol Gary Cooper. Ford summoned up his nerve and let it be known that the part was already cast. He wanted a "kid" named John Wayne to play the role. Wanger eventually

relented, although he was certain that Wayne's inability to turn *The Big Trail* into a hit proved that he would always remain a loser toiling in bottom-of-the bill oaters.

Ford and Wayne had been friends ever since the Duke had been a prop man on Ford's earlier, silent-era films. Despite their friendship, however, Ford did little to help Wayne in the industry, with the exception of having given him a few days work as an extra in some rather forgettable films. Wayne knew Ford was casting the role of Ringo, and when the director asked his opinion as to who should get the job, Wayne replied naïvely "Lloyd Nolan." Ford called Wayne a dumb S.O.B. and told him that he had already arranged for the Duke to take the role. This was to be the last civil conversation Ford would have with Wayne until the film was finished.

Shooting *Stagecoach* proved to be a nightmarish experience for Wayne. Ford berated him constantly and took characteristic delight in humiliating him in front of his co-stars. When Wayne

THE RARE ORIGINAL HERALD FOR "STAGECOACH"

commented that he thought Andy Devine held the reins of the stagecoach horses a bit too lightly to be realistic, Ford summoned the entire cast and crew to announce that Wayne felt Devine's performance was terrible. Such dictatorial mannerisms may have been intended to keep Wayne "on his feet" and not let success go to his head. Or they may just have been natural inclinations for Ford, who even his closest associates admitted had a short temper both on and off the set. Wayne bit his tongue for two reasons: he knew that isolating a powerful presence like Ford's would cement his stay in "B" Westerns and he also could not help but feel a sense of gratitude for the opportunity the crusty director had provided.

Ford filmed *Stagecoach* partly in California, with some studio work done on a giant replica of the town of Lordsburg. However, the movie is primarily noted for being the first film shot on location in Monument Valley, Arizona. Ford would return there often throughout his career, but it is no coincidence that his finest achievements were those shot on his favorite location. Monument Valley offered a stunning panorama of sheer beauty. The endless desert combined with the towering buttes made it an ideal location for a Western. Ford's extensive use of this scenery was in blatant contrast to most of the Western epics made prior to *Stagecoach*. Almost without exception these were phony-looking little "quickies" that substituted unconvincing back screen projection for actual locales. *Stagecoach* left unprepared audiences breathless with its realism and beauty.

WAYNE IS SMITTEN BY CLAIRE TREVOR

JOHN FORD'S **STAGECOACH**
Starring **JOHN WAYNE · CLAIRE TREVOR · THOMAS MITCHELL**
John Carradine · Andy Devine · George Bancroft

The movie was also unique in that Ford fulfilled his promise to Wanger of making the first "adult" Western—concentrating more on characters than mindless action sequences. The script merely puts together nine diversified passengers on a dangerous journey through Indian territory. They are a mixed bag, ranging from Claire Trevor's prostitute with a heart-of-gold, to John Carradine's slimy cardshark, to Wayne's naïve and heroic Ringo Kid. Naturally, Wayne is not the cold-blooded murderer he is taken for when he joins the stage. In fact, he has been framed for a murder and is enroute to Lordsburg to seek his father's killers. Others along for the ride include Devine's stage driver, George Bancroft's tough but soft-hearted sheriff who can't help admiring Ringo even when arresting him, Louise Platt as a pregnant woman, and others who might appear to come from the stock company of ordinary Westerns. In fact, much of *Stagecoach* appears to be somewhat cliched today, but as film historian Richard J. Anobile reminded us in a tribute to this classic, all of this was highly original in 1939. If any part of *Stagecoach* seems "old hat" today, it is because it virtually set the standard for every Western that followed.

The great pleasure of *Stagecoach* lies in the performances of the cast: there's hardly a false note played here. Claire Trevor (billed above Wayne) is totally convincing as the tragic whore who is run out of town. Thomas Mitchell won an Oscar for his endearing performance as the drunken doctor. Each member of the cast in fact is given a few good scenes to display his or her notable talents. Wayne is actually just part of the ensemble. Yet, it is clear from the first glimpse of him—dramatically stopping the stage while twirling his rifle—that his is the presence that will tower over the others. Like the young James Dean or Brando, his rugged good looks and moody underplaying would generate an immediate interest and fascination with him. From this moment on, audiences and critics knew that a major new talent was upon them. Although it took Wayne until *Red River* ten years later to prove he could have a blockbuster hit without Ford behind the camera, *Stagecoach* provided him

with a prestigious role in one of the year's most acclaimed films. In fact, all who were associated with this epic generally achieved fairly successful careers.

There are far too many memorable moments in *Stagecoach* to be recounted here. Yet, no review of the film ever fails to mention the climactic battle between the inhabitants of the stage and the attacking Indians. Shot at breathtaking speed across the desert of Monument Valley, the sequence never fails to leave viewers on the edge of their seats. It is during this scene that famed stuntman Yakima Cannutt—doubling for Wayne—makes his now classic leap from the stage onto the backs of the racing horses to retrieve the reins. It is a stunt only "Yak" himself could have topped—and he did some years later when he orchestrated the chariot race in the 1959 version of *Ben-Hur*. When asked for the umpteenth time, incidently, why the Indians simply didn't shoot the horses in order to stop the stage, Ford replied "Because they would have also stopped the picture!"

Despite its superb battle sequence, *Stagecoach* shows a great deal of restraint in that it defers most of its visual action until the very end. Throughout the movie, there is the ominous presence of the rampaging Indians behind every hill and shrub. Steven Spielberg would use a similar tactic in *Jaws*: the most terrifying parts of that blockbuster occur in the first half—wherein the shark is never actually seen.

Ford also shows restraint in the climax of the movie, in which Wayne arrives in town for the shootout with a gang of outlaws. Since little could visually top the excitement of the chase scene that immediately precedes this sequence, Ford wisely underplays the action by cutting away from the actual gun battle. We hear the shots, but it is not until moments later that we know who won.

Stagecoach, unlike so many of Ford's other films, did not have to wait years to gain the attention it deserved. It was nominated for a number of Oscars, Ford won accolades from critics everywhere, and the film proved to be a rousing success at the box-office. Sadly, when 20th Century-Fox decided to do an ill-advised

STAGECOACH

A WALTER WANGER production • directed by JOHN FORD
with CLAIRE TREVOR • JOHN WAYNE • Andy Devine • John Carradine
Thomas Mitchell • Louise Platt • George Bancroft • Donald Meek
Berton Churchill • Tim Holt   Released thru United Artists

THE CAST ENJOYS A MEAL AT THE OUTPOST

remake of this classic in 1966, they insisted that as part of the deal, the original be withdrawn commercially for a number of years. This deprived many who loved the movie of the privilege of viewing it again. Today it can be enjoyed in all its splendor on videocassette. It still is rarely shown on the large screen. In the early Seventies,

the American Film Institute began to take an active intrerest in restoring and preserving classic films. It was discovered that almost every existing 35mm print of *Stagecoach* had been irreparably damaged. Once more it was the Duke to the rescue. While looking through his garage, he located a perfect print of Ford's classic which he donated to the AFI so that new ones could be struck.

21

THE LONG VOYAGE HOME (1940)

Cast: John Wayne, Thomas Mitchell, Ian Hunter, Barry Fitzgerald, Wilfrid Lawson, Mildred Natwick, John Qualen, Ward Bond. *Director:* John Ford. *Screenplay:* Dudley Nichols, from the one-act plays by Eugene O'Neill. *Music:* Richard Hageman. *Released by* United Artists. *Running Time:* 105 Minutes.

John Wayne's role in *The Long Voyage Home* is by no means the dominant one in this brooding character study. Yet, it was one of the most important performances of his early career. The film, based on a series of one act plays by Eugene O'Neill, centers on the camaraderie among career seamen who know little of life but the hardships that merchant mariners must face on a daily basis. Wayne's role is significant for two reasons. Foremost, it precluded him from being absorbed into an endless series of minor Westerns after his sensational appearance in *Stagecoach*. Immediately following that film, offers for quality roles in major productions were conspicuously absent.

DUKE SEEKS ADVICE FROM MILDRED NATWICK

ORIGINAL ONE SHEET POSTER

The second significant factor about *The Long Voyage Home* is that it forced Wayne to gain confidence as an actor. Still uncertain about his ability to carry anything other than a "B" Western, Wayne had almost dismissed his *Stagecoach* success as a fluke. Once again, it was John Ford who rode to the rescue. Ford had been hired to direct *Voyage* and characteristically went against all conventional wisdom by insisting that Duke take on the role of Ole Olsen, a naïve young Swedish seaman.

No one was more shocked by Ford's offer than Wayne. Just as Wayne had tried to talk Ford into casting someone more "appropriate" for the role of the Ringo Kid in *Stagecoach*, so, too, did the Duke in this instance. Ford insisted that Wayne could play the part without detriment to the story, but for credibility, he also demanded that Wayne use an "authentic" Swedish accent. Despite his best efforts, the Duke could only muster a dialect of questionable quality. He argued with Ford that the accent was unnecessary, and reminded his mentor that he had been given virtually no time to prepare for the film. In fact, the crew shot around Wayne while waiting for him to finish a minor Western called *Three Faces West*. He finished working on that movie after midnight and was required to begin the role of Olsen early the next morning. His pleas for more time fell on deaf ears.

To compromise, Ford hired actress Osa Massen to teach Wayne an authentic Swedish accent. There was only one slight drawback to this plan: Massen was Danish. When this was brought to Ford's attention, he gruffly insisted that Scandanavian was Scandanavian and audiences would be none the wiser. Massen worked steadily with Wayne in preparation for a major sequence in which Duke was required to have a prolonged conversation with a bar girl. As this scene was his only lengthy "soliloquy" in the picture, he was extremely concerned that he would appear laughable. Although critics admired his performance, Wayne himself never felt overly comfortable with it. Throughout the years he mentioned that he felt his accent was uneven and not at all convincing. Ford refused to allow him to reshoot the sequence, insisting that it was perfectly

WITH CARMEN MORALES

satisfactory.

Accent aside, *The Long Voyage Home* instilled a sense of confidence in Wayne that had been missing in the previous years. He was particularly pleased when the film received critical acclaim, and always listed this among the efforts with which he was most satisfied. The movie is certainly an oddity in the Wayne canon. It is a talky melodrama that relies almost entirely on the interaction of its characters in lieu of action sequences. Fortunately, the storyline consistently holds the viewers interest because it is populated with people we come to know intimately. They are neither heroes nor villains—merely restless free spirits who know home as whatever deck they are presently standing on.

The central character in the drama is not Wayne, but Thomas Mitchell's Driscoll, a belligerent but soft hearted old salt, the motivator for

ORIGINAL TITLE CARD

the crew's actions. They both fear and love him, and everyone looks to him as their unofficial leader. It is a marvelous performance which Mitchell gives, embellishing the world-weary Driscoll with a sense of wisdom and irony. We feel as though he is not so much interested in the quality of his own life as much as he is in securing a better future for those who depend on him.

Driscoll and the other members of the crew are a close-knit bunch who profess to be tired of the seaman's way of life. After each voyage takes its toll, Driscoll and his shipmates pledge to find another means of support. The captain of the ship grudgingly pretends to believe them, but announces knowingly to his mate that "They'll be back." Indeed, he is correct. But this voyage has a tragic epilogue. The men are more cynical than ever, having barely escaped a Nazi attack on their unarmed vessel which is transporting ammunition. They realize that regardless of the risks they have little alternative but to return to the life they know so well. Yet, they are determined that Wayne's Olsen be spared this fate. They watch the naïve young crew member's every move and literally wisk him from the ship when it enters port. The men intend to "escort" Wayne to a steamer bound for his homeland so that he may realize their own elusive dream of returning to a normal life. When Wayne is "shanghaied," however, his mates must come to his rescue. This results in Driscoll taking his place, only to die aboard the freighter during a submarine attack.

There are far too many virtues pertaining to this film to list here. Suffice it to say that the melancholy storyline provides the cast with the types of richly written sequences that most actors only dream of playing. The entire cast gives a perfect example of superb ensemble acting, with no one player attempting to "chew the scenery" at the expense of anyone else. Particularly good is Ward Bond, whose touching death scene is brilliantly enacted. Likewise, Ford favorite John Qualen provides his usual light-hearted scenes as yet another bemused and bewildered Scandanavian—a role he would re-enact over the years in many of Ford's other movies. As for Wayne, his performance is perfectly acceptable, limited only by the fact that his role is not particularly large. Anyone who doubts his thespic ability would be well-advised to screen *The Long Voyage Home*. He is totally believable (despite his own reservations) in a role which took a great deal of courage for him to tackle. It is but one of the many pleasures provided by this work. One would be remiss not to mention the extraordinary work of cinematographer Gregg Toland and the sentimental strains of Richard Hageman's musical score. They are important contributions to a long-overlooked movie that for many years was forgotten because it failed at the box-office. Thanks to the video revolution, it can now be enjoyed on tape not only by enthusiasts of John Wayne, but by lovers of great movies the world over.

THEY WERE EXPENDABLE (1945)

Cast: Robert Montgomery, John Wayne, Donna Reed, Jack Holt, Ward Bond, Marshall Thompson, Paul Langton. *Director:* John Ford. *Screenplay:* Commander Frank Wead. *From the Book by* William L. White. *Music:* Herbert Stothart. *Released by* Metro-Goldwyn-Mayer. *Running Time:* 136 Minutes.

As the tide began to turn against the Axis powers during WWII, Hollywood tried to do its part to keep America's propaganda machine well oiled by churning out dozens of mostly forgettable flag wavers designed for the short term effect of rallying everyone to the common cause. Two individuals who were quite active in stirring up patriotic feelings were director John Ford and writer Frank Wead, both Lieutenant Commanders in the U.S. Navy. Ford, or "Pappy" as Duke and other intimates came to know him, volunteered to aid the war effort through his filmmaking talents. He personally did much of the camera work for the highly-acclaimed documentaries *December 7*, *The Battle of Midway*, and *We Sail at Midnight*. Ford was rewarded for his work with two Oscars, but they came at a terrible price: he was wounded in both legs while filming *The Battle of Midway*, and also lost the sight in one eye.

Wead was a hard-driven man who won praise as one of the leading proponents of modernizing the Navy after WWI. One of the great flying aces of his time, "Spig," as he was nicknamed, was influential in foreseeing the necessity for aircraft carriers and planes in keeping the U.S. fleet strong. A tragic accident left him partially paralyzed, but his grit endured and he learned to walk on crutches with such precision that the Navy agreed with his request to be placed back on active duty. (Years later, Ford was to film Wead's life as *The Wings of Eagles* with Wayne in

the lead.) At Ford's suggestion, Wead turned his skills toward screen writing. He had some notable credits, but the most prestigious of all would be the script for Ford's WWII film, *They Were Expendable*.

The story was based on a semi-fictional account of the adventures of Lt. John Bulklley and Lt. (j.g) Robert Kelly, two of the motivating forces behind the using of PT boats as assault vehicles. Bulklley and Kelly pioneered the initial battle assignments of these small vessels, which previously had been used only for light messenger duties. When the U.S. fleet was all but obliterated in the early days of the war, the naval brass finally consented to allowing PT boats to attack the Japanese fleet. These were tiny boats, lightly armed. Their sole defense was their unob-

trusive size and their rapid speed. The ships would race up to their prey, fire several torpedos and then "high-tail" it away. Casualties were inevitably high, but the boats and the courageous men who piloted them were instrumental in inflicting severe damage on the enemy.

Ford dreamed of bringing the achievements of these men to the screen. Armed with a fairly large budget and a first-rate script by Wead, he set about so doing. For the role of Bulklley, Ford cast actor Robert Montgomery, who had recently commanded a PT boat during the war. John Wayne was cast as Kelly, the more spontaneous and short-tempered of the two. Only one problem existed: despite changing the names of the characters to Brickley and Ryan, no one made an attempt to conceal the fact that Montgomery and

Wayne were portraying two very real-life counterparts. MGM was subsequently sued by Bulklley and Kelly, as well as a nurse with whom Kelly had fallen in love (portrayed on screen by Donna Reed). Both men were awarded monetary damages from the court, as was the nurse.

Wayne was said to be somewhat guilt-racked about appearing onscreen with Montgomery, who had been an officer and an actual war hero. Critics have always been quick to criticize Duke's hawkish politics, when he himself never enlisted in the "Big One." Technically, Wayne's age and family responsibilities excluded him from the draft. Depending on whether one gets his information from a Wayne friend or foe, Duke was either heartbroken that a hearing ailment kept him out of the service, or he was too hypocritical to join. Whatever the case, Wayne undoubtedly did as much good for his country by maintaining morale through his films as he would have had he worn a uniform. The legend he created was equally as important as his serving in the armed forces, as to this day the Wayne persona examplifies everything good and strong about America. The benefits which derived from his films outweighed criticisms that he was just a "paper tiger."

Ford filmed *They Were Expendable* at various sites in Florida. With a minimum of studio scenes, the drama has an authentic ring to it that eludes many of the films produced about the war. The chemistry between the soft-spoken Montgomery and the hard-bitten Wayne also adds an air of electricity to the proceedings. Things slow down a bit due to Ford's usual—and at times disturbing—propensity to include several songs courtesy of some ever-warbling servicemen. This tendency seems to make charicatures of the enlisted men, showing them to be always happy-go-lucky old salts who call each other "swell" and can't wait to race through the action in order to sing another Irish ballad. Fortunately, the script, which reflects the dark days of Pearl Harbor, features enough realism and grit to overcome the sugar-coating. In many ways, this is one of Ford's more morbid films. Many of the men we come to know intimately die. The end of the movie features a minimal

30

AS RUSTY

MANNING THE PT BOAT:

"THEY WERE EXPENDABLE" AND OTHER WWII FILMS ARE FEATURED IN THIS PUBLICITY PHOTO

amount of platitudes, perhaps because the war had already ended by the time it was released. Instead, we find Wayne and Montgomery reluctantly leaving what's left of their squad behind to return to Washington to head up efforts to produce more PT crews. There is genuine gut-wrenching emotion in these scenes, and they linger in the mind.

Ford directed the action sequences in the film with a flair seldom seen in other movies of the period. The PT attacks on Japanese warships are stunningly filmed, and are so vivid in their realism that one wonders how they were brought to the screen without resulting in injury and death to the stuntmen involved. Ford also has the good sense not to belabor Wayne's love affair with Reed. No sooner do these two fall in love than the war suddenly separates them. Although we wait for the improbable reunion, it never occurs. Nor do the lovers ever again learn of each other's fate. These developments only add to the realism of the drama.

They Were Expendable defied the predictions of those who thought that audiences would turn their backs on films about WWII once the conflict was over. To a certain extent this was true. The movie never became the enduring classic it deserved to be. However, it did much to boost the reputations of all connected with it, including Wayne, who uncharacteristically accepted second billing. His is an excellent performance, which set the stage for the fine work he would accomplish within the next few years.

FORT APACHE (1948)

Cast: John Wayne, Henry Fonda, Shirley Temple, Pedro Armendariz, John Agar, Ward Bond, Irene Rich, George O'Brien, Anna Lee, Victor McLaglen. *Director:* John Ford. *Screenplay:* Frank S. Nugent. *Based Upon the Short Story* "Massacre" by James Warner Bellah. *Music:* Richard Hageman. *Released by* RKO Radio Pictures. *Running Time:* 127 Minutes.

In the decade since Wayne had made *Stagecoach*, he had worked steadily, gradually escalating to lightweight though first rate—entertainment yarns released by major studios. The ensuing vehicles proved to be a mixed bag. Among the pluses: *Dark Command*, *Reap the Wild Wind*, *The Spoilers*, *Flying Tigers*, *The Fighting Seabees*, *Back to Bataan* and *Angel and the Badman*. There were minuses, too, like *Lady for a Night*, *Reunion in France*, *A Lady Takes a Chance*, *Without Reservations* and *Tycoon*. One of the few critically acclaimed films during this period was John Ford's *They Were Expendable*.

Predictably, it was Ford behind the camera again when Wayne was cast in what was considered to be the lead role in *Fort Apache*. It was first of Ford's famous "Cavalry Trilogy" which would eventually encompass *She Wore a Yellow Ribbon* and *Rio Grande*. Wayne gave an excellent performance as York, a veteran Army Captain assigned to deal with the problem of bringing the rebellious Cochise to justice. However, upon viewing the film it becomes quite apparent that the real star of the show is Henry Fonda, who, despite second billing to Wayne, dominates every sequence in which he appears.

32

WITH HENRY FONDA AND SHIRLEY TEMPLE

WITH GEORGE O'BRIEN, ANNA LEE AND GUY KIBBEE   *PREPARING THE TROOPS FOR AN INDIAN ASSAULT*

Fonda's Colonel Owen Thursday is without question one of Ford's most fascinating characters. A stalwart martinet, he combines sophistication and formal courteousness with an almost total disregard for human compassion. We are tempted to admire him for his unyielding convictions and later despise him for his inability to stray even slightly from the military manuals. The prissy commanding officer has often been the target of audience wrath in fiction, yet such individuals are generally presented as one-dimensional. Not so with Thursday. From the moment he arrives at Fort Apache, we are not sure what to make of him. He is weary, aggravated and uncomfortable by his reassignment to the "Wild West," yet, being the good soldier, he complies with his orders without hesitation.

At times his social manners endear him to us, and we feel certain that because the film has thus far proven to be somewhat light in tone, Thursday will eventually see the errors of his ways and become "one of the guys." To Ford's credit, this does not happen. Thursday never displays any last-moment character reversals beyond the undeniable admission that he has brought tragedy to his command.

Fort Apache might be called Ford's *Psycho*. The analogy is not as ludicrous as it may appear. With *Psycho*, Alfred Hitchcock spent the first half hour of his film letting us get familiar with the heroine. We get to see her desires, ambitions, virtues and faults until we feel we know her intimately. Then, without warning, she is murdered, leaving the audience completely shocked by the realism of the moment, and always uncertain as to what may be in store for them next. In *Fort Apache*, Ford does much the same thing. He casts the key roles with well known actors, including his stock players headed by Ward Bond and Victor McLaglen. These characters are given ample screen time to endear themselves to the audience through Ford's familiar practice of making these battle-hardened soldiers act as though at times they are merely mischievous Boy Scouts. When Thursday leads them into a Western-style version of the "Charge of the Light

35

Brigade," we are certain that Wayne's objections to the battle strategy will ultimately prevail at the last minute and enable the troop to overcome Cochise.

This never occurs. For objecting to orders, Wayne is branded a coward and relieved of his command. Playing against "type," Wayne is disgusted but does not protest. He stands by helplessly while his comrades are led into battle by Thursday. In the disaster that ensues, the entire battalion is massacred, and Thursday realizes—all too late—he has disgraced himself. Because of this realism, *Fort Apache* stands as one of Ford's most surprising and tragic works. It is also a brilliant film on almost every level.

The action sequences of the cavalry charges are superbly filmed, and one almost chokes on the dust from the racing horses. The landscapes of Monument Valley are breathtaking, and one wishes that Ford had chosen to make the film in color. Everything else about *Fort Apache* works, including a love subplot pitting John Agar against all odds to win the hand of Thursday's daughter (Shirley Temple). Usually these mandatory romances tend to slow down the action. However, in *Fort Apache*, the talk which dominates the first section of the film serves to flesh out the fascinating characters until we feel they are old friends. Although we are spared close-ups of their individual deaths during the film's climax (the entire command is obliterated with one swift Apache attack), the loss of these people makes us no less saddened.

For Wayne, *Fort Apache* was another important stepping stone in his career. The acclaim he received under Ford's direction allowed him to give a remarkable string of performances in the next year. Consider the quality of Wayne's work between 1948-50: *Fort Apache*, *Red River*, *She Wore a Yellow Ribbon*, *Sands of Iwo Jima* and *Rio Grande* (three for Ford). Perhaps only Brando has turned out such a remarkable body of work in so short a time. With *Fort Apache*, Wayne saw Henry Fonda's brilliant performance gather the lion's share of the accolades—and deservedly so, as Fonda had far more to work with. Yet, it helped Wayne gain respect as an actor—not just a guarantee for a box-office hit. Within a few years, he would utilize his new-found respect to become one of the dominant forces in Hollywood. As with *Stagecoach*, it was "Pappy" Ford who gave him the tools to work with. Yet, it is Wayne who must be credited for properly applying them to his craft in such an exemplary manner.

RED RIVER (1948)

Cast: John Wayne, Montgomery Clift, Joanne Dru, Walter Brennan, Coleen Gray, John Ireland, Noah Beery, Jr., Harry Carey, Harry Carey, Jr., Chief Yowlachie. *Director:* Howard Hawks. *Screenplay:* Borden Chase and Charles Schnee. *From the Magazine Story* "The Chisolm Trail" by Borden Chase. *Music:* Dimitri Tiomkin. *Released by* United Artists. *Running Time:* 125 Minutes.

Up until now, critics were willing to praise Wayne for his few memorable performances. However, compliments did not come easily to Duke. Throughout his career, even the positive reviews were somewhat compromised. By 1948, critics were suggesting that while Wayne could give admirable performances, it was only under John Ford's direction that this could occur. In fact, there was more than a little evidence to back

THE DRIVE!
40,000 hooves thundering across the vast plains and mighty rivers of a sprawling continent!

THE RAILROAD!
Pouring across the tracks, the herd reaches the farthest frontier of civilization!

THE AMBUSH!
Bullet against flaming arrow as blood-mad savages ride the ring of death!

IN 25 YEARS-
ONLY THREE!
"COVERED WAGON"
"CIMARRON"
AND NOW -
HOWARD HAWKS' GREAT PRODUCTION
"RED RIVER"

THE FEUD!
Vengeance . . . exploding in the fury of a desperate fight to the finish! . . . bringing new glory to a great new star— Montgomery Clift!

Monterey Productions presents
HOWARD HAWKS'   "RED RIVER"
starring JOHN WAYNE · MONTGOMERY CLIFT · WALTER BRENNAN · JOANNE DRU
with HARRY CAREY, Sr. · COLEEN GRAY · JOHN IRELAND · NOAH BEERY, Jr. · HARRY CAREY, Jr. · PAUL FIX
From the Saturday Evening Post story, "The Chisholm Trail", by Borden Chase
Screenplay by Borden Chase and Charles Schnee
Executive Producer, CHARLES K. FELDMAN · DIRECTED AND PRODUCED BY HOWARD HAWKS · RELEASED THRU UNITED ARTISTS

this up. Aside from the collaborations with Ford, Duke's films and acting had been largely unimpressive. All of this would change with *Red River*.

Director Howard Hawks was already regarded as a first-rate filmmaker by the 1940s. He felt an obsession to try a genre he was unfamiliar with: the Western. What began as disjointed effort to whip a screenplay into shape, eventually turned into the story for *Red River*. Hawks wanted this tale of a cattle drive between Texas and Missouri to be a big-budget epic, filled with gritty realism. At first he envisioned a film starring Gary Cooper as Tom Dunson, a hard-bitten, uncompromising cattle baron. Montgomery Clift—new to films—would be cast as Matt, the adopted son who eventually rebels against his father's authoritarian manner. A third key role was that of Cherry Valance a gunman who accompanies the drive. Amazingly, Hawks envisioned the dapper Cary Grant for this role.

Things began to fall apart quickly. Cooper felt

the character of Dunson was too uncompromising and left the project when Hawks refused to rewrite the script. Negotiations fell through with Cary Grant. Eventually, the role of Valance was made of secondary importance, and John Ireland was cast as the gunman.

Hawks approached Wayne, who agreed that the Dunson character should not be compromised. Wayne would play him—warts and all. The script required Duke to age several decades, with most of the action taking place when Dunson is a relatively older man. Wayne had never been called upon to stretch his acting abilities to this extent, and he was enthused about taking the role. For his services, he was paid the hefty fee of $150,000.

Hawks managed to get a budget of $3-million approved by United Artists, making it one of the most expensive Western epics ever made. He hired a virtual army of Western stunt riders, and bought over 1,000 head of cattle. All of this

WITH MONTGOMERY CLIFT

entourage was moved to a remote area of Arizona, where the production company had the misfortune of encountering the first summer rain in the area in many years. Hawks persevered, feeling—correctly—that the harsh elements would heighten the sense of realism. He was also faced with another dilemma: his original leading lady was quite pregnant by the time she arrived on the set, and had to be replaced by Joanne Dru. This accounted for even more lost time, as major portions of the script had to be rewritten.

When the finished product eventually premiered, it proved to be a box-office and critical hit, due in no small part to Wayne's towering performance. The role of Dunson fit him like a glove, and his courage in not wanting the character softened made the role one of the most fascinating of Duke's career. *Red River* is an all-around Western classic, despite the fact that it is a land-locked version of *Mutiny on the Bounty*.

When we first see Wayne, he is a young man heading west to establish himself. When he rejects his fiancée's pleas to accompany him, he soon finds he has made a mistake that will change his life. Indians raid the wagon train Duke has just left, and he learns that his lover has died in the resulting massacre. Embittered, he is not without any human emotion, however. He adopts an orphan boy named Matt and devotes his life to teaching his young son how to be successful.

The story then advances many years to find Wayne having accomplished his dream of becoming a cattle baron. Clift is now his right hand man, and the only person Wayne will trust. The two men now face their ultimate challenge—moving the massive herd to market across hundreds of miles of uncharted and dangerous terrain. Wayne tells his ranchhands they are free to stay behind, but once having signed on, no one will be allowed to quit. The trail proves harsher than anyone could have imagined. Stampedes,

BICKERING WITH WALTER BRENNAN

DUNSON SURVEYS HIS DOMAIN

torrential rains and Indian attacks combine to wear down the men's morale. Wayne refuses to let up the pace, and becomes more and more ornery as the drive drags on. The major dramatic point occurs when Duke threatens to hang a deserter. This forces Clift to rebel and seize control of the herd. Duke is sent packing, but not before vowing to kill his adopted son.

The last part of the film benefits from a good deal of tension. Although Clift and the men complete the drive successfully, we sense their nervousness at not knowing just when Wayne will reappear. Such is the power of Wayne's Tom Dunson that he can make it believable that dozens of men would fear his wrath. Wayne does appear in the tense climax. He tries to goad Clift into a gunfight, and failing this, begins to beat him mercilessly. Finally, Clift reacts and a major fight ensues. The movie was supposed to end

with Wayne dying of a gunshot wound from Cherry Valance. However, Hawks could not bear to let these two characters part so tragically. He had the script rewritten so that Joanne Dru, as Clift's girlfriend, stops the fight and gets the men to reconcile. Wayne consents, having earned respect for his protege by virtue of the fact that he has fought back. The movie ends with Wayne promising Clift half of his empire.

There has been much controversy about this ending. Most critics have stated that it remains the only weak part of *Red River*. While the climax certainly does end abruptly, to call it totally unsatisfying seems a bit harsh. By the time these last few seconds roll around, *Red River* has so completely captivated its audience that no major harm is done to the story. Much of the credit for this film's excellence rests squarely on Hawks' shoulders. With his first Western, he established himself as a major force in the genre, and it is his Westerns which would become his most financially successful works. Hawks freely admitted, however, that without Wayne's contribution, there would not have been a *Red River*.

An interesting footnote: just prior to the film's release, Hawks and United Artists were slapped with a lawsuit by Howard Hughes. Hughes claimed that the climax of *Red River* closely paralleled that of his own film *The Outlaw*. Hughes wanted an injunction forcing the ending of Hawks' film be excised. Obviously, this would have made the film unreleasable and impossible to reshoot at this late date. Wayne intervened, sensing that Hughes was motivated mostly out of hatred for Hawks, whom he never forgave for walking out on one of their joint projects some years before. Duke pleaded with Hughes to reconsider, and Hughes relented, despite the fact that he seemed to have a good case. In a bizarre way, the ultimate sucess of *Red River* might well have been due to the reclusive billionaire.

The next time you watch the film, try to look beyond the great performance of Wayne and revel in the movie's other pleasures: the sheer spectacle of the drive sequences; the nerve-wracking tension of the stampede; the excellent supporting performances, especially by Clift and Walter Brennan.

41

SHE WORE A YELLOW RIBBON (1949)

Cast: John Wayne, Joanne Dru, John Agar, Ben Johnson, Harry Carey, Jr., Victor McLaglen, Mildred Natwick, George O'Brien, Arthur Shields. *Director:* John Ford. *Screenplay:* Frank S. Nugent and Laurence Stallings. *From the Magazine Stories* "The Big Hunt" and "War Party" by James Warner Bellah. *Music:* Richard Hageman. *Released by* RKO Radio Pictures. *Running Time:* 103 Minutes.

I have always flown in the face of conventional wisdom in my opinion that *She Wore a Yellow Ribbon* is not the masterpiece many film connoisseurs proclaim it to be. Repeated viewings of the film have failed to change my mind. It is by far the weakest of the three films which comprise the Ford Cavalry Trilogy, and is most memorable as a series of interesting Western vignettes as opposed to a wholly engrossing storyline. In *Ribbon*, Ford's occasional tendency to be laid back almost makes the razor-thin plot evaporate. The movie is also quite talky, and the action sequences seem to be thrown in to satisfy the more traditional among Wayne's fans.

BANTERING WITH JOHN AGAR AND JOANNE DRU   THE USUAL BICKERING WITH VICTOR McLAGLEN

Why then include *Ribbon* in the section commemorating John Wayne's best films? The answer is that, although *Ribbon* contains some flaws, the flaws are far from fatal. Just because the movie's screenplay is weak by John Ford standards, we must remember just how high those standards are. Compared to most Westerns, *Ribbon* soars high above other films of its genre. It undoubtedly would have been among the greatest of the Ford/Wayne teamings had the plot provided something more of a "hook" to provide suspense.

Basically, this is a simple oft-told tale, although never with quite the same polish Ford and his stock company could provide.

Wayne is Captain Nathan Brittles, a career Army officer just days away from his retirement—an occasion he views with mixed pleasures. Although he welcomes the opportunity to have free time, he realizes that he has nothing in particular to accomplish. The Army is his entire life. The movie opens in the wake of Custer's battle at the Little Big Horn. Wayne receives the news that the colonel and many other friends have been massacred. He also learns that for the first time, rival Indian tribes are joining forces for a concentrated attack on local settlers. Wayne hopes to find a way to defuse the Indian strategy before his obligatory re-entry into civilian life.

Most of the story has little to do with the action, concentrating instead on the inhabitants of the fort and their relationships. Joanne Dru is cast as a flirtatious young woman who plays two rivals for her affections against each other. The men are played by Forties juvenile lead John Agar and Harry Carey, Jr., son of one of Duke's long time pals and frequent co-star, Harry Carey, who died after they made *Red River*. Then there is Ford perennial Victor McLaglen as the standard lovable lout of an Irish sergeant, who, despite his gruff nature, is more like a maternal grandmother to Wayne than a hard-bitten Army man.

In between all the talk, Wayne is frustrated by his attempts to preserve the peace. There are a few scattered incidents which allude to the Indian threat, but most such action takes place off camera. Eventually, Wayne reluctantly raids an Indian village and stampedes the horses, thus leaving the Indians no choice but to surrender. This final action sequence is technically very well done, with hundreds of horses stampeding through the Indian village. However, there are no injuries on either side, and this detracts from the realism and sense of danger.

Action is not what was on Ford's mind with this film, however. This is by far his most personal Western, and the action is merely a guise to introduce the usual fascinating array of characters that inevitably populate "Pappy's" films. Clearly, the movie's chief attribute is a brilliant performance by Wayne. It is more than a skillful job of acting. In fact, it is the centerpiece that keeps together an otherwise not very cohesive or involving plot. As a character well beyond his actual years, Wayne's Brittles is the epitome of the well-loved cavalry officer. If this is not the way such men looked and acted, it is certainly the way we like to think they did.

Wayne's performance in *Ribbon* is played with such insight and depth that it seems inconceivable that he was bypassed for an Oscar nomination. The Academy chose, instead to reward Duke for his fine—but not groundbreaking—work in *Sands of Iwo Jima*, which was released the same year. However, time has not been unkind to *Ribbon*, as both the film and Wayne have gotten their due from critics and cinema historians.

Other wonderful things to be found in the film include some of the most sensitive and touching scenes to appear in any Ford production. When Wayne visits his wife's grave and softly tells her of the events of the day, it never seems as contrived as such sequences often do in other movies. His gentle compassion is further shown in the way he relates the sad news of the deaths of people to whom they were endeared. Contrasting these moving moments are the scenes of broad comedy which abound in Ford military adventures. Most such sequences revolve around McLaglen and his drinking habits, as well as his obsession of looking after Wayne. These scenes are predictable, but, nevertheless, irresistible.

Certainly, no one can remain unmoved when, on the day of his retirement, Wayne is given a watch as a remembrance from his men, inscribed

*WITH VICTOR McLAGLEN, BEN JOHNSON
AND GEORGE O'BRIEN*

simply "Lest we forget..." We see Wayne fumble uncomfortably for his glasses as he fights to hold back his emotions. After Duke saves the day, he rides off into what was presumed to be new horizons. Ford, however, felt that an ambiguous ending for such an endearing character would not sit well with audiences. He chose—unwisely, I believe—to tack on a contrived epilogue in which Wayne is recalled to the fort and given the title of Chief of Scouts. The film is not really harmed by this sentimental gesture on Ford's part, but the ending would have been far more poignant had he stuck with the original.

Ribbon was shot in only 28 days. Filmed on location in Monument Valley, the movie is per-haps one of the most beautiful Westerns ever. Winston Hoch's camerawork is simply stunning, and earned a well-deserved Oscar. Location work on the movie was rather uncomfortable as Ford brought almost no amenities to the set. Most of the cast and crew lived in tiny adobe huts which were quickly constructed. Only one toilet and a crude, makeshift shower were provided for the entire production company—including Wayne. The movie was also not without danger. Stunt rider-turned-actor Ben Johnson was nearly stomped to death in the final stampede, and no one even noticed.

I'll stick with my conviction that *Ribbon* is a bit overrated, though it is still a joy to watch, especially for the wonderful performance by Wayne, which he understandably felt represented his finest work on the screen.

SANDS OF IWO JIMA (1949)

Cast: John Wayne, John Agar, Adele Mara, Forrest Tucker, Wally Cassell, James Brown, Richard Webb, Arthur Franz. *Director:* Allan Dwan. *Screenplay:* Harry Brown and James Edward Grant. *From a Screen Story by* Harry Brown. *Music:* Victor Young. *Released by* Republic Pictures. *Running Time:* 100 Minutes.

As war films go, many feel *Sands of Iwo Jima* set a standard that has been hard to match. I respectfully disagree on the grounds that the non-action sequences are, at least by today's standards, every bit as cliched as many of the other war films which diluted the movie industry during and immediately following WWII. What sets this film apart is its unusual honesty in showing war as dirty, unpredictable and dehumanizing. This approach was somewhat innovative for its day. Many of the war films of the era presented one-dimensional characters who perform superheroic feats to save the day. There are few such absurdities in *Sands of Iwo Jima*.

John Wayne gives a gritty performance as Sgt. Stryker, a demanding non-com who tolerates nothing but the best effort from his squad. Not surprisingly, he is resented and despised by most

WAYNE LEADS THE ASSAULT

of his men. Several try to break through Stryker's rough exterior, only to find a stone wall underneath. Only one of Wayne's confidants knows the reason for his bitterness: his wife had deserted him five years previously, taking their ten-year-old son with her. Apparently, Wayne could not succeed as a husband or father, and these faults find his character far more vulnerable than we have generally seen him. He resents most of those around him, and drives his men hard not only to make them better Marines, but also, one suspects, to alleviate some of his own anger toward the world.

Of course, the audience sees that, away from the men, Duke does have a soft side. He just doesn't want anyone else to see it. After a particularly rough battle, Wayne instructs one of his peers to see to it that his men get the Sake he has been saving for himself. However, lest they find out he has good intentions, he insists that they are told that the liquor was taken from a dead Japanese soldier. Yet, he is moved when he encounters a young mother who has to turn to prostitution in order to keep herself and her baby alive. Not only does Wayne refuse to "score" with her, but he tends to the child and winds up leaving the mother his paycheck.

Sands of Iwo Jima is also unique in that we find Wayne somewhat of a failure on the professional side as well as domestically. We learn early in the film that Wayne has been demoted, although we are never told precisely why. His men speculate that it is his inability to control his drinking, but we also see Wayne letting his emotions get the better of him by striking an enlisted man. His blatant disregard for the rule book makes him an interesting paradox. Sort of a military Jekyl and Hyde who follows every regulation on the training field, but casually puts instinct above rules at his convenience. These are pyschological traits not usually extended to the characters Wayne plays, and it helps give *Sands of Iwo Jima* a far more interesting edge than most films of this type.

There are plenty of predictable cliches along the way, however. The squad is comprised of some stock characters, only one of which is explored in any great detail. As portrayed by John Agar, this private is obsessed with a hatred of Wayne. The reasons are left annoyingly unclear, but it presumably has to do with Wayne's admiration of the young Marine's father, a career fighting man whom Agar himself despised. This premise is a bit thin to sustain the tension that is created between the two adversaries, but it does make for some dramatic moments. In one key seen, Wayne makes a last attempt to win the respect of Agar by congratulating him on becoming a new father. Agar uses this as an opportunity to humiliate Wayne and everything he stands for. In most Wayne films, Duke would simply punch the lout in the nose in order to get a rise out of the audience. Here, however, under veteran Allan Dwan's sensitive direction, Wayne merely dismisses Agar quietly. However, we see in his eyes the pain and hurt of being rejected by yet another person. It is a well written and impressively acted sequence.

Dwan also succeeds in his direction of the battle scenes. They are among the most realistic ever filmed, although one should mention that quite a bit of actual footage is skillfully edited into the action. Unlike many war movies, bombs don't stop bursting when the actors engage in a conversation. Nor is there much time for platitudes when a member of the squad is killed. The only exception occurs when the unthinkable happens: John Wayne is shot dead near the end of the battle. Differing from most of his limited screen deaths, however, Duke does not go out in a spectacular style. He is calmly talking with his men, having just gained the respect of Agar. As he reaches for a cigarette, a single shot through the back kills him. No last words, no philosophies spoken. The one concession the screenplay makes toward sentiment is a letter the men find on him addressed to his son. As the squad reads it, they—and we—are quite touched. A hint of realism is introduced in that the letter remains unfinished. The film does end with Agar giving a corny imitation of Wayne in a not so subtle attempt to tell the audience his legacy will carry on with his former adversary.

Sands of Iwo Jima was a major box-office hit. It also earned Duke his first Oscar nomination. The award itself, however, went to Broderick

Crawford for the political drama *All the King's Men*, a movie Wayne reportedly hated. It is well known that Wayne referred throughout his career to the fact that he was nominated not only for *Iwo Jima*, but for *She Wore a Yellow Ribbon* as well.

This would have been impossible, as both films were released in the same year, and, as opposed to early Academy Award years, rules preclude an actor being nominated in the same category more than once in a single year. In truth, as powerful as his performance is in *Iwo Jima*, the more subtle and memorable one was indeed in *She Wore a Yellow Ribbon*.

RIO GRANDE (1950)

Cast: John Wayne, Maureen O'Hara, Ben Johnson, Claude Jarman, Jr., Harry Carey, Jr., Chill Wills, J. Carrol Naish, Victor McLaglen, Grant Withers, Peter Ortiz. *Director:* John Ford. *Screenplay:* James Kevin McGuiness. *Based Upon the Magazine Story* "Mission With No Record" by James Warner Bellah. *Music:* Victor Young. *Released by* Republic Pictures. *Running Time:* 105 Minutes.

The last film in John Ford's "Cavalry Trilogy" casts Wayne as Col. Kirby Yorke. However, there is little indication that this is meant to be the same character Wayne played in *Fort Apache*, despite the similarity in the name. (In *Fort Apache*, Wayne's character's last name was spelled without the final "e.") Why Ford used the name twice has long been the subject for debate. If he had intended to evoke memories of the character used in his previous film, why did he change the spelling and not refer once to anything which might have linked this Colonel Yorke to the one in *Fort Apache*? Many believe this is the same character, but it is more likely that the irrascible Ford merely sought to stir up some thought-provoking controversy.

CONFLICTING EMOTIONS FOR WAYNE, O'HARA AND CLAUDE JARMAN, JR.

A Great Director-Actor Team!
JOHN FORD · JOHN WAYNE
"Stagecoach" "Fort Apache"
"She Wore A Yellow Ribbon"
"They Were Expendable" & others!

Together for the First Time!
JOHN WAYNE · MAUREEN O'HARA
The Screen's Greatest Adventure
Star and Hollywood's Most
Beautiful Woman!

HERBERT J. YATES presents
John Ford's

RIO GRANDE

starring
JOHN WAYNE · MAUREEN O'HARA

co-starring
BEN JOHNSON · CLAUDE JARMAN, Jr. · HARRY CAREY, Jr. · CHILL WILLS

featuring
J. CARROL NAISH · VICTOR McLAGLEN · GRANT WITHERS · SONS OF THE PIONEERS

Screen Play by James Kevin McGuinness   Based on a Saturday Evening Post Story by James Warner Bellah

Directed by **JOHN FORD** ·

AN ARGOSY PRODUCTION
Produced by JOHN FORD and MERIAN C. COOPER

A REPUBLIC PICTURE ·   Republic Pictures Corporation—Herbert J. Yates, President

AS COL. KIRBY YORKE

Nevertheless, Wayne's character here is quite the antithesis of the man he played previously. In *Fort Apache*, Wayne was the upstart who hated the Army's "red tape" and sought to get straight to the action. Although the finale of *Fort Apache* found him to be more polished and professional, he was certainly a more pleasant fellow at the end of that film that we find him to be at the beginning of *Rio Grande*.

Here, Wayne's Colonel Yorke is a no-nonsense, "by the book" disciplinarian who will not tolerate any hint of incompetence—even from his own son. It seems his boy has flunked out of West Point and has coincidentaly been assigned to his father's outpost, where he is part of a small contingent of soldiers who are attempting to thwart the Apaches. Wayne has not seen his son in 15 years, and there is considerable tension between the two Yorkes. This is not eased any by the arrival of Wayne's estranged wife, Maureen

O'Hara, who has never forgiven her husband for complying with orders during the Civil War which led to his burning down the family plantation.

The beginning sequences of *Rio Grande* are among the more leisurely Ford has filmed. He seems to be forestalling getting to any action, preferring to let us get to know the main characters and the ensuing subplots. Predictably, Wayne's hard-nosed attitude toward wife and son softens considerably, especially when the latter proves himself to be quite a capable and fearless trooper. Various other stories are woven into this tale, including one in which recruit Ben Johnson tries to avoid capture for a trumped-up manslaughter charge. These incidents are sufficiently interesting enough to distract us from the fact that not much of anything is happening in *Rio Grande*. Indeed, Ford's characteristic love for folksy ballads of the plains is manifest by his actual casting of the singing group, the Sons of the Pioneers. It is one thing to hear their melodious voices enhance certain sequences as they have in other Ford films. Here, however, Ford overdoes the songs by having the Pioneers pop up periodically to strum their guitars and serenade everyone in sight. They appear to be less cavalry troops than strolling minstrels. During these scenes, the plot grinds to a halt as Ford becomes uncharacteristically guilty of padding the film.

With that said, it should be noted that *Rio Grande* is certainly worthy of being ranked among Ford's classic Westerns. Its plot may be thin, but there are enough wonderful sequences and performances to more than compensate for the movie's few flaws. Chief among *Rio Grande's* attributes is Wayne's work. Sporting a mustache and small goatee, he is every bit the American hero. Small wonder that Douglas MacArthur had told him that he embodied conception of the U.S. cavalryman as much as anyone who ever wore the uniform. Wayne's performance is a multi-facted one, ranging from an insensitive, hard-as-rock bureaucrat who blindly follows orders, to a teary-eyed romanticist who almost falls to pieces at the opportunity to "court" his estranged wife. As Wayne's wife, Maureen O'Hara is cast opposite the Duke for the first of

DUKE'S TENSE REUNION WITH MAUREEN O'HARA

five times. Although this film is probably the least demanding of any of these roles in terms of acting skill, she radiates a natural warmth and beauty which makes one sympathize with Wayne when he has to leave her behind to lead an attack.

Victor McLaglen appears yet again in the familiar role of a weather-beaten, tough-as-nails Irish sergeant who's really an old softie. If the role had become a cliche by the time *Rio Grande* was released, it was certainly no less fun watching this master scene-stealer at work. Likewise, the young Ben Johnson—another member of the Ford stock company—is extremely good as the heroic trooper trying to stay one step behind the Indians and one step ahead of the hangman's noose. Claude Jarman, Jr. gives a natural and likable performance in the key role of Wayne's son.

The film builds to a climax when Wayne contradicts government policy and illegally crosses the Rio Grande into Mexico to pursue Apaches who have kidnapped a wagon filled with children. The resulting action sequences are impressively done, and some realism is added when Wayne nearly dies from an arrow. This counters one of the faults of many of Ford's battle scenes between cavalry and Indians. Although superbly directed, he generally makes the mistake of never showing any Army casualties. Despite thousands of rounds being fired, Ford usually shows only the Indians taking any losses. This often results in a lessening of suspense, as we come to believe the soldiers are invincible. Here, however, it is actually "touch and go" for a short while for Wayne, and at the film's finale, we see him uncharacteristically being dragged

55

into the fort while lying helpless on a stretcher. This adds a sense of realism that is occasionally missing from Ford's otherwise excellent battle sequences.

The filming of *Rio Grande* resulted in a widely circulated anecdote. While on location in Utah, the cast decided to put on an amateur "talent show" at a nearby high school all for the entertainment of the locals. Ford persuaded Wayne and the other cast members to join the Sons of the Pioneers in concert. Wayne, not known for his singing skills, was happily bellowing away, safe in the knowledge that his off-key voice would be masked by the more versatile professional singers. Then Ford—always the joker—signalled for the entire ensemble, except Wayne, to leave the stage. Wayne was left by himself to sing the remainder of the song solo. The joke was probably less injurious to him than it was to the audience who had to have this fate inflicted upon them. However, they responded with a standing ovation to reward Wayne's courage in not being driven from the stage in fear by Ford's practical joke.

It has also been reported that an additional scene was planned for the epilogue of the film in which Wayne would be transferred to London by the Army as punishment for entering Mexico against orders. Ford later found—probably correctly—that the scene was extraneous and therefore never actually filmed it. Although the finished movie leaves Wayne's fate unanswered, we can assume the Duke prevailed and retained his command. The Army could allow him to do no less. After all, John Wayne was responsible for winning the West single-handed. Well, at least on the screen.

THE QUIET MAN (1952)

Cast: John Wayne, Maureen O'Hara, Barry Fitzgerald, Ward Bond, Victor McLaglen, Mildred Natwick, Francis Ford, Eileen Crowe. *Director:* John Ford. *Screenplay:* Frank S. Nugent. *From the Short Story* "Green Rushes" by Maurice Walsh. *Music:* Victor Young. *Released by* Republic Pictures. *Running Time:* 129 Minutes.

All right, I'm going to say it up front and risk the wrath of millions of Wayne fans and film historians: *The Quiet Man* is NOT a great film. This statement is undoubtedly going to be equated by many as tantamount to insulting Mother Theresa. However, the movie is so completely simplistic in its storyline and execution that it never becomes overly exciting, despite its celebrated climactic brawl. In fact, much of the movie is filled with hopelessly cliched characters involved with hopelessly cliched shenanigans. Its technical merits are obvious: Winton Hoch's cinematography is stunning, and the gorgeous Technicolor processing makes *The Quiet Man* a visual treat. The performances are all top notch, and Victor Young's lush musical score haunts the mind long after the film is over. In its day, this John Ford-directed Oscar winner was obviously an innovative and inventive knee-slapper. Time, however, has hardened audiences and *The Quiet Man*'s simple virtues now appear to be somewhat old hat.

That said, it should also be stated that, simplicity aside, *The Quiet Man* is great fun to watch. One must also give Ford his due: it is unlike any of his other collaborations with John Wayne, and

he dared to bring out a tender side of the Duke that was somewhat surprising to the actor's fans. His casting of Maureen O'Hara was truly inspired, and of all their teamings on-screen, *The Quiet Man* generates the most electricity and sexuality that Wayne and O'Hara had ever been permitted to display on the screen.

Wayne is a noted prizefighter who retires to his birthplace—a tiny Irish hamlet, where he hopes to marry and work a modest farm. Rich by local standards, Wayne finds his neighbor's preoccupation with status and income disconcerting, but quickly falls in love with the town and its people. He also becomes smitten with a beautiful local girl (O'Hara) whom he is determined to wed. Her loutish brother (Victor McLaglen), however, dislikes Wayne due to some convoluted business dealings between the two, and must be tricked into approving the marriage. Learning of the deception, he refuses to pay Wayne his sister's dowry—a major insult as the marriage can never be fully recognized under Irish custom until this is done. The entire script is basically a series of incidents showing Wayne's increasing frustration with trying to placate his new wife by convincing his nemesis to pay the dowry. Finally, his tolerance of playing "by the rules" runs out, and he confronts McLaglen in one of the screen's best-orchestrated fight sequences. As with all such brawls in Wayne films, no one gets seriously injured, and the combatants inevitably become close friends at the finale, leaving everyone deliriously happy.

It is doubtful that Ford, in a virtual homage to his roots in the Old Sod, ever made a more cheerful movie than *The Quiet Man*. Its cliches may be many: the supporting cast contains every Irish stereotype known to man (including the obligatory legion of lovable priests) and the plot has the required chestnut about Wayne hiding his secret fears—his accidental killing of an opponent in the ring some years before—to fight McLaglen. However, to some degree, it is precisely because of these familiar characters and situations that *The Quiet Man* takes on a fairy-tale quality that makes it completely removed from the real world. In Ford's Ireland there are no social problems (although a fleeting reference is

THE ENRAPTURED LOVERS

made to the I.R.A.). The women are virginal and the town bully has a big heart after all. If this is not the way the world is, Ford seems to be saying, then, dammit let's at least allow ourselves the luxury of pretending it is for two hours.

If there is one thing that makes *The Quiet Man* and some of Ford's other films difficult to be appreciated by modern cinema audiences, it is his treatment of women. It is actually jarring to see the way females could be presented onscreen just a few decades ago, when such film treatment today would be greeted with ridicule or contempt. Nowhere is Ford's chauvinism more apparent than in *The Quiet Man*. Although O'Hara's

THE TROUBLED BRIDE AND GROOM

character is at all times respected and desired, she is the typical Ford woman—that is, completely subservient to the men around her. She is allowed to be spunky and moody, but in the end, her ultimate desire in life is to please her husband without losing the respect of her brother. When she exerts her independence and attempts to leave town, Wayne "resolves" the situation by pulling in the reins. He drags her over hill and dale in full view of the entire town, at one point cheerfully accepting the birch stick from a woman to be used to "beat the young lady." Naturally, O'Hara comes to enjoy this aggressive side of Wayne, and announces that she'll go home to make the supper while Duke squares off with McLaglen.

Wayne has repeated this humiliation of his leading ladies many times in his career (notably in *McLintock!* and *Donovan's Reef*) and one hates to be a prude about such matters. There is nothing wrong with such good-natured fare onscreen, but, as stated before, such chauvinism makes it a bit more difficult to relate to the plot in today's era of liberated females.

The Quiet Man was one of the most honored films of 1952. It also presented Wayne with an opportunity to broaden his acting skills, and he gives a refreshing performance as a thoughtful, rational man who resorts to violence only as a last resort. He's quite wonderful here, as are the deliciously impish performances of the other members of the Ford stock company: Ward Bond, Victor McLaglen and Francis Ford ("Pappy's" brother). There is also able support from Mildred Natwick and from Barry Fitzgerald as—surprise—a lovable Irish drunk. Ford him-

59

POLITELY REJECTED BY MAUREEN O'HARA

self won the Oscar for direction, but, sadly, Wayne was not nominated himself.

The Quiet Man marked Wayne's last association with Republic Pictures, the studio where he had worked for many years. Wayne was upset with studio head Herbert Yates, who refused to come to terms with him about financing Duke's proposed film version of *The Alamo*. Yates insisted the project be done on a low budget, whereas Wayne insisted that at least $3-million be spent to insure the kind of epic production he had in mind. When Yates balked, Wayne threatened to leave the studio. Yates called his bluff, and Wayne went to Warner Bros. where he starred in some major films of the middle phase of his career. Republic Pictures could not survive long without Wayne, and several years later, the studio closed its doors.

60

HONDO (1953)

Cast: John Wayne, Geraldine Page, Ward Bond, Michael Pate, James Arness, Rodolfo Acosta, Leo Gordon, Tom Irish, Lee Aaker, Paul Fix. *Director:* John Farrow. *Screenplay:* James Edward Grant. *From the Story* "The Gift of Cochise" by Louis L'Amour. *Music:* Emil Newman and Hugo Friedhofer. A Wayne-Fellows Production *Released by* Warner Bros. *Running Time:* 83 Minutes.

Hondo is alternately one of John Wayne's most highly acclaimed and least-seen films. It has been out of public circulation for reasons unknown since the early 1980s, when it received a single showing on CBS. Since that time, the film has all but vanished, along with such other Wayne movies as *The High and the Mighty*, *Island in the Sky* and *McLintock!* None of these films have, at this writing, surfaced on video, and it has been speculated that complications concerning the legal rights of the movies are to blame. Whatever the reason, movie lovers and Wayne fans have been deprived of again enjoying some of his best efforts.

Hondo began as a project for Glenn Ford, with the Duke producing through his production company, Wayne-Fellows. Ford had starred previously in the Wayne-produced *Plunder in the Sun*, and Duke was anxious to employ the popular star once again. Trouble arose, however, when Ford learned that *Plunder*'s director John Farrow had been signed to helm *Hondo*. Ford disliked the man, and was not eager to work with him again.

IN ACTION AS HONDO LANE

JOHN WAYNE
...They called him
"Hondo"
First she was afraid he'd stay– then she was afraid he wouldn't...
HOT BLOODED WITH THE HEAT OF THE PLAINS THAT BRED HIM -SILENT AS GUNSMOKE -A STRANGER TO ALL BUT THE SURLY DOG AT HIS SIDE...
All the vast grandeur of the Southwest shown as never before possible
IN COLOR BY WARNERCOLOR
PRESENTED BY WARNER BROS. AND INTRODUCING
GERALDINE PAGE
WITH WARD BOND · MICHAEL PATE · JAMES ARNESS
SCREEN PLAY BY JAMES EDWARD GRANT
PRODUCED BY ROBERT FELLOWS
DIRECTED BY JOHN FARROW
A WAYNE-FELLOWS PRODUCTION DISTRIBUTED BY WARNER BROS.

WAYNE AS HONDO IMMORTALIZED IN FLORIDA'S STARS HALL OF FAME

who was in the process of trying to secure a divorce from his tempestuous wife Chata. While the proceedings were dragging on, Wayne had fallen in love with future wife Pilar, whom he could not allow to visit the set for fear of stirring rumors that might affect the divorce settlement. Adding to the tension were the record temperatures, which soared occasionally to 126 degrees. Indeed, the desert sand was so hot that the dog who accompanies Wayne onscreen had to have medication placed on his paws several times a day to prevent the pooch from being scalded.

Not all of the problems were limited to weather, however. Wayne was less than fond of co-star Geraldine Page, a stage actress who had recently taken Broadway by storm. *Hondo* was her first starring film, and she and Wayne found that their acting styles clashed almost immediately. Wayne accused her of not knowing anything about the film industry, and made some not very subtle references to her alleged aversion to soap and water. The Duke also found Page's manners and habits to be quite crude, and once told Pilar that he was shocked to see Page eating mashed potatoes with her fingers. Whether any of this was actually the case will never be known, but it is safe to say that filming *Hondo* was not one of Wayne's happier experiences, despite his status as boss as well as star.

To make life a little easier on location, Wayne had brought along sons Michael and Patrick, both of whom were teenagers trying to get into some aspect of the movie business. Pat was assigned to work with the property master, whereas Michael was an apprentice to assistant director Bob Morrison. What was conspicuously absent from studio press releases was the fact that Morrison happened to be Wayne's brother. Duke had employed Bob through his production company on occasion, but the sibling had always lived his life in the shadow of his older brother. Wayne was also comforted by the presence of his co-stars Ward Bond, James Arness and Paul Fix, all of whom he considered to be close personal friends.

During the tense production of *Hondo*, Wayne was visited by John Ford, who always found it difficult not to stir up trouble on any project in

Wayne refused to fire Farrow from the project, and upon reviewing the script by old buddy James Edward Grant, found the idea of playing the title character himself to be appealing.

Location shooting began in the remote town of Carmargo, Mexico. The town itself consisted of a few shacks and a cantina, and it wasn't long before the cast and crew began counting the days until the film was finished—among them Wayne,

POSTERS

SIX-SHEET

THREE-SHEET

ONE-SHEET

ACCESSORIES

INSERT CARD

COLORED 22 x 28 (1)
Slide Also Available

COLORED 11 x 14s (8)

THEATRE IMPRINT

WINDOW CARD

40x60 Style Y
Style Z also available

Order campaign material, except where otherwise indicated, from National Screen Service Exchanges.

VARIOUS PUBLICITY POSTERS

which he was not personally involved. Ford took one look at the non-glamorous Geraldine Page, and scoffed that audiences would never buy the idea of Wayne falling head-over-heels for such a "plain Jane." Incredibly, the script was amended to include a self-deprecating line in which Page refers to herself as "homely." Duke's gallant Hondo Lane then makes like a good guy and states that there is more value to a person than his or her looks. Just how Page felt about this rather insulting amendment to the script is not known. However, she did get the last laugh by receiving the picture's sole Oscar nomination (her first of eight). Ford can also be faulted for not recognizing that it was precisely the fact that Page lacked glamour that separated the film from the countless other "horse operas" in which frontier women parade around the barnyard in designer clothes and bouffant hair-dos.

Hondo has generally been compared in quality to *Shane*, with the latter film usually reaping the lion's share of the praise. It is true that *Shane* is an infinitely more memorable film, probably because its director—George Stevens—had a far more distinctive style than did journeyman John Farrow. Yet, *Hondo* is so good on so many levels that it would be unfair not to recognize its many virtues. The plot is quite simple. Wayne is a mysterious drifter with a reputation (presumably unfair, 'natch) as a ruthless gunslinger. He encounters Angie Lowe (Page) a self-sufficient woman trying to cope with raising her small son Johnny in the absence of her husband. Wayne befriends her, but warns her that the Apaches are on the warpath. Page refuses to leave, stating she has always enjoyed a good relationship with the Indians.

Her confidence is re-enforced when Apache chief Victorio takes her son under his wing, even as he wages war against the other settlers. A subplot finds Wayne encountering Page's husband, and killing him in self-defense. In returning to Page's ranch, he is captured by Apaches and spared only when he is mistaken for the husband. When Victorio is killed, a more belligerent chief forces Page to flee with Wayne and an Army escort. A massive battle ensues, after which Wayne and Page realize they are in love and make plans for a new life in California.

The script for *Hondo* is decidely mediocre. What makes it unique is that this is a very mature

Western made in an age in which only a handful of films of the genre rose above the standard shoot-'em-up level. There are many subtleties in *Hondo* which endear the characters to the audience. Wayne's past, for instance, is hinted at just enough for us to ponder his background. We never do learn anything about him, and this mystery keeps our interest in his personality and actions. Wayne's performance is excellent indeed and, personal feelings to the contrary, he is more than matched by Page, whose acting avoids all of the cliches generally found in performances by actresses in similar roles.

The action sequences are very exciting, and there is ample stuntwork on display, particularly in a chase sequence in which Wayne must ride his horse down a sheer cliff. The supporting cast is kept in the background, with Ward Bond playing the role of "sidekick" usually enacted by Gabby Hayes or Walter Brennan. Again, we find Wayne's reputation as an Indian hater unjustified. As with most of his films, the Apaches in *Hondo* are merely defending themselves against unsavory whites who have consciously broken a treaty. Those who defame Wayne and his presentation of Indians in his films would do well to actually view movies like *Hondo*, *Fort Apache* and *Chisum*. They would undoubtedly be surprised to see that Wayne's treatment and sympathy with the Indians far outspeaks his occasional political comments to the contrary.

Hondo was filmed in 3-D, and during the action scenes there are a few obvious shots that were designed to make audiences duck for cover. To director Farrow's credit, however, there are no irrelevant or superfluous scenes included simply to take advantage of the 3-D process. Despite improvements in the viewing process for 3-D films, audiences had tired of the gimmick by the time *Hondo* was released. It played for a short while in 3-D, but most theaters presented it in a standard "flat" version. The movie was nonetheless a big hit at the box-office, and, despite the difficulty in viewing it today, it remains one of Wayne's best remembered movies.

TRIVIA NOTE: As an inside joke, Wayne portrayed a drifter named Lane to Ann-Margret's Mrs. Lowe in the 1973 film The *Train Robbers*.

THE SEARCHERS (1956)

Cast: John Wayne, Jeffrey Hunter, Vera Miles, Ward Bond, Natalie Wood, John Qualen, Olive Carey, Henry Brandon, Ken Curtis, Harry Carey, Jr., Pippa Scott, Walter Coy, Hank Worden. *Director:* John Ford. *Screenplay:* Frank S. Nugent, *Based Upon the Novel by* Alan LeMay. *Music:* Max Steiner. *Released by* Warner Bros. *Running Time:* 119 Minutes.

The word "masterpiece" should not be used too casually in reviewing films, for if it is, it might dilute the impact of reserving that designation for the relatively small number of cinematic works

deserving the label. *The Searchers* is a masterpiece. At least by the standards of most people who know something about the art of moviemaking. It certainly is the highpoint of the collaborative efforts of John Wayne and John Ford, and could easily be acclaimed as the best film of either man's career.

Yet, *The Searchers* was not regarded in its time as the classic it has become. The film received generally positive—and sometimes ecstatic—reviews, as well as a healthy box-office gross. Yet, it remained relatively undiscussed and ignored throughout the years following its release. In

DUKE IS DEPUTIZED BY WARD BOND

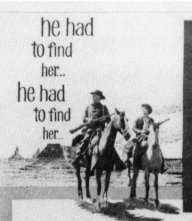

WAYNE AS ETHAN EDWARDS—ONE OF THE ALL-TIME GREAT SCREEN PERFORMANCES

fact, it was not until the early Seventies that a younger generation of film critics began to do more than dismiss Ford and Wayne's work as indistinguishable horse operas. Almost overnight, it was chic to admire both men, and eventually *The Searchers* began popping up on critics' listings of the ten greatest movies produced.

Although Wayne would eventually win the Oscar for his performance as Rooster Cogburn in *True Grit*, it might be argued that the award was more appropriate for his work in *The Searchers*. Certainly, the character of Ethan Edwards ranks as one of the most fascinating and perplexing roles ever undertaken by an actor. Wayne plays the part beautifully, and, as with *Red River*'s Tom

Dunson, it is to his credit that he was not afraid to portray an unsympathetic character. Wayne himself described Edwards as "a man dedicated to the wrong cause." He is all but heartless, and displays few redeeming values.

The film begins with a stunning shot of a cabin door opening to reveal a lone rider slowly approaching a farm house. As a woman strains her eyes to see who the visitor might be, the beautiful theme music by Max Steiner provides enough atmosphere that, within seconds, we feel as though we, too, are living the lonely experience of life on the plains. The rider turns out to be Ethan Edwards, about whom little is revealed throughout the course of the story. As portrayed by Wayne, there is every indication he is a man with a past, but is too dangerous to be questioned about it. Wayne has returned from parts unknown to be reconciled with his brother's family. We get the impression that Wayne does not want to be there, but apparently had nowhere else to go. After a cautious welcome, it becomes clear that Wayne is not exactly welcomed by his brother Aaron (Walter Coy). His obstinence in revealing anything about his actions during the years of his absence troubles those around him, and there are plenty of hints that he may be wanted for crimes.

Much about Wayne's character is of fascination to the family and to those of us in the audience. Ford is wise not to reveal very much, leaving the character all the more interesting for what we do not know. It is implied that at one point Wayne and his sister-in-law were in love, and there are indications the emotions remain. Again, nothing is blatantly stated, but the underlying tension that remains unspoken by the people in the house is obviously the result of rather strained relationships.

Wayne is immediately regarded as a "know-it-all" and is idolized by the children of the family, in contrast to their more traditional, hard-working but ultimately vulnerable father. Wayne makes a fatal mistake, however, by joining a posse to investigate some cattle rustling. Once they are far from the ranch, there is a sickening realization by Wayne and the others that they have been duped by Indians into leaving the ranch un-

DON'T ASK HIM WHAT HE SAW. DON'T EVER ASK HIM WHAT HE SAW. JOHN WAYNE— AND A GIRL HE HAD TO FIND! WARNER BROS. PRESENT THE C. V. WHITNEY PICTURE, DIRECTED BY 4-TIME ACADEMY AWARD WINNER JOHN FORD, "THE SEARCHERS"

Co-Starring *Jeffrey Hunter Vera Miles • Ward Bond Natalie Wood • Screen Play by Frank S. Nugent Executive Producer Merian C. Cooper Associate Producer Patrick Ford VistaVision and Technicolor*

TEASER POSTER

protected and vulnerable to a raid. Wayne's performance hits its peak here. There are just a few seconds in which the camera records his reaction at the precise moment of the recognition that his error has doomed his family. Outwardly, he reacts cooly, but one can see a look of sheer despair and anger reflected in his eyes. It is a poignant and moving moment.

The attack on the ranch is loaded with tension as Aaron tries to forestall his families' realization of their impending doom. We never see the

70

approaching Indians, but feel gut-wrenching panic as the family tries fruitlessly to shield their house from the savage onslaught. Your heart breaks as the parents push their little girl out of the window and instruct her to hide. The girl obliges and in her innocence cannot recognize the fate of parents and siblings. The assault is never shown, and yet it remains a devastingly suspenseful scene.

Wayne returns home in the company of Martin Pawley (Jeffrey Hunter), a half-breed whom Wayne had saved from an Indian massacre some years before. As the family's adopted son, Hunter is shattered by the slaughter. Both he and Wayne vow to track the Indians responsible and vent their own brand of justice. Wayne, however, is not an easy man to ride with. He disavows working with a posse, because he can't tolerate taking orders from its leader (Ward Bond). He detests Hunter because of his Indian blood, and makes no pretenses about his standing as an all-around bigot. Following the massacre, Wayne's mission on the surface is to rescue the only members of the family to survive: his two nieces, played by Natalie Wood and Pippa Scott. However, as the months turn to years, it becomes clear that he is also driven as much by the desire to spill Indian blood.

Wayne's resolve is strengthened when he finds Scott butchered. He begins to insinuate that even if Wood is still alive, she is by now no better than an Indian and should be put out of her misery. Hunter continues to plod along on a seemingly hopeless cause, partly to insure that Wayne does not murder his own niece.

Eventually, Wood is located, but Indians prevent Wayne from fulfilling his vow to shoot her. He continues to press on, determined to kill the war party chief responsible for his obsession. When the tribe is located, Wayne and Bond lead a cavalry raid, during which Wood runs desperately from her would-be murderer. When she is finally cornered, she hides her head and prepares to die. Instead, in one of the screen's great

moments, Wayne gently picks her up and tells her it's time to go home. The next few minutes have no dialogue, only Steiner's theme music and the Sons of the Pioneers singing the title ballad. We watch in a brilliantly directed sequence as Wayne reunites both Natalie Wood and Jeffrey Hunter with friends of the family. As all of the others walk into the house, Wayne is left standing alone—already a forgotten figure. Knowing he has no place with these people, he pauses, and then turns to walk toward his horse. As he prepares to ride off to destinations unknown, the cabin door which opened to greet him at the beginning of the film, slowly swings shut one final time, excluding Wayne from the lives of those around him forever. I believe this, coupled with the climactic scene in which Wayne chooses to save rather than murder Wood, to be among the most moving and superbly directed sequences in any film.

Wayne dominates *The Searchers* with a powerhouse performance that makes it inconceivable that he was ignored again at Oscar time. Wayne felt so good about his work in this film, that his youngest son was named Ethan in honor of the central character. Duke gets excellent support from all the cast, with Hunter giving his best performance as the perfect foil for Wayne. As with all Ford films, the stock company is ever-present and better than ever. Particularly good are Ward Bond and John Qualen.

Of the 250 technicians involved with this film, over 100 of them had worked with Ford at least five times. They all seemed to try a little harder on this effort. Monument Valley has never looked so magnificent, and John Ford's skill behind the camera has never been more apparent. In fact, "Pappy" considered *The Searchers* to be so good that he seriously considered retiring from films rather than attempting to top it. Happily, this never occurred. Although Ford would never actually exceed the quality of *The Searchers*, his efforts in his remaining years proved to be very valuable contributions to the cinema.

TRIVIA NOTE: Singer Buddy Holly was said to be so impressed by Wayne's performance as Ethan Edwards that he was inspired to write his song classic "That'll Be the Day." The title of the song was taken from Wayne's catch phrase which is used extensively in the film.

RIO BRAVO (1959)

Cast: John Wayne, Dean Martin, Angie Dickinson, Ricky Nelson, Walter Brennan, Ward Bond, John Russell, Claude Akins, Harry Carey, Jr., *Director:* Howard Hawks. *Screenplay:* Jules Furthman and Leigh Brackett, *From a Short Story by* B.H.McCampell. *Music:* Dimitri Tiomkin. *Released by* Warner Bros. *Running Time:* 141 Minutes.

Among the major career achievements of all involved, *Rio Bravo* must certainly rank high on everyone's list. It is that rarest of gems: a virtually perfect motion picture entertainment. Despite its abnormally long running time, the film is so good on every level that we are generally sorry to see it end. The pace is leisurely, but director Howard Hawks uses his time wisely to let his audience identify with a fascinating cast of characters.

For this writer, *Rio Bravo* represents the quintessential John Wayne movie. He has never looked better on screen, and his troubled and subdued performance lends an aura of mystery to this loner. We constantly want to know more about him, but never succeed in doing so. As with the most memorable Western heroes, the more that is left to our imaginations, the more haunting the character becomes.

Rio Bravo presents Wayne as John T. Chance, the silent, but strong-willed sheriff of a small town on the Mexican border. The film opens with a stunning and innovative sequence as we see a drunken gunman (Claude Akins) murder a man in a saloon. Wayne enters to arrest him and is knocked unconscious by the town drunk, who obviously has reason to resent him. This entire sequence, we realize later, is played without dialogue, and none is needed. Hawks heightens the tension and sense of foreboding by concentrating on Dimitri Tiomkin's music and Russell Harlan's camerawork. The scene next switches to the drunk helping Wayne arrest the culprit.

ON THE SET

We later learn that the drunk is named Dude (played by Dean Martin) and he had been Wayne's deputy before allowing girl troubles to drive him to drink. When the influential brother of the murderer in Wayne's jail cell vows to use a virtual army to free him, Wayne is reluctantly forced to accept Martin's offer to clean himself up and help.

Help is something the Duke can use, as his

JOHN WAYNE | **DEAN MARTIN** | **RICKY NELSON** | **RIO BRAVO** | ANGIE DICKINSON · WALTER BRENNAN WARD BOND · JOHN ____ RUSSELL

TECHNICOLOR® from WARNER BROS.

WAYNE AND BRENNAN WAGE WAR ON THE VILLAINS

only other deputy is Stumpy (who else but Walter Brennan), a cantankerous, crippled old man who is nonetheless fearless and quite competent when wielding a double-barreled shotgun. It is interesting to note that in many ways these early scenes in *Rio Bravo* could be viewed as Wayne's answer to *High Noon*. The Duke openly denounced that earlier film as un-American. He resented the storyline in which the only honorable person in town is the sheriff, who finds to his disappointment that not a single friend or neighbor will come to his aid against a group of killers. In *Rio Bravo*, pains are taken to show that while Wayne is hopelessly outnumbered, it is not for lack of courage on the part of the local citizenry. Ward Bond appears as an old friend

and cattle owner who volunteers to help out before being gunned down for his efforts. This causes his protegé, Colorado (Ricky Nelson), a young gunslinger, to reluctantly join the cause. Wayne is also aided by Feathers (Angie Dickinson), a beautiful saloon girl along with the meek owner of a local hotel (Pedro Gonzalez-Gonzalez.) Hawks eventually cut out another scene in which Harry Carey, Jr., appeared as a willing, but inept volunteer.

The rest of the film depicts the efforts of the principal characters to keep their prisoner under guard until a federal judge arrives for a trial. Meanwhile, the bad guys are assembling an entire army to wage war on the lawmen. It is this element of hopelessness that gives *Rio Bravo* the

JOHN WAYNE | DEAN MARTIN | RICKY NELSON | RIO BRAVO   ANGIE DICKINSON · WALTER BRENNAN
WARD BOND · JOHN   RUSSELL
TECHNICOLOR® from WARNER BROS

WAYNE IS TRICKED INTO LEAVING THE JAIL

suspenseful edge lacking in most westerns. While we strongly suspect none of the heroes is going to meet an untimely end, we can never be too sure. Wayne plays somewhat against type by being an all-too-fallible human being. He even allows himself to be lured out of the jail in an obvious and successful attempt to kidnap him. For once we feel Wayne is totally helpless, as he must lead the villains back to the jail to free the prisoner. One suspects Wayne's character might actually have to do this in defiance of all his principles. However, we soon see there is method to his madness as he knows that Brennan would rather see him perish before betraying any convictions. It is the "old cripple" who saves the day by blasting Wayne's captors with his trusty shotgun. It is just one of a series of memorable sequences in this superb film.

There is a great deal of action in *Rio Bravo*, but, surprisingly, some of the best moments are the quieter scenes. Wayne's awkward and romantic plays for Dickinson are for once realistic and convincing. Hawks keeps him from overplaying such sequences, as Wayne has been guilty of doing under less persuasive directors. Likewise, there are marvelous moments in which literally nothing happens, such as the scene in which all the principals listen intently as Dean and Ricky pass the time singing cowboy songs. Wayne doesn't join in, but the look in his eyes shows the quiet pride he has in this small but brave group of men who are willing to die in order to help him.

WAYNE AND RICKY NELSON ELIMINATE SOME COMPETITION

The film comes to a crackling climax in which Wayne and company wage war on their adversaries who have commandeered a farmhouse. As Brennan tosses sticks of dynamite at the house, Duke, Dean and Ricky ignite them with gunshots causing the complete destruction of the premises. This is the most entertaining part of the film due very much to the appearance of Brennan's Stumpy. Cackling and barking orders and insults at Wayne, he is absolutely hilarious. Brennan's endearing performance in *Rio Bravo* is not only one of the best supporting performances in a Wayne film, but it should have been nominated for an Oscar.

There are plenty of other individuals who deserve praise for their work in this landmark Western. Angie Dickinson gives a terrific performance as the bad girl with a heart of gold. For once the role is not sanitized, and we really come to believe this is a woman who not only enjoys sex, but has absolutely no regrets about it. Dean Martin had already quieted skeptics who assumed he would fade into oblivion after he and Jerry Lewis went their separate ways. His performances the previous year opposite Marlon Brando in *The Young Lions* and Frank Sinatra in *Some Come Running* proved that, if anything, the partnership with Lewis was holding back some considerable acting skills. Fortunately, these are again quite evident in *Rio Bravo*. As the pathetic drunk who regains his pride, Martin is alternately sympathetic and strong or weak-willed and incompetent. The scene in which he describes to Wayne the tortures of going "cold turkey" from liquor are among the dramatic highlights of Martin's career.

If there is a weak link in the casting it is Ricky Nelson, who was obviously given the role of Colorado to capitalize on his fame as a teenage idol of the late 1950s. He handles his role competently, but he is far too gentle looking to be taken seriously as a notorious gunslinger. Yet, one must give him credit for holding his own among the heavyweight cast. At no time is his performance distracting or harmful to the proceedings.

Sadly, *Rio Bravo* (which Wayne and Hawks would virtually remake a decade later as *Rio Lobo*) would mark the last motion picture teaming of Duke and longtime friend and frequent co-star Ward Bond. The two men would later appear in an episode of Bond's hit TV series *Wagon Train*, in which Wayne would make a cameo appearance. Appropriately, that episode—titled "The Colter Craven Story"—would be directed by John Ford. It would mark the final collaboration of these three men, as Bond died of a heart attack shortly thereafter, leaving both Wayne and Ford devastated by the loss and the inescapable knowledge that they, too, were entering their twilight years.

THE HORSE SOLDIERS (1959)

Cast: John Wayne, William Holden, Constance Towers, Althea Gibson, Hoot Gibson, Anna Lee, Russell Simpson, Stan Jones, Hank Worden, Carleton Young. *Director:* John Ford. *Screenplay:* John Lee Mahin and Martin Rackin. *From the Novel by* Harold Sinclair. *Music:* David Buttolph. *Released by* United Artists. *Running Time:* 119 Minutes.

Life has always held three great mysteries for me: (1) what is the origin of the pyramids? (2) what, if anything, is the meaning of life itself? and (3) why is *The Horse Soldiers* consistently dismissed in any examination of the great works of John Ford and John Wayne? The first two questions might be more important than the last, but the point is that *The Horse Soldiers* is a major achievement for

AS COL. MARLOWE

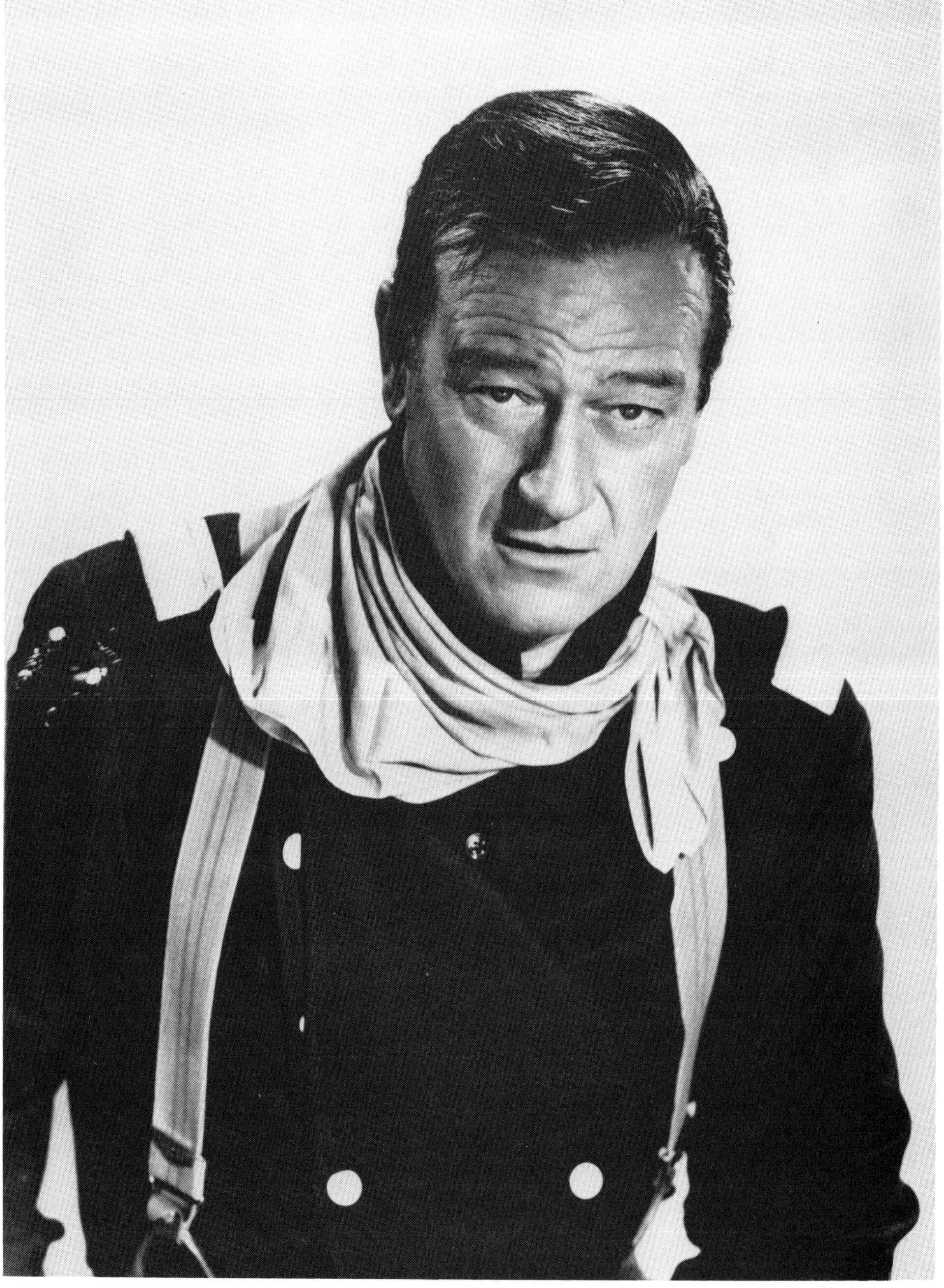

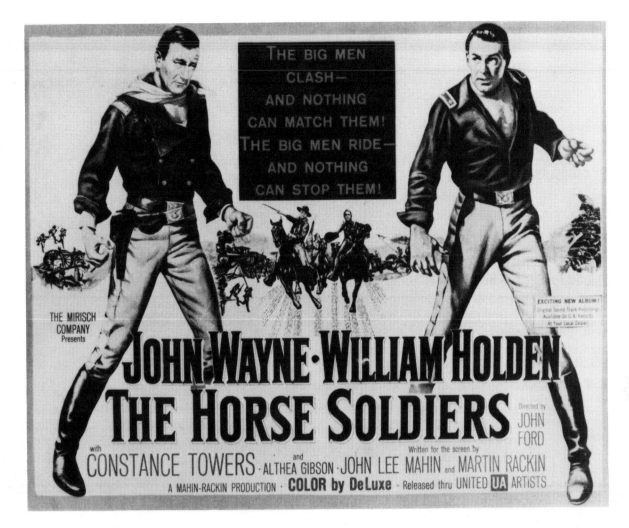

THE BIG MEN
CLASH—
AND NOTHING
CAN MATCH THEM!
THE BIG MEN RIDE—
AND NOTHING
CAN STOP THEM!

THE MIRISCH
COMPANY
Presents

JOHN WAYNE · WILLIAM HOLDEN
THE HORSE SOLDIERS

Directed by
JOHN FORD

with
CONSTANCE TOWERS · ALTHEA GIBSON · JOHN LEE MAHIN and MARTIN RACKIN

Written for the screen by

A MAHIN-RACKIN PRODUCTION · COLOR by DeLuxe · Released thru UNITED UA ARTISTS

EXCITING NEW ALBUM!
Original Sound Track Recording
Available On U.A. Records
At Your Local Dealer

both men and yet it is rarely discussed in any detail by film historians.

I'll admit I have a sentimental attraction to the movie because it is the first Wayne film I can recall seeing. However, despite my prejudice, I believe this ranks with the very best work of both Wayne and Ford's careers. The movie did not come about easily. Wayne had his own production company, as did Ford. When William Holden signed on as Wayne's co-star, it became even more entangled as he, too, insisted on becoming involved in the technicalities of the contract. This caused major headaches for the producers, but eventually a compromise made everyone happy. In her book *Duke: My Life With John Wayne*, Pilar Wayne relates that the resulting contract for the principals was so lengthy that it ran over 250 pages. Both Wayne and Holden

were "hot" at the box-office. Holden, in particular, was riding a wave of popularity due to his starring role in *The Bridge on the River Kwai*. This pairing of superstars did not come cheap for United Artists. Wayne and Holden each demanded—and received—$750,000 plus a percentage of the profits. The salaries made headlines, as few other actors had ever before been paid so handsomely for a single performance.

The movie details a factual Union raid on Confederate territory during the early days of the Civil War. With the Union armies hurting from the underestimated resolve of the Southern troops, General Grant assigns Wayne's Colonel Marlowe the dubious task of "sneaking" 800 men through the Deep South to destroy the supply depot at Newton Station, Louisiana. It is vital to cut Rebel supply lines if Grant is to succeed in his most important goal—the capture of Richmond.

Wayne's Marlowe is a hard-bitten character almost devoid of the kind of sentimentalism which is usually shown to soften Duke's image. He is tough with his men and his peers, and rarely cracks a smile. Things don't improve much when he learns his streamlined force is to be "burdened" with surgeon Holden. It appears Wayne despises all doctors since his wife died as the result of a mis-diagnosis some years before. The two men are at odds immediately, with Holden failing to be intimidated by his superior.

When the regiment arrives in the South, they commandeer the plantation of Hannah Hunter (Constance Towers), a flirtatious belle who tries to charm Wayne and Holden with an all-too-obvious "helpless female" act. When Holden discovers that Towers has overheard Wayne's strategies for destroying Newton Station, the "damned Yankees" have no choice but to take her along, accompanied by her slave Lukey (played by Olympic star Althea Gibson in her acting debut).

Towers proves to be rather independent, and almost alerts passing Rebel troops on a couple of occasions. Her hatred of Wayne softens a bit when she realizes that he hates the war and carnage as much as she does. The destruction of Newton Station is accomplished, but not before Wayne regretfully must fight off a determined, but out-gunned Confederate raid. With Rebel troops closing in for the kill, Duke and company prepare to make a daring and desperate charge against a fortified bridge, their only escape route. At this point, all loose ends come together. As Wayne prepares to leave Towers behind, he expresses the love for her that he had been hiding. He also learns to respect Holden when he sees the latter's professional ethics lead him to stay behind with the wounded, despite certain imprisonment at Andersonville. Wayne leads the inevitable charge and emerges victorious. He says goodbye to the heartbroken Towers, but not before tying her kerchief around his neck as a remembrance.

It is difficult to know where to begin listing all

WITH WILLIAM HOLDEN IN WASHINGTON D.C.
TO RECEIVE A COMMENDATION FROM THE CIVIL
WAR CENTENNIAL COMMISSION

of the great elements in *The Horse Soldiers*. Foremost, it should be said that the chemistry between Wayne and Holden is every bit as good as anyone might have expected. Their characters' mutual animosity gives the film an air of suspense and tension. Both men do very well with their roles, and the dialogue between them is most impressive and occasionally amusing. Towers is quite good, although her initial Southern belle routine is so overdone that not even a schoolboy would be duped by her. The supporting cast is conspicuously absent of the Wayne and Ford stock company members, although Hank Worden appears as his by now traditional demented but lovable eccentric.

'The Horse Soldiers' Roaring Civil War Drama Stars John Wayne, William Holden

Colorful Film Tells of Bold, Heroic Six-Hundred Mile Raid

Still HS-X-1   Mat 14
John Payne and William Holden are starred in a stirring Civil War drama, "The Horse Soldiers," which tells of a daring raid deep in Confederate territory. The picture, filmed in DeLuxe color, and directed by John Ford, opens .... at the .... Theatre through United Artists release.

Still HS-P7-G7   Mat 2A
John Wayne plays Lt. Colonel Marlowe who led a daring raid against a Confederate railroad stronghold and turned the tide of the Civil War. "The Horse Soldiers," filmed on location in DeLuxe color, will open .... at the .... Theatre through United Artists release.

(Advance Production Feature)

One of the most dramatic and exciting incidents of the Civil War supplies the fabric for the story of "The Horse Soldiers," the $6,500,000 epic production opening on .... at the .... Theatre through United Artists release.

This was the incredibly bold and heroic six-hundred mile raid through Confederate territory of Colonel Benjamin Grierson and his brigade of Union cavalry. Historians have credited this remarkable feat with having mercifully shortened the conflict by as much as a full year, with the saving of perhaps 150,000 lives.

John Wayne and William Holden are starred in "The Horse Soldiers," and two famous Gibsons—Hoot, the great cowboy star of yesteryear, and Althea, the awe-inspiring young Negro girl athlete—are featured. A lovely newcomer to pictures, Constance Towers makes her film debut in the drama.

Filmed in DeLuxe color on location in Mississippi and Louisiana, in the actual country through which Grierson's column made its famous raid, "The Horse Soldiers" is a Mirisch Company presentation. John Lee Mahin and Martin Rackin produced the film, and also wrote the screenplay, an adaptation of Harold Sinclair's best-selling novel.

'The Horse Soldiers'—John Ford's Most Lavish Film

(Prepared Review)

John Ford, Hollywood's foremost director of action spectacles, has outdone himself in the most lavish drama of thunderous adventure in his unreal career. It is "The Horse Soldiers," filmed in blazing color by DeLuxe, and tells the heroic story of Colonel Benjamin Grierson (in the picture he is called Marlowe) raid through 600 miles of Confederate territory to destroy Newton Station and thus become the turning point for the Northern victory in the Civil War. The picture which opened yesterday at the .... Theatre through United Artists release, captures all the gallantry, bravery and rough fighting of that time during of military operations.

Starred in the picture are John Wayne, as Marlowe, William Holden, as a medic attached to Marlowe's troop, and a newcomer to the screen, lovely Constance Towers, as a southern lady whose mansion is commandeered by Marlowe, and who subsequently is obliged to accompany his troops to Newton station. Also a newcomer to movies but already established

in the world of sports, Althea Gibson, gives a fine, warm portrayal as Miss Towers' companion on the hazardous journeys.

Wayne is an exceptional leader turned destroyer. His conflict on the screen is with himself as well as with Holden and Constance Towers, for his training and the ethics lead him to abhor all that war calls for. Holden has the same slant of inner conflict. As a doctor, the miraculousness of war and its destruction of mankind goes against everything he has stood and lived for. The two men clash from the start, for each stands at an opposite pole—one destroys, the other saves. It is a conflict between two strong personalities.

When Constance Towers enters the scene, the conflict becomes even more intense. She is a southerner, completely outraged by the invasion of her land. She cannot help for light everything Wayne stands for and tries to accomplish even when, as a woman, completely feminine, she finds herself drawn to a strong and determined man.

'The Horse Soldiers' Reconstructs Raid

(Production Feature)

Gen. Ulysses S. Grant, in April, 1863, was sitting before Vicksburg. He'd been looking at it for a year, and getting sick with the sight of it. Vicksburg was a troubler that the South with her men and her resources had fought that North to a near standstill. Grant knew that if he didn't take Vicksburg by that summer, he might not be able to take it at all, thus losing the war.

It was then he conceived the idea of sending a Union Cavalry Brigade from La Grange, Tennessee, through Mississippi to Newton Station 600 miles inside Confederate Territory. Newton Station was the supply center for Vicksburg. With Newton Station destroyed, Grant could take Vicksburg. With Vicksburg in Union hands, Grant could have Tennessee. Sherman loose in a notch to the sea, the Confederacy would be cut in two, and the war could be over, with the North victorious.

And that is the story told when "The Horse Soldiers" a movie set representing Newton Station, was reconstructed on a levee along side the Cane River near Natchitoches, Louisiana, is burned to the ground. "The Horse Soldiers" filmed in Color by DeLuxe and starring John Wayne and William Holden, will open .... at the .... Theatre through United Artists release.

For the record, the set depicting Newton Station, Mississippi, was an exact replica of the real Mc—, as it was on Saturday, April 24, 1863, the ninth day of Grierson's Raid, when the Union Garrison destroyed two trains, a large store of supplies, telegraph lines and all railroad yards and station.

"The Horse Soldiers" is one of the most elaborately produced films in recent years. Next to the salaries of the stars, the biggest slice of the budget was taken by the amazing trip. Hundreds of people actors, technicians, stunt men, administrative personnel—hundreds of horses, and uncounted tons of valuable equipment had to be trucked overland from Hollywood to the location site. And this story

Still WH-1   Mat 2G
William Holden is cast as a doctor attached to Lt. Colonel Marlowe's (John Wayne) cavalry troops on their daring raid deep into Confederate territory. "The Horse Soldiers," in color by DeLuxe, will open .... at the .... Theatre, through United Artists release.

The author of Grierson's raid was, actually, none other than General Ulysses S. Grant. In April of 1863, Vicksburg was under siege. Grant had been trying to take the river city for some ten months without success. At the time, the war was going badly for the North in the field. In Washington and in the newspapers it was said that Vicksburg be taken before the summer rolled, or that Grant could launch his called drive to overwhelm the Confederacy.

In desperation, the General conceived the scheme of sending a brigade of cavalry through hundreds of miles of rebel-held territory to attempt to destroy Newton Station, the all-important supply center for Vicksburg. He called Grierson in, outlined his plan, and the rest is history—some of the most exciting history of the entire colorful and tragic Civil War.

Good Reasons, All

Members of Hollywood's .... live in a blue, and a trick, or a trick .... indeed, they wonder why John Ford went to Louisiana to film scenes for "The Horse Soldiers," a Mirisch-Rackin Production for United Artists release, with John Wayne and William Holden in the starring roles. The picture, in color by DeLuxe, opens .... at the .... Theatre.

The answer could point out several things. The facts are different there than that furnished by Central Casting. About any weeping willows, but at last not in California to ride. And there are the guidelines found, but even more important is that in little has changed in the hinterland from the days of the Civil War.

An outstanding example with the telegraph lines. They are strung exactly as the telegraph lines were strung when Col. Grierson marched his Union cavalry column through Mississippi to Baton Rouge is one of the most daring military moves of history. No Civil War "raid" can point to the wires strung along the lines of march and use "if it wasn't so in the old days, because it be did. It's only since last generation.

"The Horse Soldiers" introduces blonde beauty Constance Towers to the screen. It is a screen version of the book of the same title which was a famed account of an actual event that took place when the War

Still HS-P13-G13   Mat 2D
Attractive, blonde Constance Towers makes her film debut as a southern lady taken prisoner by an invading Union Army. "The ....

A major "plus" in this film is William Clothier's beautiful cinematography and David Buttolph's fine musical score. Of all the music used in Ford's films, *The Horse Soldiers* boasts perhaps the finest soundtrack. There are also memorable ballads written for the film by Stan Jones. It is the action sequences that are generally the best things about a Ford film, and this one proves no exception. The raid on Newton Station is a veritable slaughter as a motley army of Confederates steadfastly run a gauntlet of Union firepower which decimates their ranks. Such scenes give you the impression that for all the violence in a John Ford Western, the director was well aware of the horrible side of war and its consequences. The other great sequence in the film is one in which a Confederate military school mobilizes its "troops," consisting of young boys who are told to do whatever they can to slow Wayne's advance on Newton Station. Unlike the ragtag army actually fighting for the Southern cause on the battlefields, the boys represent the illusion of how the South really envisioned the war—with pride and hope. Long columns of youngsters in pristine uniforms follow their elderly headmaster to the battlefield while an incredulous Union Army watches. The joke wears thin when the bullets start to fly. Wayne,

of course, will not combat the "enemy" and seems to enjoy retreating so that the boys can brag in the future about the day they "whipped the Yankees." When one of his men captures a drummer boy, Wayne instructs him to "spank the prisoner." It's a marvelous moment in an altogether splendid film.

Ironically, *The Horse Soldiers* was a box-office disappointment. It received fair-to-good reviews and was backed by a gigantic ad campaign, but audiences did not respond in high numbers. Ford himself had unpleasant memories of the film, as he was deeply depressed by the accidental death of a stuntman in one of the film's action sequences. It is my belief, however, that it is the last great epic to involve both Wayne and Ford. *The Man Who Shot Liberty Valance* would follow in 1962, and is also a classic. However, that film would be a much more intimate if violent drama, devoid of the great landscapes and sweeping action sequences that characterized most of the Ford/Wayne collaborations. Despite the fact that the film never received its due from critics or audiences, *The Horse Soldiers* was an appropriate vehicle to symbolize the end of the type of Western on which Ford and Wayne built their careers.

THE ALAMO (1960)

Cast: John Wayne, Richard Widmark, Laurence Harvey, Richard Boone, Frankie Avalon, Patrick Wayne, Linda Cristal, Joan O'Brien, Chill Wills, Joseph Calleia, Ken Curtis, Carlos Arruza. *Producer and Director:* John Wayne. *Screenplay:* James Edward Grant. *Music:* Dimitri Tiomkin. *Released by:* United Artists. *Running Time:* 161½ minutes. (original roadshow version: 192 minutes).

The Alamo is unique among John Wayne's films in that the incredible logistics of bringing this epic to the screen, along with the ensuing controversies following its release, have been given far greater voice than the merits or faults of the finished product. Because *The Alamo* is of interest not only to Wayne fans, but also to the large number of people who consider themselves afi-

cionados of anything to do with the historic battle, it is safe to say that few, if any, films have been so thoroughly examined in every way.

The story behind the making of this movie has been retold many times, and any book concerning the career of the Duke is likely to devote more space to *The Alamo* than any other film. On the assumption that most of the readers of this book have at least a peripheral knowledge of Wayne's dream to bring the story to the screen, I will summarize only the basics behind the difficulties *The Alamo* inspired. Indeed, with so many Alamo buffs analyzing everything written about the subject, it is unlikely that any exploration of the minute details which went into the movie would meet with everyone's satisfaction. There are plenty of people still around who were part of the film, but each one has such varying descrip-

tions of what happened, you have to wonder if they weren't working on different movies.

This much is undisputed: It was John Wayne's dream since the early Fifties to bring to the screen the heroic battle of the Alamo. Wayne saw the courage of the fort's defenders as indicative of the spirit which made America great. His interest became an obsession, and many of the mediocre films he did in the 1950s were seen as merely convenient ways for Duke to raise the cash he needed to film *The Alamo*. From the beginning, he envisioned it as an elaborate spectacle that would rival anything ever filmed for sheer sweep and pagentry. There would be no phony sets or rear-screen projections to save money. Additionally, Wayne wanted total artistic control, and was most interested in making this vehicle his debut as director. His own production company,

DIRECTING THE SIEGE

84

RARE STUDIO CONTACT SHEET SHOWING WAYNE IN REHEARSAL

Batjac, would produce, and it was his intention to play a cameo role as General Sam Houston.

For years, Wayne tried to get a studio to help him finance the film. Even with the Walt Disney Davy Crockett rage which swept the country in the Fifties, he could find no backers. He was rejected by Republic Studios because they were not proponents of big-budget films. Jack Warner refused to help out, saying audiences would reject the film because they knew, ultimately, all the heroes had to die. Eventually, Duke struck a deal with United Artists which gave him creative control and financial backing. As early as 1957, elaborate plans were made to ensure that the replica of the Alamo was correct in every way. Although Wayne had originally considered filming in Panama, he later found what he felt was the perfect location in a remote area of Texas called Brackettville. Here, he leased a large spread from a gentleman known as "Happy"

Shanahan, and set construction began. (The Wayne "Alamo" set remains a major tourist attraction.)

While the site was excellent for keeping the distractions of civilization away, it soon became apparent that getting supplies to the location would be a logistical nightmare. A very detailed listing of just what Duke had to import can be found in *The John Wayne Reference Book* (Citadel). Suffice it to say that the cost of housing and feeding hundreds of people made money disappear into thin air. It literally cost more money to film *The Alamo* than it did to finance the entire Mexican-American war. Before long, the entire budget had been spent. Wayne asked United Artists for more financial help, but the studio declined. Rather than "skimp" on costs, Duke mortgaged everything he had, and found—to his dismay—that his longtime business manager had lost most of Wayne's money through bad invest-

DESPITE AD CLAIMS, "THE ALAMO" WAS NOT SURE FIRE AT THE BOX-OFFICE

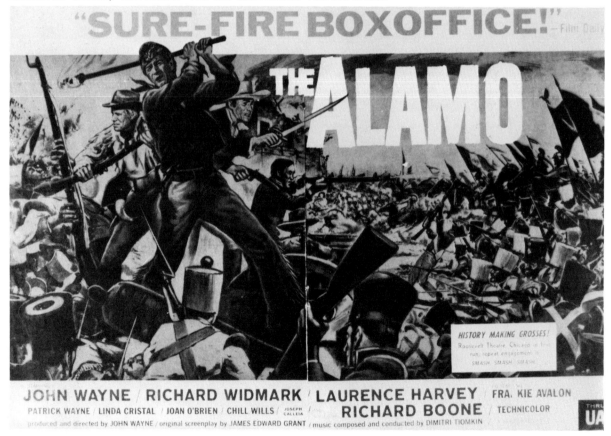

ments. Scraping together whatever he could, Duke poured the remaining fruits of a lifetime of work into this single project. In the end, the budget would top $12-million—an enormous amount of money for its day.

Adding to Wayne's pressure was United Artists insistence that, for box-office appeal, Duke had to take a starring role. He reluctantly agreed to play Davy Crockett, and between the time spent both in front of and behind the cameras, he managed to get only a few hours sleep a night. He had been able to attract an impresive cast, most notably Richard Widmark as Jim Bowie and Laurence Harvey as Col. William Travis, commander of the Alamo. The Sam Houston role Wayne originally wanted to play eventually went to Richard Boone, who refused to take a salary, settling instead for keeping the beautiful leather coat he wore in the film. It's been said that Wayne was so touched by Boone's selflessness,

that he eventually sent him a car as a token of his appreciation.

No such camaraderie existed between Wayne and Richard Widmark, however. When Widmark was signed for the film, Duke took out a full page ad in *Variety* which read "Welcome aboard, Dick!" When Widmark arrived on the set he admonished Wayne, dourly declaring "The name is RICHARD!" Things went downhill from that point, although their frequent fights were kept in check by each man's devotion to making *The Alamo* an artistic success. Surprisingly, Wayne had a wonderful time working and socializing with Laurence Harvey. Many felt the aristocratic and somewhat effete actor would also rub Duke the wrong way. Instead, Harvey proved to be a down to earth gentleman who enjoyed telling ribald stories and drinking with the guys. This, despite his penchant for importing everything from expensive wines to caviar to the set for his

CROCKETT'S ARRIVAL AT THE ALAMO

personal consumption. Duke was further impressed with his professionalism when a cannon rolled over Harvey's foot and broke it. Despite horrendous pain, Harvey did not flinch until the scene was completed.

In spite of the enormous pressure, Wayne enjoyed much of his work on *The Alamo*, possibly because it was one of the few locations in which his entire family was present. Pilar flew in with daughter Aissa, who, although only four years old, had a part in the film. In fact, Pilar herself appears with Duke's daughter Toni as extras in one sequence. Michael Wayne was in charge of production, along with Duke's brother Bob Morrison. Patrick Wayne was given a small but key role as one of the Alamo defenders. Nepotism was rampant, but no one could complain, as Duke was footing most of the bill himself.

Incredibly, Wayne managed to shoot the entire film in 81 days. Those present stated he seemed to be everywhere at once, making sure the film was exactly as he had envisioned it. It was reported that once on the set, Duke was so familiar with the script that he never once had to consult it. Trouble arose, however, when John Ford arrived on location. Ordinarily, Duke would have been thrilled to have "Pappy"'s guidance and company. *The Alamo*, however, was John Wayne's dream, and he would take all the credit or blame. Immediately, Duke's worse fear began to materialize. Ford began to "advise" Wayne how to shoot scenes, and it became apparent that he thought of himself as a consultant. Rumors began to fly that Wayne had asked Ford to come to the set to bail him out of trouble. Wayne thought too highly of his mentor to hurt his feelings, but he wanted him out of the way. He spent over $250,000 of his own money to send Pappy out shooting second unit action sequences that he had no intention of using. The ruse worked, and Ford left after feeling he had contributed in an important way. Although it is widely reported that not a single frame of Ford's footage remains in *The Alamo*, a player recently told "The Alamo Society" journal that a few frames of the battle sequence in which he appears were actually directed by Ford. Aside from this assertion, there is no other corraboration to date

that even these few seconds remain in the film.

Eventually, filming was completed and Wayne was left with a weight loss of 30 pounds and a five-pack-a-day cigarette habit. He was also left with over 500,000 feet of celluloid which had to be cut. He supervised every aspect of the post-production work, including working with the film's composer Dimitri Tiomkin. Finally, a 192-minute version was ready for exhibition. Filmed in 70mm Todd-AO, the movie was scheduled for limited—or "roadshow"—release in the nation's most prestigious threatres. Wayne held his breath as his dream was ready to be unveiled.

Contrary to popular belief, *The Alamo* was neither a critical or box-office disaster. It has generally been lumped into the same "overblown" epic category with the likes of three other unfairly maligned films, *Cleopatra*, the 1962 remake of *Mutiny on the Bounty*, and *Heaven's Gate*. To be certain, many critics attacked the film savagely, but just as many others defended the final product, even if such defense was less than enthusiastic. As with all big budget blockbusters, *The Alamo* was a prime target for reviewers who critique the budget and not the film. Does it really matter to the audience if *The Alamo* or *Heaven's Gate* were worth their exorbitant costs? Spending too much on a film is a matter best left for studio executives and accountants.

The Alamo does have its flaws. For one thing, Wayne just about put the kiss of death on the project by hiring long time favorite screenwriter James Edward Grant to take sole responsibility for the script. This was an unfortunate choice, as there are lines in the film that are unspeakably corny. (Wayne to Linda Cristal: "I want you to listen tight..." and "You may be walkin' around, but you're deader than a beaver hat!") Such platitudes sound even worse than they read. In Grant's script, there is little room for understating an issue. Scroungy mountain men and pioneers are seen delivering lines of dialogue worthy of Shakespeare, and you feel like rooting for the Mexicans when, on the eve of the battle, there is a long-winded and ponderous discussion by the Alamo's defenders about the meaning of God. Dialogue like this is almost an endorsement for the American Athiest movement.

WIDMARK, HARVEY AND WAYNE PLAN THEIR STRATEGY

Many have also criticized Wayne's performance as Davy Crockett, and not without some justification. British film historian Allen Eyles wrote that Andy Griffith would have been a more ideal choice for the role. He has a point, but as stiff as Wayne may have been in a few of the dramatic sequences, he was at his peak in the action ones. Indeed, it would be difficult to envision *The Alamo* without Wayne as the star. His performance is a bit forced at times, but ultimately it's a respectable acting job that holds up well alongside his prestigious co-stars.

Both Widmark and Harvey excel in their roles, and it is truly shameful that the latter did not receive an Oscar nomination. As Travis, Harvey avoids many of the phony heroics found in other interpretations of the role. He is seen as stubborn, hardheaded and not very likable. This image does not change much throughout the course of the film, although we—and the onscreen defenders of the Alamo—come to admire his principals and his unfledging courage. One of the best moments in the film depicts his quiet pride at the fact that, given a choice to leave the doomed garrison, not a man decides to abandon Travis. His eyes swell with tears, and he says not a word. Yet, you can feel the emotion far more than had the script provided a lengthy speech for Harvey. It's one of the few times in *The Alamo* that James Edward Grant used the correct judgment.

Much of the movie crawls at a snails pace, but for some reason, it is never boring. This is because *The Alamo* is one of those rare spectacles that takes the time for the audience to become familiar with the characters. By the movies end,

89

we feel as though we are intimately familiar with all these people. It makes their inevitable fate all the more meaningful and difficult to deal with.

The real star of the film, of course, is the battle scene. After waiting so long to get to this final set-piece, Wayne does not disappoint his audience. Even critics of the dramatic portions of the movie were quick to credit Wayne with directing some of the most spectacular sequences ever filmed. Look, for example, at the moments before the first siege. Literally thousands of Mexican soldiers surround the tiny fortress, as the eyes of the defenders reflect the reality of just how hopeless their cause actually is. When the battle itself begins, it is a stunning mosaic of charging cavalry, blazing cannons and massive explosions. Wave after wave of Mexicans are slaughtered until, inevitably, the Alamo is overrun. Harvey is killed defending his post, and Widmark dies heroically while confined to a hospital bed. With the aid of a mini-blunderbuss, he takes down quite a few opponents. Wayne is mortally wounded by a Mexican lance, but dies spectacularly by igniting the ammunition dump. When the

battle ends, there is a touching, brilliantly directed sequence in which the few survivors (a woman and several children) walk solemnly through ranks of Mexican troops who salute the spirit of the defenders of the Alamo. The scene is made all the more memorable by having it accompanied by Dimitri Tiomkin's *The Green Leaves of Summer*, among the great themes to accompany any motion picture.

When *The Alamo* opened, its initial grosses were impressive, but not spectacular. In one of those classic cases of movie exhibitors compromising art in order to add another showing each day, the studio was pressured into having the film's running time shortened. Wayne was heartsick over the prospect, but eventually relented. Among sequences removed were: a birthday party for the girl played by Aissa Wayne (rumored to be Duke's favorite sequence); the deathbed scene of a character called "Parson"; the arrival of Alamo reinforcements from a town called Gonzalez; the death early in the story of a villain named Emil Sand (who simply vanishes in the prints shown today); two full-length songs (which still remain on the soundtrack album), and an inspirational talk by Laurence Harvey referred to by Alamo aficionados as "The Jeffersonian Speech." Ultimately, the widely released version of the film ran 161.5 minutes, which is the version seen today on videocassette. (Television stations inevitably run an even more truncated 142-minute version to allow for a three-hour time slot).

The first edition of this book, printed in 1989, concluded that all evidence pointed to the missing footage from *The Alamo* as having been completely destroyed. The book featured this author's plea to the public to come forward if anyone had any information regarding the whereabouts of the missing footage. This lead to a series of dramatic developments. Canadian Wayne fan Bob Bryden recalled seeing a 70mm print of the complete version in the 1970s at a theater in Toronto. Bryden contacted Ohio native Ashley Ward, widely recognized as one of the foremost experts on the film and a man who was dedicated to finding the missing sequences. On a hunch, Ward contacted the United Artists film rental office in Canada and rented a 70mm print of *The Alamo* for a private viewing at Toronto's Elginton theater, in November 1990. Although the film canisters were marked as being the standard, truncated version, Ward was heartened when he saw the film open with the long-missing "Todd A-O" logo. His optimism was well placed, as the select few in the audience then saw—for the first time in decades—the complete 70mm version of *The Alamo*. For Wayne aficionados this was akin to discovering the Holy Grail.

Inspired by the find, Ward notified MGM/UA in the hopes that the studio would invest in a full restoration of the film through a new 70mm print. The studio declined, but, bowing to the importance of the lost footage, the home video division intercut the missing sequences with an existing print of the film. For the first time since its initial theatrical release, the public could see John Wayne's true version of *The Alamo*. Best of all, MGM gave the film the deluxe treatment on the laser disc edition, highlighting separate chapter stops so viewers could tell which footage had been restored. Additionally, filmmaker Brian Huberman contributed a superb documentary about the making of the film, comprised of rare home movie footage shot on the set along with recent interviews with cast and crew alumni. Ironically, the "Alamo curse" struck again in the year 2000 with the first release of the film on DVD. Fans were shocked to find that the edited version was used for this wide release, presumably because MGM had concerns about the quality of the missing footage matching that of the master print. Sadly, the studio did not even include the missing scenes as stand-alone "extras" on the DVD. Once again, the studio which helped bring Wayne's vision to life also contributed to taking his director's cut out of wide circulation. Whether or not the full version is ever released again on home video or restored for theatrical re-release remains unknown at this time. (For an in-depth study of the fascinating story behind this legendary film, the author would highly recommend *The Making of John Wayne's* The Alamo, by Don Clark and Christopher Andersen [Citadel Press].)

THE COMANCHEROS (1961)

Cast: John Wayne, Stuart Whitman, Ina Balin, Nehemiah Persoff, Lee Marvin, Michael Ansara, Pat Wayne, Bruce Cabot, Joan O'Brien, Jack Elam, Edgar Buchanan, Aissa Wayne. *Director:* Michael Curtiz. *Screenplay:* James Edward Grant and Clair Huffaker. *Music:* Elmer Bernstein. *Released by:* 20th Century-Fox. *Running Time:* 122 minutes.

With *The Comancheros*, John Wayne entered the twilight of his career. Unlike many stars who steadfastly refuse to acknowledge their age and foolishly continue to portray romantic leading actors, Wayne knew that he must modify his image if he was to remain popular. In this film, he makes that transition subtly but effectively. The romantic lead is actually played by Stuart Whitman, whose chemistry with Wayne is so good that it makes one wonder why these actors did not team again onscreen (although both would have supporting roles in *The Longest Day*). In fact, the chemistry between everyone involved with *The Comancheros*—onscreen as well as off—is so enjoyable that it is almost impossible to find a fault with this film.

The story presents Whitman as a debonair ladies' man and scoundrel who is forced into a duel with a rival. When Whitman kills the man, a price is put on his head and he flees to Texas, which is not yet a state. He feels the murder charge cannot be enforced in this region of the country, and he makes no attempt to be discreet. On a riverboat, Whitman is seduced by a rich, independent woman played by Ina Balin, but the next morning, he finds she has left the boat without a word. Actually, the character portrayed by Balin was quite daring for the time in which the movie was made. Her dialogue with Whitman leaves little doubt that she considers it great sport to pick up strange men, use them sexually and then discard them. The script does not attempt to soften her character in these early

scenes, either. Although Whitman becomes emotionally involved, it is obvious that she regards him as a physical plaything.

Whitman's troubles don't end there, as he is taken by surprise and arrested by no-nonsense Texas Ranger John Wayne, who tells him that Texas now has an extradition treaty with the States. The dialogue between the men in their first meeting is extremely well-written. While we know they are adversaries, we can also tell that they find great amusement in each other's personality, despite the fact that Wayne is trying to ensure that Whitman hangs. Enroute home, the men encounter a ranch devastated by Indians and Comancheros—white men who ride with the tribes and supply them with liquor and guns. After burying the dead settlers, some of whom have been grotesquely tortured, Whitman uses a shovel to knock Wayne out and escapes, leaving Wayne to return to the taunts of his fellow rangers.

Bruce Cabot, as the leader of the rangers, informs Wayne that his next assignment is to pose as a gunrunner to meet a contact who will sell the weapons to the Comancheros. Wayne is given a wagon of guns confiscated from a real gunrunner, and sets off to find his prey. The man in question turns out to be Lee Marvin as a hideously scarred gunslinger named Crow, who explains that he fell into league with the Comancheros when they prevented Indians from scalping him—although they were halfway through the job by then. Marvin's Crow is hot-tempered and wild, and the brief scenes between the two are among the most enjoyable of either man's career. (They would again work together on several films.)

When Marvin accuses Wayne of cheating in a card game, the latter is forced to kill him before

DUKE AIDS WHITMAN AGAINST AN ADVERSARY

IN ACTION WITH PATRICK WAYNE AND STUART WHITMAN

he (Duke) can be lead to the Comancheros. Wayne also encounters Whitman at the game and arrests him again. Enroute to the ranger station, they stop at a ranch owned by friends of Wayne's in time to help fight off a Comanchero attack. When things begin to go badly for Wayne and friends, Whitman gallantly escapes the fracas, and goes for reinforcements from the rangers. He is rewarded for this by having all charges dropped and being made a Texas Ranger. He and Duke, armed with the guns, immediately set off to find and infiltrate the Comanchero camp.

Eventually, they encounter Indians who bring them to a hidden valley ruled over by a wheelchair-bound tyrant played by Nehemiah Persoff, excellent in the role. He reminds one of one of those ultra-civilized madmen found in the James Bond films, the type who makes wonderful small

talk about how he will torture .007 to death, but not before elaborately wining and dining him. Persoff ruins Duke's plan to build a gunrunning network with the Comancheros. He simply confiscates the weapons and sentences the lawmen to a slow death.

At the last minute they are spared by Persoff's daughter, who just happens to be Ina Balin. She still has an interest in Whitman, as well as a desire to escape her father's empire. She aids Wayne and Whitman in plotting an escape, by sneaking her captive father and herself out of the valley and away from the army of Comancheros. The plan goes awry, however, and they are pursued by dozens of Comancheros. In the blazing battle that follows, Persoff is killed and things look grim for Duke and company. But, conveniently, Bruce Cabot and the Texas Rangers

JOHN WAYNE "THE COMANCHEROS"

STUART WHITMAN · INA BALIN · NEHEMIAH PERSOFF · LEE MARVIN as CROW   PRODUCED BY GEORGE SHERMAN · MICHAEL CURTIZ   CINEMASCOPE · COLOR BY DE LUXE   SCREENPLAY BY JAMES EDWARD GRANT and CLAIR HUFFAKER · BASED ON THE NOVEL BY PAUL I. WELLMAN

WAYNE AND WHITMAN ARE IN THE COMANCHERO CAMP

arrive on the scene, decimate the bad guys, and leave Whitman and Balin to pursue their romance as they head toward Mexico.

The most admirable thing about *The Comancheros* is the crispness of the dialogue. It is next to impossible to believe that the "Tower of Babble," James Edward Grant, actually co-wrote the script. One is tempted to credit Clair Huffaker with the better things we find in the story, but that would be unfair. Among the film's other assets are some superbly choreographed action scenes by second unit director Cliff Lyons, and the overall compatibility of the cast. In addition to his frequent co-stars, Duke gave plum roles to son Pat and little daughter Aissa. Even Ina Balin's character's name is that of Duke's wife Pilar. The producer is George Sherman, who directed Wayne in earlier "B" Westerns. In

all, *The Comancheros* was a family affair.

Sadly, director Michael Curtiz, the man who can be credited for much of the richness of this film, did not live long enough to see the results of his efforts. He was ill throughout the entire production, and both Wayne and Cliff Lyons are known to have directed certain sequences. The veteran director passed away immediately following the film's completion.

Shot in Utah, *The Comancheros* offers beautiful panoramic views of the West that remind one of John Ford's epics which were shot in Monument Valley. William Clothier's cinematography is superb, as is a typically lush Elmer Bernstein score. *The Comancheros* is not often discussed as a masterpiece, and perhaps it isn't. However, it would be difficult to find a Western that is more enjoyable to watch.

THE MAN WHO SHOT LIBERTY VALANCE (1962)

Cast: John Wayne, James Stewart, Vera Miles, Lee Marvin, Edmond O'Brien, Andy Devine, Ken Murray, John Carradine. *Director:* John Ford. *Screenplay:* Willis Goldbeck and James Warner Bellah. *From the short story* by Dorothy M. Johnson. *Music:* Cyril J. Mockridge. *Released by:* Paramount Pictures. *Running Time:* 122 minutes.

In his foreword to director Peter Bogdanovich's book about filmmakers, *Pieces of Time*, Harold Hayes writes: "For my money, *The Man Who Shot Liberty Valance* is one of the worst movies ever made. Peter Bogdanovich thinks it is one of the best. We have argued this difference over the past twelve years...(and) I suppose if Bogdanovich wants to go on making a ninny of himself over *Liberty Valance*, he has, I suppose, earned the right."

This type of dispute over John Ford's brooding and off-beat Western was not uncommon at the time of its release, and remains a point of debate among film historians. There have been many theories and speculations about what Ford really meant to say, and one is tempted to simply discard them all and leave it at "He just wanted to make a small scale Western with people he liked in the twilight of his career." And yet, *Valance* virtually pleads for analyzation. There are still many who consider it somewhat talky and plodding, but almost everyone agrees its concept and execution make it one of Ford's more interesting films.

The plot could be written on the head of a pin. Ford had adopted the basics of a short story which had appeared in a 1949 issue of *Cosmopolitan*. He was quite liberal about adding and deleting characters and, to no one's surprise, used the opportunity to cast familiar faces from

WITH JAMES STEWART

his stock company to flesh out the roles. In fact, *Valance* was to be the last hurrah for so many longtime Ford luminaries. Because many of these regulars realized that this was obviously the end of an era, a sense of melancholy pervades the entire film.

"THE MAN WHO SHOT
LIBERTY VALANCE"...

A MASTER MOVIEMAKER
LIKE JOHN FORD DOES WHAT
HE KNOWS BEST...

like making the classic "Stagecoach"...or the
masterpiece, "The Informer"...or "Grapes of Wrath,"
that reflected the anger and the conscience of its time
or the immortal blend of power and tenderness in
"How Green Was My Valley"...as he gained a
quartet of Academy Awards in the process...

or like bringing America's frontier to heroic life
again in his latest picture, "THE MAN WHO SHOT
LIBERTY VALANCE," filmed against a breathtaking
sweep of mountain, sand and sky, as he brings
two great stars together for the first time to
enact the most powerful scenes that ever came
out of the West—or a motion picture camera.

JAMES STEWART
JOHN WAYNE IN A

JOHN FORD PRODUCTION
The Man Who Shot
Liberty Valance

VERA MILES · LEE MARVIN · EDMOND O'BRIEN   ANDY DEVINE · KEN MURRAY   JOHN FORD   WILLIS GOLDBECK   JAMES WARNER BELLAH and WILLIS GOLDBECK   A PARAMOUNT RELEASE

WITH STROTHER MARTIN, LEE MARVIN AND JAMES STEWART

The screenplay finds James Stewart as Ranse Stoddard, a tenderfoot attorney who arrives in the lawless town of Shinbone to bring law, order and education to its inhabitants. Before he even reaches town, he is robbed and humiliated by Lee Marvin's Liberty Valance, a pyschopath who remains one of filmdom's more despicable villains.

The script concentrates on Stewart's determination not to resort to primal methods to oust his longtime nemesis. Wayne appears as Tom Doniphon, a hard-as-nails rancher who reluc-

tantly befriends Stewart and attempts to convince him that his methods are inappropriate to the saving of the West. A love triangle ensues when Vera Miles, previously Wayne's "gal," falls for Stewart's gentleness and intellectualism. Wayne now knows that his era is over, and he and his type have no place in the New West. When Stewart angrily is goaded into an ill-advised shootout with Valance, Wayne hides in the shadows and guns down the outlaw, leaving Stewart to reap the praise. Years later, after Wayne's death and having established himself successfully in politics on the basis of being "the man who shot Liberty Valance," Stewart confesses the truth to the press. Amazingly, they are not interested, prefering to let the story remain as people prefer to hear it. In the now classic line, a newspaper editor tells Stewart "When the legend becomes fact, print the legend."

One could argue that *Valance* is a combination of John Ford and Ingmar Bergman. There are so many subtleties to its very basic storyline that one is almost never aware of the fact that not much happens. This is due to the fact that the characters presented are all complex and fascinating people. Stewart's motivation for pursuing his somewhat insane dream of taming the West with a lawbook is never fully explained. Yet, despite his endless humiliations, we feel he is the true hero of the story. It is one of the first times that Ford seems to agree that civilization in the West was ultimately brought by patience and education, not guns.

Wayne's Tom Doniphon is an enigma. For all intents and purposes, he is a chauvinist hothead who takes no particular interest in helping rid the population of the menace of Liberty Valance, although he is clearly the only man in town with the capabilities of doing so. He professes a disdain of Stewart and everything the "dude" stands for, yet finds himself incapable of ignoring Stewart's plight when the latter is desperately in need of help. Each time he comes to Stewart's aid, he puts another nail into his own coffin. He despises the end of the West he loves, but realizes that he has become a dinosaur on the verge of extinction. He tries to let Stewart self-destruct, but cannot overlook the fact that because the lawyer is a physical "milquetoast," he (Stewart) is actually the braver of the two men.

The love triangle in *Valance* is equally compelling. Vera Miles is a simple woman when we first meet her—obedient to men and illiterate. She is exactly what Wayne wants, and he announces that he plans to marry her shortly. Yet, for precisely the same reason as Wayne, Miles is drawn to Stewart—his intrinsic bravery and stubbornness makes him a man to be admired by all. Stewart is too naïve to realize his presence has destroyed Wayne's dreams of a life with

Miles, and he does not reject her advances when her intentions become clear. Wayne dies a bitter old man filled with anger, certainly one of the more tragic figures he has ever portrayed.

Ford came under some criticism for casting Stewart and Wayne in roles that were obviously suited for much younger men. However, they never appear foolish in their parts, and the towering presence of both compensates for the fact that they may have been a little "over the hill." In fact, *Valance* presents two major acting triumphs.

Wayne and Stewart are supported by a superb entourage of fine actors. Particularly good is Edmond O'Brien as the courageous editor who uses his paper to attack Valance. Andy Devine is the film's comic relief as a cowardly sheriff whose fear of Valance results in some genuinely funny sequences. Woody Strode is solid as Wayne's loyal servant, and John Carradine appears late in the film in a characteristically hammy but thoroughly delightful performance. Lee Marvin is riveting as the vicious gunman of the title.

Valance is a disconcerting film to see when one is used to grand epics about the West. Indeed, it would not be difficult to imagine this story being translated into a play. By Ford standards, the sets are positively claustrophobic. Few sequences are filmed outside and the cinematography gives the film a dark, foreboding look. Yet, these are the virtues which make *Liberty Valance* one of the all time great Westerns. Do not get sidetracked about the hidden meaning of Ford's intentions or the subliminal significances of the casting decisions. This film is a major work of art. It is increasingly fascinating on the subsequent viewings, and, unlike many of Wayne's efforts, finally seems to be enjoying the praise it deserved when it opened to mixed reviews and mediocre box-office results. Chalk one up for Bogdanovich and all the others whose attention to *Valance*'s virtues insured that time did not obscure its importance among the major films of our time. In answer to the trivia buffs who have tried to locate the sequence in which Gene Pitney's best-selling title song appears: stop looking and listening. It doesn't.

THE LONGEST DAY (1962)

Cast: John Wayne, Henry Fonda, Robert Mitchum, Curt Jurgens, Richard Burton, Red Buttons, Sean Connery, Peter Lawford, Robert Ryan, Sal Mineo, Rod Steiger, Robert Wagner, Stuart Whitman, Eddie Albert, Jeffrey Hunter, Fabian, Mel Ferrer, Richard Beymer. *Directors:* Ken Annakin, Andrew Marton, Bernhard Wicki, Darryl F. Zanuck. *Screenplay:* Cornelius Ryan. *Based upon his book. Music:* Maurice Jarre. *Released by:* 20th Century-Fox. *Running Time:* 180 minutes.

If every a film deserved the label "epic," producer Darryl F. Zanuck's *The Longest Day* is it. When he first read the Cornelius Ryan's bestseller recounting the Normandy D-Day invasion, Zanuck became obsessed with the mammoth undertaking of bringing this tale of 20th century heroics to the screen. One of Hollywood's legendary forces, Zanuck knew the toll in manpower and money would be astronomical. Yet nothing would dissuade him from spending whatever it took to fulfill his ambition.

BARKING ORDERS IN FRANCE

1969 REISSUE POSTER

The logistics of filming *The Longest Day* remain awesome even by today's mega-budget standard. When one remembers what a single dollar could buy in 1961, the movie's $10 million final cost made it one of the most expensive epics to ever go before the cameras. Zanuck accumulated a virtual army of high priced talent both in front of the camera and behind the scenes. He hired four directors, and helmed the American-based sequences himself. At one point, he had two full units shooting in different locations with hundreds of actors on each set. Filming was done on location at Normandy, as well as Corsica. For the studio shots, Zanuck utilized Studio Boulogne in Paris, where he commissioned the largest set in French film history. Forty-eight technical advisors were employed to ensure that every single aspect of the story was accurate. He even arranged for many of the actors to meet with the real-life characters whom they were portraying so that they might get the proper "feel" for the role.

In all, 31 different locations were utilized. $800,000 was spent on sets—an incredible sum at that time. 63,000 hot meals were served and 155,000 bottles of beverages were consumed. As if these statistics are not overwhelming enough, consider that 9,900 pounds of nails were needed, as well as 120,000 pounds of plastics, 3,600 gallons of paint, 110,000 pounds of plaster, 25,000 old tires (to create smoke for special effects), and 100,000 gallons of gasoline (enough to keep the average car running for 25 years). Added to this mix was the cost of hiring over 40 international stars.

Zanuck had hoped to save money by having each star appear occasionally throughout the film, thus making their roles extended cameos. The policy in such cases was that no matter how well known an actor was he could expect only a token salary. The real reward, producers argued, was the chance to appear in a popular epic which would reap prestige for all concerned. Zanuck got virtually everyone he wanted under the conditions he demanded. The key word here is "Virtually," because the biggest catch almost got away... Duke Wayne.

Wayne had admired Zanuck for many years

ENJOYING A LAUGH ON THE SET

and considered him to be a friend. This came to an end after the release of *The Alamo*. In a printed interview, Zanuck went on a tirade against actors who were exerting increasing control over screenplays, directors, and salaries by forming their own production companies. Among those he cited an ingrates to the producers who helped establish them as stars were Burt Lancaster, Marlon Brando, Kirk Douglas and... John Wayne. Zanuck was particularly critical of the Duke, saying bluntly he had no "right" to produce, direct AND star in *The Alamo*. He told the world he pitied "poor old Duke Wayne" for what he felt was incompetent producing talents, and stated that Wayne wouldn't see "a nickel" for all of his efforts. Although Zanuck was proven right

DISCUSSING INVASION PLANS WITH ROBERT RYAN

about the last, Wayne hastily responded with a public announcement that the film of "poor old Duke Wayne" was breaking box-office records. Deep inside, however, he was severely hurt by the unprovoked attack by his good friend.

One can imagine Wayne's secret delight when Zanuck approached him to play the part of Colonel Vandervoot, who led the heroic 82nd Airborne Division through the invasion. The role had originally been set for William Holden (whose studio biographies throughout his career mistakenly continued to credit this film). When Holden withdrew from the project, Zanuck knew whom he wanted as replacement. With hat in hand, he came to Wayne only to be told that the Duke couldn't be less interested. Zanuck tried to appeal to Wayne's sense of patriotism to no avail. After several weeks of stringing Zanuck along, Wayne said he would consider the possibility of joining the cast. He intended to get Zanuck's hopes up, only to blow the entire deal by asking for a ridiculous salary. Zanuck offered Wayne $30,000. Wayne demanded $250,000 for four days work with the stipulation that he could delay filming if his pregnant wife gave birth. To Duke's amazement, Zanuck swallowed his pride and paid up.

With the cast complete, Zanuck resumed his duties as director/producer, working as much as 18 hours a day. He would demand that scenes featuring the French and German actors be shot simultaneously in their native languages not only to insure realism, but also to broaden the film's appeal in these countries. At the French village of Ste. Mare Eglise, he recreated Vandervoot's paratroopers' ill-fated landing in the town square, and their subsequent massacre. So realistic was this depiction that some villagers stoned actors dressed as Nazi soldiers. To further the sense of authenticity, Zanuck located and refurbished actual Spitfires and Messerschmitts for the aerial sequences. As both planes were rarities at the time of shooting, this added considerable expense to the production.

When all was said and done, however, Zanuck had the satisfaction of having brought to the screen what may be the most impressive war movie to date. It is absolutely riveting every step

of the way. One would think that the large number of directors, each working independently in a different style, would create a wildly uneven mess (witness the fate of the James Bond spoof *Casino Royale* several years later). Incredibly, the narrative structure of *The Longest Day* is completely consistent, and the suspense in certain sequences is almost unbearable as we come to know each of the principals involved and sympathize with these brave men who are to face death.

Wayne's screen time lasted only 12 minutes. Yet, due to excellent editing, his scenes are used sparingly, giving the viewer the impression he is onscreen a great deal more than he actually is. Despite a cast filled with genuine superstars, each of whom has several memorable scenes, it is Wayne who dominates the film and provides much of the "glue" that holds the narrative together. The look of sadness and disgust on his face when he observes his massacred men is one of the most poignant moments of the film—and Wayne's career.

The Longest Day was a critical success and box-office smash. For many years it was listed as the top-grossing black and white film ever made. (Zanuck had decided to shoot in black and white after noting that the color screen tests he did left the film without the somber look he desired.) The movie was nominated for many major Oscars, and won a variety of prestigious awards within the film industry. Wayne's name was considered enough of a draw that, although the other actors are billed alphabetically, Wayne gets a special listing after everyone else.

Did Duke ever feel guilty about playing hardball and getting that excessive salary from Zanuck? Years later he commented, "Poor old Zanuck, I shouldn't have been that rotten, I guess. The other cameos, they were getting maybe $25,000 the most. I always liked that son-of-a-bitch...But I was goddam mad at his attack on me. But you know, it was nice that when I got over there on location, old Zanuck was decent to me. He was so pleasant that I kinda wished I hadn't charged him that much money. That had to be the most expensive interview a movie producer ever gave."

HOW THE WEST WAS WON (1963)

Cast: James Stewart, Debbie Reynolds, John Wayne, Gregory Peck, Henry Fonda, Karl Malden, Richard Widmark, Lee J. Cobb, George Peppard, Robert Preston, Carolyn Jones, Eli Wallach, Walter Brennan, Carroll Baker, Andy Devine. *Directors:* George Marshall ("The Railroad" sequence); Henry Hathaway ("The Rivers," "The Plains," "The Outlaws" sequences); John Ford ("The Civil War" sequence). Richard Thorpe directed (uncredited) the transitional historical scenes. *Screenplay:* James R. Webb, with John Gay (uncredited). *Music:* Alfred Newman, Ken Darby. *Narrator:* Spencer Tracy. *Released by:* Metro-Goldwyn-Mayer. *Running Time:* 162 minutes.

How the West Was Won was one of Hollywood's gargantuan epics. In the early 1960s, the studios were heavily promoting the process of Cinerama, and this expensive tale of the West was to be the last word in bringing the big-screen process the critical acclaim it had lacked to date. Cinerama required three cameras to simultaneously film the action. The result was shown on specially-equipped theatre screens which curved to such a degree that the audience felt they were literally surrounded by the events onscreen. For all its technical achievements, Cinerama was generally snubbed by critics who complained that most of the films done for exhibition in this process were

SHERMAN AND GRANT DISCUSS THE HORRORS OF WAR

WITH HARRY MORGAN

weak on story and long on irrelevant special effects designed to make viewers gasp with astonishment.

Metro-Goldwyn-Mayer was determined to give audiences a "thinking man's" spectacle, and was willing to spare no expense. The screenplay for *How the West Was Won"* is a rambling tale which shows the story of the founding of the West through the eyes of several generations of a pioneer family. Their triumphs and tragedies are mirrored through the historical events of the day, which brings an air of intimacy to sequences which had been done—less spectacularly—many times before. The studio enlisted an army of actors and technicians to bring the story to the screen. Over 12,000 roles were cast over the eleven months of filming. The movie was meticulously researched, and 87 volumes of historical notes provided the basis for even the smallest

details. When it was discovered that close-ups of the actor's wardrobes revealed machine-stitched garments, every article of clothing was ordered to be hand-sewn. More than 100 wagons were built, most of which were accurate to the last detail. For the railroad sequence, an authentic 1870 locomotive was shipped via 13 different railroads to the location in South Dakota. More than 350 Indians were employed for a scene depicting a raid on a wagon train. Seventy-one full-time vehicles used for production logged over a million miles in bringing equipment to locations throughout the United States. For a scene in which stampeding buffalo destroy a town, 1,500 bison were rounded up in a national park—the largest remaining herd in the country.

The cast consisted of a "Who's Who in Hollywood" with nearly every major available star involved. Wayne elected to play a short cameo sequence as General Sherman in the Civil War episode, directed by old crony John Ford. The remaining scenes from the film were directed by George Marshall and Henry Hathaway. As with *The Longest Day*, Wayne demanded—and received—a large compensation for his work. His $25,000 fee was only a tenth of what he had demanded from Darryl F. Zanuck for the former film, but it was still highly impressive when one considers that he only worked six days and appears onscreen for under four minutes.

Dramatically, *How the West Was Won* works very well indeed. Its plot rambles somewhat in trying to cover so many years of American history within the course of one film, but it never bores its audience. Furthermore, the styles of each director mesh perfectly, thus allowing the movie to be enjoyed without the disruptions of individual techniques sabotaging the narrative flow. The screenplay is intelligent, although it is indisputably the action scenes which give the film its memorable moments. A journey down the rapids turns into a tortuous tragedy for a pioneer family in one of the movie's most riveting sequences. Likewise, the spectacle of the Indian attack on the wagon train and the buffalo stampede are so realistically filmed, that one wonders how the stuntmen avoided death. The film's climax finds George Peppard in a blazing battle with outlaws aboard a runaway train. It is thrilling, and at times, breathtaking filmmaking. As for Wayne's contribution, one can only say that, unlike *The Longest Day*, he is not the "glue" which holds the parts together. His appearance is disturbingly brief, and even the role he portrays is secondary to Harry Morgan's General Grant. It must be said, however, that this episode was the most critically acclaimed section of the film. Ford turns away from battle sequences, and allows us to see the full horror of the Civil War through the eyes of a young recruit (played by Peppard). Following a bloody battle, Peppard encounters a young Confederate soldier whom he befriends. The two boys realize they are not natural enemies and strike up a close bond in a short period of time. This is tragically interrupted when the two observe Sherman and Grant talking by the campfire, reflecting on the tragic, human cost of the battle. The Confederate instinctively rises to shoot Grant, necessitating Peppard to kill his new-found friend. It is a poignant and low-keyed sequence which succeeds in its attempt to demonstrate the futility of war. One only wishes that Wayne's involvement could have been more extensive.

How the West Was Won succeeded in becoming both a critical and box-office hit. It's sure-fire combination of the most popular names in the movie industry insured that its production costs would be earned back in short order. The film was nominated for Best Picture and succeeded in winning several technical Oscars as well. Sadly, the Cinerama process was to be short-lived due to the expense of using three cameras, as well as the prohibitive costs of equipping theatres with the special curved screens. When the film was re-issued in 1970, it was seen exclusively in its "flat" version. Beware, however, when viewing the movie on TV or video. By necessity, much of the movie has been visually "cropped" to fit onto the small screen. This not only robs the film of much of its periphreal imagery, but also makes the "seams" from the three cameras quite obvious, and in the river sequence an actual vertical line can be seen running the length of the picture.

IN HARM'S WAY (1965)

Cast: John Wayne, Kirk Douglas, Patricia Neal, Tom Tryon, Paula Prentiss, Jill Haworth, Brandon de Wilde, Dana Andrews, Stanley Holloway, Burgess Meredith, Franchot Tone, Henry Fonda, Patrick O'Neal, Carroll O'Connor, Slim Pickens, James Mitchum, George Kennedy, Bruce Cabot, Barbara Bouchet, Hugh O'Brian. *Director:* Otto Preminger. *Screenplay:* Wendall Mayes. *From the novel* "Harm's Way" *by* James Bassett. *Music:* Jerry Goldsmith. *Released by:* Paramount Pictures. *Running Time:* 167 minutes.

Among the later films of Wayne's career, *In Harm's Way* can best be described as a movie for people who don't generally like John Wayne movies. Despite its sprawling plotline, exotic locales (filmed on location in Hawaii) and all-star cast, this film is basically a soap opera peppered with some obligatory action sequences. The thought of Wayne as a primary force in a soap opera is enough to instill anyone with a case of the giggles. However, everyone involved with this epic deserves high praise for keeping the

THE LOVERS PREPARE TO GO IN HARM'S WAY

movies' lengthy running time consistently engrossing and never overly-melodramatic.

One critic remarked that the film's central message seemed to be "You can't kill John Wayne," and indeed it seems a fairly accurate assessment, at least on the surface. Wayne is a hard-luck Naval officer in Hawaii at the outbreak of World War II. He runs afoul of his superiors, ignores regulations and leads his ship into a disasterous engagement. For this he is stripped of his command. Throughout the course of the movie, he also endures the death of his son, the suicide of his would-be daughter-in-law, the disgrace and untimely death of his best friend, a broken arm, and a leg amputation. Only rarely has Wayne played a role which left him so vulnerable.

And yet, *In Harm's Way* is only peripherally about Wayne. It is vast in its scope, and the screenplay incorporates quite a few separate storylines which are intelligently interwoven with each other. Consequently, the film never becomes one of those cardboard all-star melodramas like *Airport* or *Earthquake*. Everyone plays his role with restraint, and considering some of the egos involved, it was miraculous that director Otto Preminger could make such a film without having the on-set fireworks eclipse the World War II battles depicted onscreen.

When Wayne was signed for the lead, pundits quipped that either he or Preminger would walk off the project before a week had elapsed. Preminger was notoriously temperamental, and prided himself at getting performances he wanted from his actors by literally terrorizing them into submission. Hollywood held its collective breath waiting for the war of words when the ultra-conservative Wayne met with the ultra-liberal Preminger. Otto had a reputation for being the sole boss on the set, and Wayne had been known to take more than a passive hand in directing many of his directors. Alarmists were to be disappointed, however. No eruptions of temperament were observed. Preminger was duly impressed with Wayne's knowledge of literature and politics, and was equally enchanted by his professionalism. Characteristically, Wayne remained on the set long after receiving permission to leave for the day. He was always early and knew every actor's lines. More importantly, he

FIRST DATE WITH PATRICIA NEAL

respected Preminger as the power behind the throne and only made a few simple suggestions for the script, which Preminger was delighted to accept.

Adding to the potentially volatile chemistry of these two giants was the casting of Kirk Douglas as Wayne's Chief of Staff and confidant. Douglas was also known to be less than willing to take orders from temperamental directors. The one thing he had in common with Preminger was an alliance with liberal political causes in contrast to Wayne's well-known conservative bent. The two actors had never co-starred before, and no one knew what to expect when the two legendary leading men met for the first time. Again, there was plenty of respect all around and no animosity. Douglas reported years later in his autobiography, *The Ragman's Son*, that although he and Wayne rarely socialized off the set and never did reconcile their political differences, the Duke seemed to have the utmost admiration for his fellow superstar. Douglas never seemed able to quite explain why Wayne had more tolerance for his views than he did for many others'. Yet, Wayne proved his loyalty to Kirk by playing a

major role in getting financing approved the next year for Douglas' highly dramatic film *Cast a Giant Shadow*. The two men would team yet again in the near future for *The War Wagon*.

The plot of *In Harm's Way* is far too rambling to recount here. In summary, however, Wayne is reinstated as an Admiral and plans a daring and risky operation to destroy the Japanese stronghold in the Pacific. In between he gets to play some very touching and believable love scenes with nurse Patricia Neal (the two had co-starred in another Navy picture, *Operation Pacific*) as well as try to reconcile with his estranged son, Brandon de Wilde. These are among the most dramatic sequences Wayne has played, and his uncharacteristic underplaying only enhances the excellence of his performance.

Douglas has a major role as a maverick chief-of-staff to Wayne, who is a brilliant and daring strategist, but also a magnet for trouble. His inability to adjust to the death of his nymphomaniac wife leads him to rape de Wilde's fiancée, Jill Haworth, which results in her suicide. Unable to confront Wayne, he goes out in style by flying a suicidal reconnaissance mission

THE LOVERS MEET

AS ROCKWELL TORRANCE

which helps win the ultimate victory. As always, Douglas is never less than fascinating, breathing fire into what could have been a one-dimensional role.

The rest of the casting is equally meticulous, with even minor roles played by such luminaries as Carroll O'Connor, Burgess Meredith, Dana Andrews, Patrick O'Neal and Hugh O'Brian. The screenplay covers a lot of ground but due to excellent editing never becomes bogged down. In addition there are the brief, but intriguing appearances by Henry Fonda, Loyal Griggs' top-notch black and white cinematography (which earned an Oscar nomination), and Jerry Goldsmith's superb score.

Wayne himself expressed admiration for the film as a whole, but felt the storyline was ultimately robbed of its emotional punch by Preminger's insistence upon using obvious models for the climactic sea battle. He commented,

"I thought the story played beautifully right up to the end of the battle...All an audience has to do is get out of identity with that scene and the picture's done. It would have been better just to have the ship start in and then come with the things that says 'Come next Thursday,' and they'd like the picture. The finish was just so poorly done." Douglas also argued against the miniatures, but both men's pleas fell on deaf ears. Sadly, their predictions proved correct. Many critics panned the film on the basis of the several minutes of unconvincing action sequences. The unfortunate part of the entire episode is that *In Harm's Way* was in sum a film of which all concerned could take pride. Although fairly popular box-office performer, the movie has yet to reap the praise it deserves.

Two significant notes concerning *In Harm's Way*: It was the last black and white Wayne film, and it was during the production of this movie that Wayne began suffering from the symptoms which lead to his lung cancer operation in 1965.

112

THE SONS OF KATIE ELDER (1965)

Cast: John Wayne, Dean Martin, Martha Hyer, Michael Anderson, Jr., Earl Holliman, Jeremy Slate, James Gregory, Paul Fix, George Kennedy, Dennis Hopper. *Director:* Henry Hathaway. *Screenplay:* William H. Wright, Allan Weiss and Harry Essex. *From a story by* Talbot Jennings. *Music:* Elmer Bernstein. *Released by:* Paramount Pictures. *Running Time:* 122 minutes.

The Sons of Katie Elder is probably most memorable for the story behind the film than the actual finished product which appeared onscreen. Fol-

lowing several weeks shooting on *In Harm's Way,* Wayne had been plagued by a deep chronic cough. When the Preminger picture was completed, Duke's wife Pilar begged him to undergo a physical, which he reluctantly agreed to do. This decision undoubtedly saved Wayne's life. He was diagnosed as having lung cancer and was scheduled for emergency surgery which resulted in the removal of his left lung. Skeptics doubted he would even survive the operation, let alone work again.

As we all know, Wayne not only survived, but

QUIET MOMENT WITH MARTHA HYER

113

SPECIAL AD

FOR

MULTIPLE

RUNS

3 COLS. x { 85 LINES . . . . 255 LINES
              6 inches . . . . 18 inches

MAT 301

TWO DIFFERENT AD CAMPAIGNS FROM THE PRESSBOOK

ignored his business people's initial advice not to publicize the true nature of his ailment. They reasoned that it would tarnish Duke's "invincible" image to let it be known that his five pack a day cigarette habit had made him vulnerable to a deadly disease. Dismissing their advice, Wayne went to the press with his story as a way to encourage other people who also suffered from cancer. To prove that one can survive against insurmountable odds, Wayne steadfastly—and perhaps foolishly—insisted upon making his next film, *The Sons of Katie Elder,* on schedule. Pilar tried frantically to convince Duke to take an extended recuperation period, but he refused. Fourteen weeks after facing "the Big C," Wayne arrived on location in Durango, Mexico, to see if he could prove to himself and the world that the old John Wayne was as vibrant and vigorous as ever.

Press coverage for *Katie Elder* exceeded that given to *The Alamo.* While the public clamored for Wayne to triumph in his return to the screen, many felt the press was merely there to record any sign whatsoever that Duke was faltering. His appearance in the film is often described as weak and sickly, but nothing could be further from the truth. Wayne looked slimmer and leaner, but certainly not sickly. In fact, he appears to be in better shape than he was in his previous few films. Despite this, there is no doubt that the location work took its toll on Wayne, and Duke himself admitted he might have staged his "comeback" a bit prematurely.

Directing the film was Wayne's old friend Henry Hathaway, whom Duke apparently forgave for the haphazard handling of a fire sequence in *Circus World* which almost cost Wayne his life. Hathaway had himself survived a critical operation, and drove Wayne hard in the belief that self-pity leads to self-destruction. Nothing in the script was toned down to make things easier on Wayne, and characteristically, he refused to use a double in scenes in which the reality might suffer by doing so. The press had a field day covering Duke's first action scene. In it, he and his onscreen brothers have a free-for-all in an icy stream. Hathaway agreed to shoot this difficult sequence in one take, and had posi-

THE ELDERS: WAYNE, MICHAEL ANDERSON, JR.,
DEAN MARTIN AND EARL HOLLIMAN

tioned many cameras to record various angles. The cameras rolled, and Duke fought it out for a full five minutes. When the take was over, he almost collapsed from exhaustion and had to rely on the oxygen supply he always had on hand. While some members of the press took sadistic delight in reporting Wayne was at death's door, many others rallied to his side because of the courage he displayed. *Life* Magazine put his photo on the cover with the slogan "I kicked the Big C."

Sadly, with all this attention to Wayne's health, it has been difficult to examine *Katie Elder* solely as a film. This is unfortunate, because this proves to be a superb Western with a terrific cast, each of whom is in top form. Beginning with Elmer Bernstein's exciting muscial score, we know this is going to be special film throughout.

LIFE SPOTLIGHTS JOHN WAYNE ON LOCATION FOR "KATIE ELDER"

Cover Story is Rousing Tribute

Life Magazine dramatically captures the rough and tough figure of John Wayne as he appears during the location filming of "The Sons of Katie Elder" in Durango, Mexico. Highlighted by a full page portrait on the magazine's front cover, the pictorial article stretches across six pages.

Rugged Wayne, clothed in his western-styled "Katie Elder" outfit, is seen between scenes, on and off the set, and with his family. The unusual and behind-the-scenes coverage provide a moving portrait of a man who has always stood for action and masculinity.

DUKE'S RETURN TO THE SCREEN
LANDED HIM ON THE COVER OF "LIFE"

The story presents the four Elder brothers, John (Wayne), Tom (Dean Martin), Matt (Earl Holliman) and Bud (Michael Anderson, Jr.), as estranged siblings who are reunited at the funeral of their mother Katie.

We learn that despite this woman's being regarded as a saint by all who knew her, she had been abandoned by her sons, three of whom were trouble-prone drifters. Only the youngest, Anderson, had any recent contact with Katie before she spent her life savings to send him to college. The brothers immediately regret their treatment of their mother, and decide to do whatever it takes to make sure Anderson finishes school, a decision that the young man objects to, wanting to drift around with his brothers and find excitement.

Events unfold rapidly. The Elders learn that their father was murdered, and a local land baron (James Gregory) had cheated Katie out of the family ranch. The Elders suspect Gregory was behind the murder, and as their investigation intensifies, so, too, does Gregory's attempts to stop them before they can prove the truth. When the local sheriff (Paul Fix) comes to their aid, he is murdered and the Elders are framed for the crime. They barely escape a bloody ambush in which Holliman is mortally wounded. Wayne and Martin hide out in a barn in town, and in a furious climax, bring about Gregory's destruction.

Much of this story seems old hat, and it is true there is nothing very original here. That is precisely the point. In an age where the movies had begun to change rapidly, *Katie Elder* represented one of the last of the first class, traditional family Westerns. Almost everything about it reflects good, solid filmmaking. Wayne plays his

116

FROM THE FOUR WINDS THEY CAME...

role with a conviction and intensity not displayed since *Liberty Valance*. His action sequences are among the most convincing of his career. His character is refreshing, also. We never learn much about his past, but we know he's the blackest sheep of an entire family of black sheep. For once, he is not a know-it-all, and displays sensitivity and sadness at the fact that he is helpless to make amends to the mother he shunned so cruelly.

Wayne is more than matched by Dean Martin, reunited with Duke for the first time since *Rio Bravo*. Martin characteristically plays a wise guy here, but his eagerness to duck a fight whenever possible contrasts well with Wayne's tough image. There is a prolonged, quite hilarious sequence in a bar in which Martin cons the patrons into bidding for a phony glass eye. The rest of the cast do justice to the overall quality of the picture, and Hathaway's direction is excellent.

There are a couple of slow moments, and the screenplay makes the Katie Elder character too angelic to believe. In fact, at times the picture threatens to become a frontier version of *Psycho*, as the character of mom is so consistently interwoven throughout the script that it comes almost as a jarring shock when we realize we have never seen her at all. Also stretching credibility is the casting of Michael Anderson, Jr., as Wayne's kid brother. While Anderson's performance is perfectly fine, I estimate that at the time of filming, Wayne was slightly older than his onscreen sibling—by 36 years! It's to Duke's credit that his appearance was so impressive that one does not find this oddity a distraction.

The Sons of Katie Elder proved to be a major box-office hit, and erased any doubts that John Wayne would be back in the saddle for a good long time.

117

CAST A GIANT SHADOW (1966)

Cast: Kirk Douglas, Senta Berger, Angie Dickinson, Luther Adler, Stathis Giallelis, James Donald, Gordon Jackson, Topol, Ruth White. *Special Appearances by:* Yul Brynner, Frank Sinatra and John Wayne. *Written and Directed by:* Melville Shavelson. *Produced by:* Melville Shavelson and Michael Wayne. *Music:* Elmer Bernstein. A Mirisch/Llenroc/Batjac Production. *Released by:* United Artists. *Running Time:* 141 minutes.

Cast a Giant Shadow is not a good John Wayne film. Rather, it is a good film in which John Wayne makes occasional appearances. The significance of his scenes in the actual movie may be minimal, but it can safely be said that had it not been for Wayne's influence and belief in the project, the cameras might never have rolled.

There are many in the industry who undoubtedly feel that such an occurrence would not have been entirely negative, for *Cast a Giant Shadow* was not a box-office success and is among the least-discussed films in which Wayne had appeared. This is truly a shame, because, despite the movie's many flaws, it is a rousing and often inspiring film that attempts to bring to the public the story of one of this century's more neglected heroes: Mickey Marcus.

If that name doesn't ring a bell with most

AT DACHAU WITH KIRK DOUGLAS

OUTNUMBERED— UNARMED— UNPREPARED—

they stunned the world with their incredible victory!

"CAST A GIANT SHADOW"

STARRING KIRK
DOUGLAS

SENTA
BERGER

CO STARRING

ANGIE DICKINSON · JAMES DONALD
STATHIS GIALLELIS · LUTHER ADLER

AND SPECIAL APPEARANCES BY

FRANK SINATRA
YUL BRYNNER AS ASHER
JOHN WAYNE AS THE GENERAL

A MIRISCH CORPORATION PRESENTATION
A FILM BY MELVILLE SHAVELSON

Written for the Screen and Directed by MELVILLE SHAVELSON
Co producer — MICHAEL WAYNE · Music — ELMER BERNSTEIN
Produced by MIRISCH-LLENROC-BATJAC

COLOR by DeLuxe · **PANAVISION** Released thru UNITED ARTISTS

readers, it is because Marcus, an American Jew, and his noble deeds are best known in Israel. Prior to that country's declaration of independence in 1948, the soon-to-be active Israeli government was justifiably concerned about Arab threats to crush the new nation with a massive invasion on the very eve of its birth. Virtually friendless among the nations of the world, Israel turned to WWII hero Mickey Marcus, a nonpracticing Jew and career U.S. Army officer, with a desperate plea to help organize and mobilize its own pathetically ill-equipped army.

Marcus reluctantly accepted this nearly impossible assignment, and almost immediately regretted his decision. He found a ragtag army that was more intent on fighting each other than the enemy. Nevertheless, he succeeded against all odds, and helped lead the Israelis to victory in the ensuing conflict. Ironically, Marcus was killed in a tragic accident when he was shot by one of his own men. In fact, he was the last official casualty of the 1948 Arab-Israeli war.

For many years, writer/director Melville Shavelson had sought to give Marcus his due by putting his exploits on the big screen. Shavelson had difficulty obtaining major studio backing, however, as the inside word was that the film was too ethnic to be of enough interest to justify the large budget it would require. In desperation, Shavelson sought to "sweeten the pot" by in some way involving the world's biggest box-office star, John Wayne.

Shavelson thought his chances were slim. He later recalled, "If God had set out to print a million photographs of Jewishness, he would have used John Wayne as the negative." He also expected to be ignored due to a rather heated dispute he had with Wayne on one of Duke's earlier films, *Trouble Along the Way*, which Shavelson had co-written and produced.

Wayne stunned Shavelson by claiming the idea of a man like Marcus helping a small nation fight for independence proved that the film was more of a traditional American story than an ethnic one. On the basis of reading the first 35 pages of Shavelson's script, Wayne not only agreed to co-produce through his Batjac production company, but also to take a supporting role as an American

general who helps Marcus gain diplomatic recognition for Israel on the night of independence.

With Wayne involved, the entire scenario changed. Kirk Douglas was persuaded to take the lead role after conferring with Wayne. United Artists agreed to provide the funding, and even Yul Brynner and Frank Sinatra asked to play extended cameo roles. Alas, however, *Cast a Giant Shadow* was to prove to be Shavelson's own *Alamo*.

Shot on location in Israel, Shavelson encountered every major set back imaginable, from the 126 degree heat which left equipment ruined, to the constant squabbling among the cast and crew which caused the budget to skyrocket. The film eventually came in at over $1 million above its original estimate, and left Shavelson much more frustrated for his efforts at bringing this story to the screen. Years later, however, he did write a humorous recounting of his many tribulations in his book, *How to Make a Jewish Movie*, a project which probably earned him more than the film itself. (Shavelson had to take a considerable salary cut in order to get Douglas for the lead.)

Yet, the film itself is one of those drastically underrated epics that are usually dismissed in serious critics circles. Despite some moments of Hollywood schlock apparent in the obligatory love scenes between Douglas and on screen wife Angie Dickinson and between Douglas and mistress Senta Berger, Shavelson fashioned a highly involving adventure which at least dared to educate us about an important historical figure who has remained nearly unknown in his native land.

There are impressive battle scenes, and some moments of emotional punch that are hard to ignore. The scene of the proud Israelis declaring their independence in the face of possible annihilation is deeply affecting, and the movie benefits from an enigmatic performance by Kirk Douglas, who commands each scene in which he appears.

Although Wayne appears only for 11 minutes throughout the film, his sequences are quite memorable and well-acted. In fact, Wayne is such a forceful presence that it appears to the audience that he is onscreen far more than he actually is. Particularly affecting is a flashback scene in which the skeptical Wayne is "enlightened" to the

WAYNE AND ANGIE DICKINSON
WATCH KIRK DOUGLAS RECEIVE A DECORATION   *UNDER FIRE WITH KIRK DOUGLAS*

true horrors of Naziism when Douglas shames him into personally inspecting Dachau. Here, Wayne says little, but the look in his eyes speaks volumes as he physically retches after viewing the carnage. It's a fine example of Wayne proving he could do what so many doubted he could achieve: play a sequence with a great deal of subtlety.

Other highlights are the fine contributions of Brynner as a hard-headed commander often at odds with Marcus, and Frank Sinatra in a very

brief but amusing appearance as a mercenary pilot who tries to stop Egyptian tanks with seltzer bottles. Well, you'd have to see the movie to understand why.

Upon its release, United Artists played up the stars, and hid the fact that the film dealt in any way with Israel. From the ads it appeared to be a World War II movie, and despite some fine early reviews, audiences stayed away. Here again, however, is the opportunity for the curious to appreciate the film as it is available now on videocassette. For some inexplicable reason, the movie was cut by five minutes for distribution in Great Britain.

122

EL DORADO (1967)

Cast: John Wayne, Robert Mitchum, James Caan, Charlene Holt, Michele Carey, Arthur Hunnicut, R.G. Armstrong, Edward Asner, Paul Fix, Christopher George. *Director:* Howard Hawks. *Screenplay:* Leigh Brackett. *From the novel* "The Stars in Their Courses" by Harry Brown. *Music:* Nelson Riddle. *Released by:* Paramount Pictures. *Running Time:* 127 minutes.

El Dorado represented the fourth teaming of John Wayne and Howard Hawks. Previously, Wayne had starred under Hawks direction in the classics *Red River* and *Rio Bravo*, not to mention the less impressive *Hatari!* Their fourth collaboration, *El Dorado*, is interesting, partly because it represents Hawks at the laziest year of his career. It is clear that in his twilight years, he became less inspired in choosing his films, preferring to constantly remake *Rio Bravo*, and *El Dorado* is a film with enough similarities to the earlier movie to be justifiably classified as an actual remake, although Hawks never admitted as much, other than stating he was not adverse to repeating a successful scene in another film.

The criticism leveled at Hawks for not being more original with the script for *El Dorado* did not in fact deter him from remaking *Rio Bravo* yet again, this time in the guise of Wayne's 1971 effort *Rio Lobo*. Neither that film or *El Dorado* is as good as *Bravo*, but both have their merits, with *El Dorado* emerging as the more effective.

The script of *El Dorado* finds Wayne as a gunslinger who has been summoned by land baron Edward Asner. When Wayne discovers that his assignment is to terrorize a rancher who won't sell his valuable land to Asner, he bitterly rejects his prospective employer. In town, Wayne meets sheriff Robert Mitchum, an old friend with a history of alcoholism. Both men decide to help the rancher (played by R. G. Armstrong) and his family in the face of Asner's army of hired guns.

WITH ROBERT MITCHUM AND ARTHUR HUNNICUT

Based on Leigh Brackett's *The Stars in Their Courses*, the film weaves a predictable tale of good vs. evil in the Old West. In less capable hands, the result would be a standard oater. However, Wayne, Mitchum, James Caan and Arthur Hunnicut exert the special camaraderie that audiences came to expect of a Hawk's film. The result is an exciting but light-hearted and occasionally, very funny Western.

Most of the fun derives from watching Wayne and Mitchum poke fun at each other's "he-man" image. The actors blatantly play upon the fact

123

IT'S THE
BIG ONE
WITH
THE BIG
TWO!

HOWARD HAWKS presents
JOHN WAYNE
IS THE GUNFIGHTER
ROBERT MITCHUM
IS THE SHERIFF

EL DORADO

TECHNICOLOR®

"I'm girl enough
for both of you..."

CO-STARRING
JAMES CAAN · CHARLENE HOLT · PAUL FIX · ARTHUR HUNNICUTT · MICHELE CAREY

SCREENPLAY BY
LEIGH BRACKETT

Based on the novel
THE STARS IN THEIR COURSES
by Harry Brown

DIRECTED AND PRODUCED BY
HOWARD HAWKS

MUSIC SCORED BY
NELSON RIDDLE

PARAMOUNT
PICTURE

AD FROM THE PRESSBOOK

WAYNE'S HAND IS STRICKEN WITH PARALYSIS

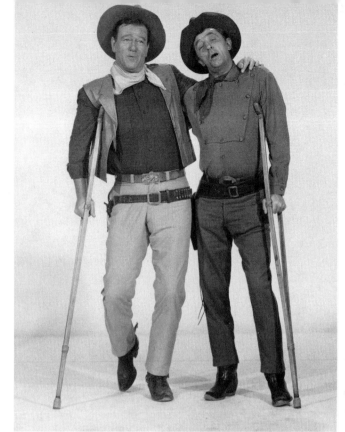

CHARLENE HOLT HAS THE BEST OF BOTH WORLDS   RARE STUDIO PUBLICITY STILL OF WAYNE AND MITCHUM

that they are well beyond their prime. Mitchum resorts to the bottle and spends a good deal of the film as a pathetic burden. Wayne shows some unusual vulnerability by collapsing at key moments from paralysis resulting from an untreated bullet wound. In fact, as the film nears its climax, Wayne's gunhand is paralyzed and Mitchum is on crutches.

There are several memorable segments from *El Dorado*. Wayne's cold rejection of Asner's threats is a tense and suspenseful sequence. Mitchum's theatrics while drunk and Wayne and company's subsequent attempts to sober him up are extremely amusing bits. Arthur Hunnicut (in the Walter Brennan role of *Rio Bravo*) does not have the opportunity to match his predecessor's classic performance, but he remains quite funny nonetheless. One of the memorable scenes from the movie finds Mitchum sobering up enough to hunt out a killer in the town saloon. He uses the opportunity to get revenge on those who scorned and mocked his drunkeness in the past. The sequence is played well, but it must be admitted, it was lifted almost intact from *Rio Bravo*.

Among the other little gems in *El Dorado* is the

witty banter between Wayne and James Caan as a rebellious kid who is proficient with a knife, but useless with a gun. In an amusing scene, Wayne asks Caan if he managed to hit a fleeing assailant with a shotgun blast. "I think so," says Caan. "He was limping when he left here." To which Duke replies, "He was limping when he GOT here!" There is also a well played cameo by Hawks' favorite sculptor of Western artwork, Olaf Weighorst, who is hilarious as a non-plussed gunsmith.

El Dorado also provides an intriguing villain in the person of gunslinger Christopher George as a mercenary hired to kill Wayne. Even when locked in a duel to the death, the men genuinely feel there are no hard feelings, as it's just business. Also interesting is George's obvious resemblance to Jack Palance in *Shane*. The climactic ending is very well directed, and Wayne's shoot-out with George is exciting. *El Dorado* may be uninspired, but Hawks and Wayne even at their most lethargic were several notches above almost anyone else making Westerns.

THE WAR WAGON (1967)

Cast: John Wayne, Kirk Douglas, Howard Keel, Robert Walker, Keenan Wynn, Bruce Cabot, Joanna Barnes, Gene Evans, Bruce Dern. *Director:* Burt Kennedy. *Screenplay:* Clair Huffaker. *Based upon his novel* "Bad Man." *Music:* Dimitri Tiomkin. *Released by:* Universal Pictures. *Running Time:* 101 minutes.

On a technical level, this film is standard. It was not Oscar-caliber material, nor did it break any new ground in Wayne's acting career. What it did offer was yet another co-starring role with Kirk Douglas, with whom Wayne had worked in *Cast a Giant Shadow* and *In Harm's Way*. In this, their third (and last) collaboration almost in succession, the two men are at the peak of their chemistry together. At least their joint efforts ended on a high note.

The War Wagon is a tongue-in-cheek Western, a standard, but involving "caper" film with Wayne

A TYPICAL "QUIET" MOMENT WITH FOE KIRK DOUGLAS

THE WAR WAGON ROLLS AND THE SCREEN EXPLODES!

JOHN WAYNE   **KIRK DOUGLAS**

"THE WAR WAGON"

CO-STARRING

HOWARD KEEL · ROBERT WALKER
KEENAN WYNN · BRUCE CABOT · JOANNA BARNES

TECHNICOLOR/PANAVISION

Music by
DIMITRI TIOMKIN · Screenplay by CLAIR HUFFAKER Based on his book "Badman" · Directed by BURT KENNEDY · Produced by MARVIN SCHWARTZ · A BATJAC PRESENTATION · A MARVIN SCHWARTZ PRODUCTION

A Universal Picture

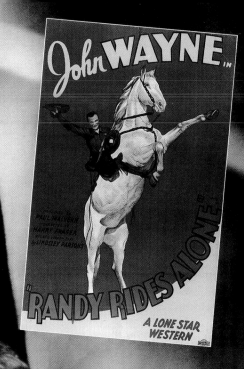

John WAYNE in

"RANDY RIDES ALONE"

A LONE STAR WESTERN

John Wayne as Cord McNally
in *Rio Lobo* (1971)

(*Inset*) Vintage poster for
Randy Rides Alone (1934)

(Above) Reissue title card for *Blue Steel* (1934)

(Left) Reissue title card for *The Star Packer* (1934)

(Above) Title card for *The Sea Spoilers* (1936)

(Left) Original window card poster for *Stagecoach* (1939)

Harold Bell Wright's

THE SHEPHERD OF THE HILLS

COLOR BY TECHNICOLOR

Starring

JOHN
WAYNE

BETTY
FIELD

HARRY
CAREY

with

BEULAH BONDI

JAMES BARTON

SAMUEL S. HINDS

MARJORIE MAIN

MARC LAWRENCF

Screen Play by Grover Jones

Based on the Novel by Harold L

Directed by HENRY HATHAWA

A PARAMOUNT RE-REL

COUNTRY OF ORIGIN U. S. A.

Property of National Screen Service Corp. Licensed for display only in connection with the exhibition of this picture at your theatre. Mur* be returned immediately thereafter.

R55-403

(Above) Lobby card for *Shepherd of the Hills* (1941)

(Left) One sheet for *Oregon Trail* (1936)

(Above) Title card for *War of the Wildcats* (1943), which was originally released under the title *In Old Oklahoma*.

(Right) Belgian poster for *Red River* (1948)

HERBERT J. YATES
presenta el MAS grande triunfo de
JOHN FORD

El Hombre Quieto
THE QUIET MAN

JOHN   **MAUREEN**   **BARRY**
WAYNE   **O'HARA**   **FITZGERALD**
Con WARD BOND · VICTOR · McLAGLEN · MILDRED NATWICK

en Color *por* TECHNICOLOR

DIRECTOR
JOHN FORD

MERIAN C. COOPER *una producción* **ARGOSY**

Dist. por DISTRIBUIDORA SOTOMAYOR, S.A.

(Above)
Mexican lobby
card for *The Quiet Man*
(1952)

(Opposite top left) Spanish poster for
The Searchers (1956), acclaimed by
many as the greatest western ever
made.

MARINE AIR-DEVILS IN HOT PURSUIT . . . BLOOD-RED TRAILS STREAK THE SKY!

•YOU haven't got
the guts to point
your finger at a
guy and say:
Go get killed!•

HOWARD HUGHES *presents*

JOHN WAYNE · ROBERT RYAN
in
FLYING LEATHERNECKS
COLOR BY TECHNICOLOR

with DON TAYLOR · JANIS CARTER · JAY C. FLIPPEN · WILLIAM HARRIGAN

JOAN: "When he comes home
. . . I forget he's a soldier . . . I
just remember he's my man!"

BARES
THE HEARTS
OF
THE WOMEN
WHO WAIT!

NORA: "I'm glad I'm going
to have a baby . . . whatever happens I'll have
something to live for!"

ANNABELLE: "The boys
need cheering up . . . to
cheer 'em . . . it's the
patriotic thing to do!"

VIRGINIA: "There's so little
time together . . . you've
got to make every min-
ute he's with you count!"

JEANNE: "People are talk-
ing . . . but can I help
it? He's away and I'm
alone . . . and lonesome!"

LOIS: "When wounded
kids grin . . . it gets you
down . . . but somehow it
keeps you going too!"

AN **EDMUND GRAINGER** *production* · NICHOLAS RAY · EDMUND GRAINGER · JAMES EDWARD GRANT

This is a facsimile of the full page advertisement in four
colors appearing in COLLIER'S and THE SATURDAY EVE-
NING POST; double pages in full color appear in LIFE and
LOOK and the 23 newspapers distributing the AMERICAN
WEEKLY; and full pages in color appear in THIS WEEK,
distributed by 28 newspapers. Your patrons have been alerted
to the coming of "FLYING LEATHERNECKS" by this extensive blanket of colored advertising published prior to your
presentation of this attraction.

Total Circulation of 35,366,332

EXHIBITORS MANUAL

(Right) Pressbook
advertisement for
Flying Leathernecks
(1951)

(Opposite top right) Shopping bag promoting the home video relase of
Fighting Kentuckian (1949)

(Opposite below) Pressbook artwork
for *Legend of the Lost* (1957)

(Left) Title card for *The Barbarian and the Geisha* (1958)

(Below) Pressbook art for *The Horse Soldiers* (1959)

(Above) 1967 reissue lobby card showcasing the all-star cast of *The Alamo*

(Right) Original release Japanese program for *The Alamo* (1960)

(Below) Belgian poster for *The Man Who Shot Liberty Valance* (1961)

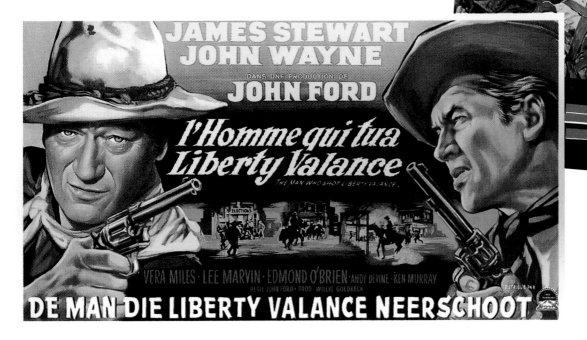

(Right) Lobby Card for the Spanish release of *The Wings of Eagles* (1957)

QUE HOMBRE ESE WAYNE! UN AUDAZ PILOTO QUE ARRIESGA LA VIDA CON UNA SONRISA

METRO-GOLDWYN-MAYER presenta
EN METROCOLOR

JOHN WAYNE
DAN DAILEY
MAUREEN O'HARA
CO-ESTRELLA WARD BOND
ARGUMENTO FRANK FENTON Y WILLIAM WISTER HAINES
DIRECTOR JOHN FORD · PRODUCTOR CHARLES SCHNEE

ALAS DE AGUILA

(Below) One sheet poster for *McLintock*

WALLOPS THE DAYLIGHTS OUT OF
EVERY WESTERN YOU'VE EVER SEEN!

JOHN WAYNE + MAUREEN O'HARA

"McLINTOCK!"
IS McNIFICENT!

McLintock! He put his brand on the territory and every woman in it!
McLintock! The brawl-for-fun who put a town on the map—and hung his name on it!

Look! You get three Waynes for the Price of One! John, Pat and Mike"

Co-starring PATRICK WAYNE / STEFANIE POWERS / JACK KRUSCHEN / CHILL WILLS / And Guest Star YVONNE DE CARLO
Written by JAMES EDWARD GRANT / Directed by ANDREW V. McLAGLEN / Produced by MICHAEL WAYNE A BATJAC PRODUCTION
TECHNICOLOR® PANAVISION® Released thru UNITED ARTISTS

危険な道

(Right) Japanese souvenir program of Otto Preminger's epic *In Harm's Way* (1965)

(Above) Lobby card for *The Sons of Katie Elder* (1965), Duke's first film following his operation for lung cancer.

(Below) A.B.C. TV telop slide promoting showing of *El Dorado* (1967)

(Above) Half sheet poster for *El Dorado* (1967)

(Above) Duke and Maureen O'Hara reunited for the last time in *Big Jake* (1971)

(Left) Duke in action for *Big Jake* (1971)

JOHN WAYNE

in

A Howard Hawks
Production

"RIO LOBO"

A Cinema Center Films Presentation

Co-starring Jorge Rivero · Jennifer O'Neil · Jack Elam · Victor French · Susana Dosamantes
Screenplay by Burton Wohl and Leigh Brackett · Story by Burton Wohl · Music by Jerry Goldsmith
Directed by Howard Hawks · Technicolor · A National General Picture Release G All Ages Admitted / General Audiences ➔

7

Property of National Screen Service Corp. Licensed for display only in connection with the exhibition of this picture at the theatre licensing this property. Licensee agrees not to sublease, trade, sell, give away or permit others to receive or use this material. Immediately after complion of display, revised material must be returned and leased material either returned or destroyed.

71/5

THE TRAIN ROBBERS

大列車強盗

(Above) Lobby card for *Rio Lobo* (1971)

(Opposite above) Lobby card for *McQ* (1974),
Duke's answer to Dirty Harry.

(Opposite below) In action as *Cahill, U.S. Marshall* (1973)

(Left) Japanese souvenir program for *The Train Robbers* (1973)

WAYNE
ON
WHEELS...

JOHN WAYNE
"McQ"

A BATJAC AND LEVY-GARDNER PRODUCTION

EDDIE ALBERT · DIANA MULDAUR · COLLEEN DEWHURST · CLU GULAGER · DAVID HUDDLESTON · AL LETTIERI as "Santiago"

TECHNICOLOR® PANAVISION® · Music by ELMER BERNSTEIN · Executive Producer MICHAEL A WAYNE · Written and Co-Produced by LAWRENCE ROMAN
Produced by JULES LEVY and ARTHUR GARDNER · Directed by JOHN STURGES · from Warner Bros. A Warner Communications Company   PG

Five killers robbed
the Valentine bank.

The lucky ones
got caught.

The rest got Cahill.

MARSHAL

CAHILL UNITED STATES MARSHAL

JOHN WAYNE in A BATJAC PRODUCTION "CAHILL: UNITED STATES MARSHAL" Also Starring GARY GRIMES · NEVILLE BRAND and GEORGE KENNEDY as Fraser
Screenplay by HARRY JULIAN FINK and RITA M. FINK · Music—ELMER BERNSTEIN · Produced by MICHAEL WAYNE · Directed by ANDREW V. McLAGLEN · PANAVISION® · TECHNICOLOR®   PG PARENTAL GUIDANCE SUGGESTED   Celebrating Warner Bros. 50th Anniversary A Warner Communications Company

73/210

Duke with his
coveted Oscar
for *True Grit*
(1970)

ON THE SET WITH SON ETHAN

as an embittered rancher who has served time for a trumped up murder charge, courtesy of Bruce Cabot, playing the local evil land baron (aren't land barons ever good?). Cabot has framed Duke so that he could confiscate his land and mine the gold reserves on the property. When Wayne returns to town, Cabot immediately tries to find ways to prevent Duke from reclaiming his ranch.

What Cabot doesn't know is that Duke's motives go far beyond getting his land back. He is out to steal a million dollar gold shipment Cabot is personally escorting through the desert. Getting to the loot isn't easy, as Cabot is transporting the gold in a steelplated contraption called "The War Wagon," which resembles a prototype of a modern day tank, complete with a deadly Gat-

WAYNE IN THE BARROOM BRAWL

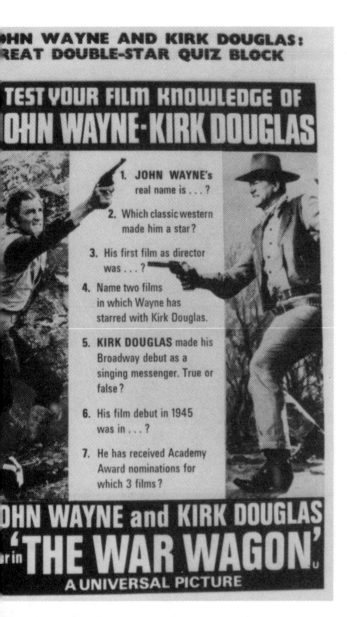

TEST YOUR FILM KNOWLEDGE OF
JOHN WAYNE-KIRK DOUGLAS

1. JOHN WAYNE's
real name is . . . ?

2. Which classic western
made him a star?

3. His first film as director
was . . . ?

4. Name two films
in which Wayne has
starred with Kirk Douglas.

5. KIRK DOUGLAS made his
Broadway debut as a
singing messenger. True or
false?

6. His film debut in 1945
was in . . . ?

7. He has received Academy
Award nominations for
which 3 films?

JOHN WAYNE and KIRK DOUGLAS
in 'THE WAR WAGON'
A UNIVERSAL PICTURE

TRIVIA QUIZ FROM THE BRITISH PRESSBOOK

ling gun.

Wayne assembles a motley crew to help him carry out his scheme. Robert Walker (Jr.) appears as the town drunk who has the assignment of using nitro to blow up a bridge. Keenan Wynn is a cantankerous old goat whose possessiveness of his young wife causes friction all around. Howard Keel, in an unusual casting choice, is a wise-cracking Indian more obsessed with personal enrichment than the "stupid" tribe which has let Cabot run them off their land.

Wayne's main co-conspirator is Douglas. The relationship is uneasy from the beginning, as Douglas had nearly succeeded in killing Wayne years before. Now Duke needs his skill with a gun, and it is only Douglas' desire for money that prevents these men from going at each other in round two. Eventually, their elaborate scheme is carried out, and the war wagon is destroyed. In an ironic scene inspired by *The Treasure of the Sierra Madre*, however, most of the gold is scattered to the wind as Indians loot the barrels in which the gold is hidden, thinking it is flour.

The best part of *The War Wagon* is the perception that Wayne and Douglas are having such a great time together. Their constant insults and taunting one another are often quite funny, thanks to Clair Huffaker's humorous screenplay. When Wayne takes Douglas to a remote location to introduce him to his friend Keel, they see a man chained to a giant rock with banditos shooting at him for target practice. Douglas sighs, and asks rhetorically: "Don't tell me, let me guess which one is your friend." Another witty exchange occurs when the two rivals gun down a pair of would-be assassins. "Mine hit the ground first," exclaims Douglas. To which Duke calmly replies, "Mine was taller!"

Under Burt Kennedy's solid direction, there is seldom a dull moment in *The War Wagon*. The supporting performances are competent, but unremarkable, although it is always good to see old buddies Wayne and Bruce Cabot on screen together. The last 20 minutes or so are tense, exciting and skillfully directed, but it is the dialogue that puts this film a notch above most other Westerns.

The War Wagon was shot in Durango, Mexico, as so many of Duke's other films had been. Released by Universal, it represented the first time that studio had employed Wayne since the Forties. The wait was worth it, as the film proved to be a box-office hit. The studio intended to release John Wayne films for a long time to come, but Duke severed his ties with the studio once more after their refusal to honor a commitment to back one of his personal projects *The Green Berets*. Wayne would only appear in two more films for Universal: *Hellfighters* and *Rooster Cogburn*.

TRUE GRIT (1969)

Cast: John Wayne, Glen Campbell, Kim Darby, Robert Duvall, Jeremy Slate, Dennis Hopper, Alfred Ryder, Strother Martin, Jeff Corey. *Director:* Henry Hathaway. *Screenplay:* Marguerite Roberts, *from the novel by* Charles Portis. *Music:* Elmer Bernstein. *Released by:* Paramount Pictures. *Running Time:* 128 Minutes.

After decades, John Wayne finally got the attention and recognition he so richly deserved from his peers, an Oscar as Best Actor for his memorable performance in *True Grit*. Wayne had been more enthused about *Grit* than he had been about any other prospective film in many years. He had read the Charles Portis novel while still in galley form, and instructed his son Michael to immediately bid for the screen rights, only to learn that he was outbid by legendary producer Hal Wallis. Heartbroken at perhaps not having the opportunity to play the film's central hero, Rooster Cogburn, he uncharacteristically went to the producer hat in hand and asked to play the part, which he felt would fit him like a glove.

Happily for Wayne, Wallis was in complete agreement. He signed Duke for the role, and hired one of Wayne's favorite directors, Henry Hathaway to direct. Ironically, the screen adaptation would be written by Marguerite Roberts, a previously blacklisted writer whose political leanings would doubtlessly have placed her on Wayne's enemies list a decade before. Rounding out the talent was a wonderful supporting cast headed by Robert Duvall as the chief bad guy, Kim Darby as the story's heroine Mattie Ross, and Glen Campbell as the Texas Ranger named LeBoeuf, who matches wit and insults with boozing, one-eyed Marshal Rooster Cogburn.

The script follows the book in impeccable detail, and the few changes that are made are generally improvements. Hathaway and Roberts opted to retain the distinctive language of the book, which although hardly natural, added a

WITH KIM DARBY

great deal of charm to the story. The plot centers on Mattie Ross, a 14-year-old tomboy who is determined to hunt down a man named Chaney (Jeff Corey) who robbed and murdered her father. When the more reliable lawmen cannot spare her any time, she reluctantly hires the alcoholic, cantankerous, over-the-hill Cogburn to track the killer and bring him to justice.

It is apparent from the start that the character portrayed by Wayne is slovenly and untrustworthy, and has justifiably earned the scorn of all those who know him. Wayne initially scoffs at the girl's request for aid, but comes around when she offers a fat reward. He also reluctantly accepts the help of Campbell as a Texas Ranger

132

RARE RADIO CITY MUSIC HALL POSTER

also on Corey's trail, and the two men immediately come into conflict.

Much to Wayne's chagrin, Darby insists on going on the manhunt. She's not overly fond of Wayne, but comes to gain a bit of respect for him as he spins intriguing tales of his glory days as a lawman. The trio learns that Corey has joined a notorious band of outlaws headed by Duvall. When Darby locates Corey, she is captured and held by her dad's killer as Duvall and several accomplices attempt to flee on horseback. In what is probably Wayne's greatest screen moment, the bandits encounter Duke's solitary figure astride his horse in an open meadow. When they scoff at his order to throw down their guns Wayne shouts, "Fill your hand, you son-of-a-bitch!" and rides into the entire gang in a manner described by at least one film critic as that of a knight in a jousting tournament. With pistol in one hand, rifle in the other, and the reins

133

*ORIGINAL PROGRAM FROM RADIO
CITY MUSIC HALL PREMIERE*

*ON THE SET WITH MR. AND MRS.
HENRY HATHAWAY*

between his teeth, Wayne decimates the group.

A tragic twist occurs when Campbell is killed
by Corey, and the murderer, in turn, is gunned
down by Wayne. At this point Duke must also
rescue Darby from a deep pit filled with snakes,
one of which succeeds in biting her. Determined
to save the teenager's life, Wayne drives their
horse to death and walks miles before comman-

134

WITH KIM DARBY AND GLEN CAMPBELL

THE SEQUENCE WHICH STANDS AS
WAYNE'S FINEST MOMENT ONSCREEN

deering a wagon to get her medical help. The final frames of the film depict Wayne and Darby respectfully bidding each other goodbye. Wayne invites her to "come see a fat old man sometime!" and rides off into the sunset, jumping a four rail fence to prove he still has *True Grit*. With the possible exception of the finale of *The Searchers*, it is the most poignant and moving ending for any Wayne movie.

True Grit was the kind of movie Wayne felt he would never again see in his career. So unanimous was the praise for the film and his performance, that many of the "liberal press" which crucified him in print for *The Green Berets* actively hyped Wayne for the Oscar and placed the film on their Ten Best lists. Wayne clearly relished the attention, and with good reason. Although it is fashionable to say that he was merely capitalizing on the sentiment of a press which unjustly ignored him for so long, this was clearly not the case. Wayne's performance as Cogburn is a brilliant piece of movie acting. Period. And *True Grit* deserves its status as one of the screen's classic Westerns.

Wayne cannot take all the credit for the movie's success. He is aided immeasurably by a wonderful performance by Kim Darby as the stalwart heroine. Although Darby and Wayne did not get along well on the set, it in no way affected their work. In fact, the animosity between their characters might have been helped by the tension between the actors. Excellent, too, is Robert Duvall as Ned Pepper, the outlaw leader. Duvall, however, did not particularly agree with Hathaway, which added additional fuel to the fire.

Singer Glen Campbell made his acting debut in this film (he starred in only one other), and although his performance is the weakest of the central characters, it grows stronger through the film and he deserved praise for holding his own against a heavyweight cast. Wayne and Campbell got along well, and remained close friends. There is also a sterling supporting performance by veteran character actor Strother Martin that makes *True Grit* a joy to behold. High praise should also go to cinematographer Lucien Ballard and composer Elmer Bernstein, both of whom are operating in peak form.

CHISUM (1970)

Cast: John Wayne, Forrest Tucker, Christopher George, Pamela McMyler, Geoffrey Deuel, Ben Johnson, Glenn Corbett, Bruce Cabot, Andrew Prine, Patric Knowles, Richard Jaeckel. *Director:* Andrew V. McLaglen. *Screenplay:* Andrew J. Fenady. *Music:* Dominic Frontiere. *Released by:* Warner Bros. *Running Time:* 110 Minutes.

Following Duke's triumph in *True Grit*, the actor went immediately to work on *The Undefeated*, a large-scale Western co-starring Rock Hudson. Despite some impressive scenary and action, the film was basically a routine hoss opera that does not rank among Wayne's more memorable movies. Fans wondered if he would begin to slip into making the kind of mediocre films which had immediately preceded *True Grit*. The worries proved to be groundless. Whether by coincidence or design, most of Duke's post-*Grit* films would be both entertaining and impressive. His next feature following *The Undefeated* was titled *Chisum*, and it proved to be, in the words of *Cue* Magazine critic William Wolf, "a real gem worth treasuring."

For *Chisum*, Duke teamed again with director Andrew V. McLaglen, the son of Wayne's long-time pal, colleague and drinking pal, Victor McLaglen. Andy's track record with Wayne thus far was "1 win, 2 losses," having directed the popular and successful *McLintock!* and the mediocre *Hellfighters* and *The Undefeated*. The two would team again in 1973 for the sluggish, *Cahill: U.S. Marshal*. For all intents and purposes, *Chisum* would prove to be the highpoint of the duo's semi-frequent collaborations.

The story is based loosely on the life of cattle baron John Simpson Chisum, whose kingdom became the focal point of the legendary Lincoln County War. That event helped to perpetrate the legend of Billy the Kid, and the young gunman plays a prominent part in this tale. Things get off to an impressive start, as McLaglen uses the

WITH FOES FORREST TUCKER AND BRUCE CABOT

DOUBLING FOR DUKE, STUNTMAN CHUCK ROBERSON CRASHES INTO MURPHY'S HIDEOUT

136

EINE BATJAC PRODUKTION

JOHN WAYNE
ALS
CHISUM

Darsteller:

John Chisum	John Wayne	Sheriff Brady	Bruce Cabot
Lawrence Murphy	Forrest Tucker	Henry Tunstall	Patric Knowles
Dan Nodeen	Christopher George	Jess Evans	Richard Jaeckel
James Pepper	Ben Johnson	Sue McSween	Lynda Day
Pat Garrett	Glenn Corbett	Gouverneur Axtell	Alan Baxter
Alexander McSween	Andrew Prine	Billy „The Kid" Bonney	Geoffrey Deuel
		Sallie Chisum	Pamela McMyler

Regie: Andrew V. McLaglen
Drehbuch: Andrew J. Fenady
Kamera: William H. Clothier, A.S.C.
Musik: Dominic Frontiere
Herstellungsleitung:
Michael Wayne
Produktion: Andrew J. Fenady

WB
A KINNEY COMPANY

EIN FARBFILM IN TECHNICOLOR UND PANAVISION IM VERLEIH DER WARNER BROS.

GERMAN PRESSBOOK AD

CHISUM AND MURPHY IN THE FILM'S CLIMAX   GIVING FORREST TUCKER A TASTE OF HIS OWN MEDICINE

technique of showing the credits over some distinctive paintings of life on the prairie to reflect the events Chisum had to endure in order to gain his success. Accompanied by a corny, yet catchy driving theme song, the credits fade and the movie opens with an impressive shot of Duke alone on a mountaintop at sunset surveying his domain.

When we first meet Wayne, we see he is a tough, but reasonable businessman who has no intention of relinquishing one bit of the land he fought so hard to own. This comes as disturbing news to his rival, in the person of Forrest Tucker. The two men are vying for control of the choicest land, and Tucker is not above using unscrupulous means to get what he covets—Chisum's cattle empire and spread. Into this tense atmosphere rides Billy Bonney (aka Billy the Kid), who is trying desperately to put his scandalous past behind him by becoming a trusted employee of Duke's neighboring cattle baron, played by Patric Knowles.

The peaceful atmosphere soon erupts, as events unfold rapidly. Billy (Geoffrey Deuel) falls for Wayne's niece (Pamela McMyler), to the dismay of Duke, who likes the boy personally, but distrusts his instinctive reactions toward violence. Tucker eventually declares all-out war on Wayne, leading to the murder of Knowles. When this occurs, Deuel decides it's time for Billy the Kid to do what he does best—shoot. He guns down the corrupt sheriff (Bruce Cabot) as well as Knowles' killers. Wayne informs Deuel he will not tolerate his lawlessness, and tells him to leave the territory. Deuel refuses, and along with a few accomplices, gets trapped in a building by Tucker and a veritable army of thugs. A blazing gunbattle erupts in which innocent people are murdered. Wayne is then faced with the choice of waiting for "due process" or taking action. To no one's surprise, he chooses the latter, telling sidekick Ben Johnson he's going to do "what I woulda' done 25 years ago."

This sets the stage for the spectacular climax of *Chisum*, which culminates in what one critic called "the busiest 40 seconds of any John Wayne movie." In a wonderfully staged action sequence, Duke and his men smash through a barricade in the middle of town by stampeding a herd of cattle. As dozens of men engage in a thrilling gun battle, Wayne crashes his horse through a store window to get at Tucker. The two aging rivals then engage in a terrifically exciting fist fight, which leads to Tucker being impaled on a set of cattle horns. The war is over, John Simpson Chisum resumes his quiet life, and Billy the Kid heads off for the pages of history.

There are a great many things to admire in *Chisum*. For one thing it presents a solid storyline and does not hurry through the dialogue to get to the next shootout. There's plenty of action, but never at the expense of the characterizations. Wayne is excellent in the title role, conveying a sensitive side rarely seen in his films. He is more than matched, however, by Forrest Tucker, whose interpretation of the despicable, yet charming rival to Wayne probably represents the best performance of his career. The supporting cast is less impressive, though it would be unfair to say that any performance was actually unsatisfactory. The weakest link is Deuel's Billy the Kid. He is simply too much of a lightweight to provide the insights associated with the character. The portrayal is adequate, but nothing more.

Seasoned pros like Ben Johnson and Bruce Cabot are far more watchable, having been part of the Wayne stock company for many years. The screenplay bogs down a bit with the needless romantic entanglements between Deuel and McMyler, and there are a couple of mediocre love songs thrown in as part of one of those dreadful but seemingly obligatory "montages" of couples in love. Yet, for its few flaws, *Chisum* was a superior Western in every way. Audiences agreed, making it one of the most successful films of 1970. The film was also a major stepping stone for Andy McLaglen, who became a leading director of action films, including the superb movie *The Wild Geese*. Much fanfare was generated shortly after *Chisum*'s release when Richard Nixon declared it to be one of his all-time favorite movies. Perhaps he was a bit too inspired by Duke's two-fisted way of imposing his views, as shortly after seeing *Chisum*, the President ordered military action in Cambodia.

BIG JAKE (1971)

Cast: John Wayne, Richard Boone, Maureen O'Hara, Patrick Wayne, Chris Mitchum, Bobby Vinton, Bruce Cabot, Glenn Corbett, Harry Carey, Jr., John Doucette, John Ethan Wayne, Jim Davis, John Agar. *Directed by:* George Sherman. *Screenplay:* Harry Julian Fink and R.M. Fink. *Music:* Elmer Bernstein. A Batjac Production. *Released by:* National General for Cinema Center Films. *Running Time:* 110 minutes.

Big Jake more than any other John Wayne film of the Seventies remains the actor's most underrated work. Although a popular success at the box-office, it was attacked by critics for its admittedly brutal action sequences and bloodletting. Some years earlier, many of these critics were quick to classify Sam Peckinpah's *The Wild Bunch* as the classic it was, despite its then-shockingly realistic depiction of violence. Although *Big Jake* is a far less sadistic film—and one which dilutes its violence through its use of frequent humor—critics accused Wayne of betraying his basic family audience.

His fans apparently had no such reservations, and *Big Jake* remains one of Wayne's most enjoyable latter-day films. Originally titled, *The Million Dollar Kidnapping*, the movie is an unending pleasure, moreso even today, as we realize that many of the cronies who appear with Wayne on screen and off are doing so for the last time. Sentimentally, it teams Wayne and Maureen O'hara for the first (and last) time since *McLintock!* (1963), and it's an impressive screen swan song for the couple. Wayne looked extremely well in this film, and had yet to show the wear of the medical crises he would face over the next few years. O'Hara is absolutely stunning, and appears not to have aged since her last outing with Wayne. One wishes they had more screen time together, but *Big Jake* is above all an action film, and we all know romance generally takes a back seat to keeping the story moving.

A PENSIVE MOMENT FOR WAYNE

The movie was directed by George Sherman, who helmed some of Wayne's *Three Mesquiteer* serials in the 1930s. By 1971, he had lost none of his touch, as demonstrated with his first-rate direction of an impressive cast. Wayne is re-teamed with *Alamo* co-star Richard Boone, here seen as one of the slimiest of all Wayne villains. Duke also co-stars for the last time with son Patrick and for the first time with youngest son Ethan. Sadly, *Big Jake* marks the last cinematic teaming of Wayne and Bruce Cabot, who appears quite fit, but would soon die of cancer.

The movie opens with a *Butch Cassidy*-inspired montage of old stills and newsreels depicting life in the West during the early part of the century. We then see Boone and his motley band of outlaws lay siege to O'Hara's cattle empire, brutally killing almost everyone. It is a shocking and effective scene, culminating in the kidnapping of

WITH ETHAN WAYNE, MAUREEN
O'HARA AND (FIRST ROW): L TO R:
PATRICK WAYNE, BOBBY VINTON AND
CHRISTOPHER MITCHUM

WAYNE BELTS CHRIS MITCHUM

O'Hara's grandson (Ethan Wayne) who is to be held for $1 million ransom. O'Hara and her sons (Patrick Wayne and Chris Mitchum) reluctantly call upon the Duke's Big Jake McCandles, O'Hara's estranged husband, to rescue the boy.

What follows is somewhat predictable, but extremely entertaining as Wayne continues the type of badgering with his family that led to his leaving some 20 years before. Aided by Indian sidekick Cabot, Wayne and sons confront Boone and his men in a bloody, suspenseful showdown.

While the action sequences are excellent, the real joy of watching *Big Jake* lies in the chemistry between the stars. Wayne has a rollicking good time opposite his son and young Mitchum, quite possibly because he gets to play the old "know-it-all" who consistently upstages his "young whippersnapper sons." The chemistry carries over into the confrontations with Boone, and the banter between the two adversaries is priceless. Between the bloody shootings, there is added sentimentality between Wayne and Cabot. As

they prepare to enter what they believe to be a suicidal showdown with Boone, there is a brief moment in which the two men make vague plans to hunt again in the future. Yet, we know that they realize these plans will never come to fruition. They are now too old, and this is their last chance to live out the adventures of their youth. The scene takes on all the more sentiment as we now know that this was the last teaming between the two co-stars—a fact they probably realized at the time.

Big Jake has so many virtues it is difficult to find faults. Still, they exist. Certain sequences bog down and become long-winded, such as Boone's ambush of a posse of "horseless carriages." The scene drags on as we watch Mitchum utilize a motorcycle in an improbable series of stunts. Also, the film seems to have left quite a few loose ends. For one, Bobby Vinton is seen early in the film as one of Wayne's sons who is severely wounded by Boone. By the end of the story, however, his fate is never told. It would also have been nice to see O'hara's reaction to Duke's successful rescue of their grandson, but she does not reappear following the opening sequences. Another fault is Wayne's reaction to the dramatic death of Cabot, who perishes saving his old friend's life. Wayne does not utter a single word of remorse, and the movie abruptly ends on an upbeat note.

Every other aspect of *Big Jake* works very well indeed and there are classic moments to remember: Wayne's frequent knock-abouts with his "boys"; the sentiment in his eyes as he sees his grandson for the first time; his amusing assault on a pool hall bully; his casual shooting of another villain from a shower stall; and most gratifying, the movie's superbly directed climax which builds to sharp suspense—an attribute not generally found in a Wayne Western.

Throughout the film, Wayne is told by friend and foe alike that he has been presumed dead for many years. "Not hardly" is his response. The line works well in the context of the film, but one suspects that Duke had a Freudian delight in using it to address his critics, who time and again predicted audience rejection of his films as he continued to battle age and medical problems.

142

THE COWBOYS (1972)

Cast: John Wayne, Roscoe Lee Brown, Bruce Dern, Colleen Dewhurst, Slim Pickens, Lonny Chapman, Charles Tyner, A Martinez, Robert Carradine. *Director:* Mark Rydell. *Screenplay:* Irving Ravetch and Harriet Frank, Jr. and William Dale Jennings. *Based on the novel by* Jennings. *Music:* John Williams. *Released by:* Warner Bros. *Running Time:* 128 Minutes.

The Cowboys was an unusual film for John Wayne. Unusual in the sense that it represented one of the rare times in his twilight years in which he was employed simply as an actor. Director Mark Rydell insisted that he only wanted Duke, not his entourage of favorite actors, his son Michael as producer, or any interference from Batjac. Fortunately, Duke agreed to the terms because there was literally no other actor in the world as appropriate for the role of aging rancher Wil Andersen.

Filming began in April 1971 in New Mexico and Colorado. The shooting schedule lasted 12 weeks on location, with two more weeks of interiors in Hollywood. It was a hectic schedule, as an actors' strike was looming that could have jeopardized the production. The cast and crew worked strenuously seven days a week. Wayne was 64 years old when he began filming *The Cowboys* and there was concern that the rugged locations and fast pace might endanger his health. Yet, he kept his tradition of being on the set even when not required. He insisted upon doing most of his own stunts, including the rugged riding scenes that are shown during the credit sequence at the beginning of the film. He also endured a brutally realistic fight scene in which he was "mutilated" on screen, in the words of his makeup man, Dave Grayson.

Many were skeptical that Wayne could keep his temper in control on the set. Certainly there were enough elements present to cause an explosion. For one thing, one-time actor Mark Rydell

JOHN WAYNE & THE COWBOYS

A MARK RYDELL FILM

was a young man who had no experience directing Westerns (in fact, he'd only made three other films). It was feared that Duke's well-known penchant for "advising" even seasoned directors like Ford and Hawks might not be appreciated by Rydell. Other elements adding potential fuel to the fire was the casting of Roscoe Lee Brown and Bruce Dern. Brown is a classically-trained black actor who was well known for his liberal views. Dern, who specialized at the time in psychos and slimy villains, was the co-star of many anti-establishment films which undoubtedly did not head up Duke's list of all time favorites.

Almost in amazement, Rydell reported how all on the set loved Duke. To the surprise of many, they discovered Wayne was a well-read man who had great tolerance for the views of others. Rydell was impressed by Wayne's acknowledgement that, on the set, the director is the only boss. Rydell said he never got over the fact that the legendary Wayne referred to him constantly as "Sir." As for Brown, the men predictably agreed on nothing. However, they had such mutual admiration that, in the words of Rydell, "They can't get off the phone with each other."

The boys in the film were a talented group of youngsters, many of whom had never acted before. Conversely, the professional actors among them had no experience on a ranch. This posed a problem for Rydell. In addition to teaching the novices acting lessons, he also had to have the "city kids" instructed on how to handle horses and cattle. A special event occurred on the set, when John Ford visited Duke on location. The aging director was recovering from injuries sustained in a fall. He was driven to the set by his grandson Dan, who was working on the TV special *The American West of John Ford*. The men chatted awhile and posed for a few photos together before "Pappy" departed. It would be one of their last meetings. (In 1973, when Duke was on location for *McQ*, he would be summoned to Ford's house. A gravely ill "Pappy" asked Wayne, "Here for the death watch, Duke?" Wayne replied, "Hell, you'll bury us all." A few hours later, John Ford departed into "that good night," thus bringing to an end one of the most successful collaborative efforts in film.)

As for *The Cowboys* as a movie, it can be said that it is probably one of Wayne's more controversial Westerns. The story shows Wayne's Andersen as a tough man of principal who is left

144

WAYNE HITS BRUCE DERN...

IS STRUCK DOWN...

BUT EARNS A SHORT-LIVED VICTORY BY GAINING THE UPPER HAND

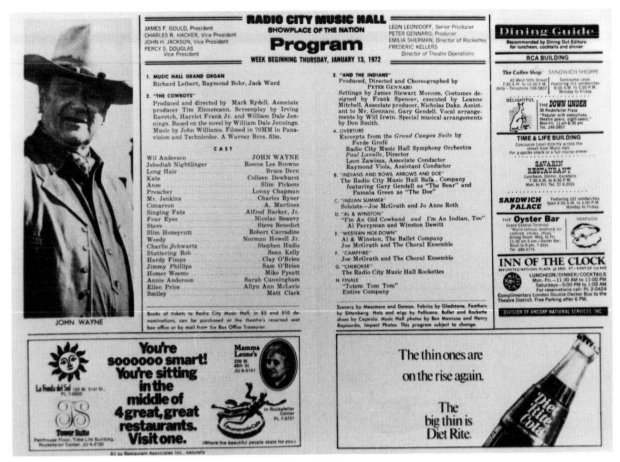

ORIGINAL PROGRAM USED EXCLUSIVELY AT RADIO CITY MUSIC HALL

"high and dry" when his ranchers run off to a gold strike. In order to get his cattle to market, he reluctantly hires a group of 11 boys with no experience to get the job done. Along the way, the group—accompanied by Roscoe Lee Brown as the cook—encounters hardship, friendship, laughter and tragedy, forcing the boys quickly to mature beyond their years. Wayne drives them mercilessly, but learns to respect them individually as they grow to like "the old man."

The movie grows realistic when, three quarters of the way into the story, Wayne and the boys are overtaken by Dern and his band of scroungy cattle thieves. In an effort to distract his attention from the boys and save their lives, Wayne goads Dern into a brutal fistfight in which both men are battered severely. Wayne wins the battle, but loses the war when Dern, to the shock of the audience, shoots Duke in the back. The boys,

lead by Brown, then avenge his death by killing all the villains in an elaborately staged battle at the film's conclusion.

None of the above accurately describes the real value of *The Cowboys*. Although it is an exciting, lively film, its best moments are the quiet ones in which characterizations are allowed to develop. In a short period of time, we really get to know each of the kids, as well as gain a full understanding of Wayne and Brown. You feel as though you are along for the drive.

Among the highlights of *The Cowboys* are:

• Wayne talking gently with his wife about the hardships of the life they have lived together, and his appreciation of her quiet acceptance of his failures.

• Duke surveying his spread on the eve of the

drive, with all the worry and concern reflected in his eyes as he allows his horses to run free before the drive begins.

- The wonderful chemistry between Wayne and Brown, who as trail cook Jebediah Nightlinger gives a top-notch performance as a man who has seen and lived almost too much in his lifetime.

- The unexpected and tragic death of one of the boys, and Duke's short but touching speech at the gravesite.

- Wayne's silent but moving visit to the graves of his sons who "went wrong on him."

- The boys' encounter with town madame Colleen Dewhurst's "girls" and Brown's gentlemanly manner of persuading them not to entice the youngsters.

All of these scenes are wonderfully directed and enacted. Rydell proved to have an exceptional flair for both the quiet and solemn scenes as well as those containing action. Clearly, the film's highlight is the fight between Wayne and Dern. We suspect it will end tragically, but not in the brutal way in which Dern disposes of the world's Number One movie star. The fight is graphic and bloody, but superbly staged and directed. Oddly, Wayne himself complained that it was too realistic, and considered the sequence—and the film itself—to be disappointing. The movie does suffer following the scene, as it truly is the film's climax. However, since no one would want the bad guys to go unpunished, the contrived ending is put in to boost audience acceptance.

Regardless of Duke's own feelings, I consider *The Cowboys* to be a brilliant film, with Wayne giving what many feel to be the best performance of his career. Certainly, he and Brown should have been nominated for Oscars, along with Rydell and composer John Williams, whose beautiful score lingers in the mind. Robert Surtees cinematography is also a vision to behold, and so gritty we almost feel the dust in our faces as we watch the film.

Critics were positive about the acting and technical aspects of the films, but many felt the sight of children handling guns was distasteful. Nevertheless, *The Cowboys* was a major box-office hit. Next to *The Shootist*, I consider it to be the last great film of John Wayne's career.

146

McQ (1974)

Cast: John Wayne, Eddie Albert, Diana Muldaur, Colleen Dewhurst, Clu Gulager, David Huddleston, Al Lettieri, Julie Adams. *Director:* John Sturges. *Screenplay:* Lawrence Roman. *Music:* Elmer Bernstein. *Released by* Warner Bros. *Running Time:* 116 Minutes.

Considering the reputation John Sturges had as a director of first rate action adventures and Westerns, it is surprising that he and John Wayne had not teamed up for a film until 1974, when both men were in the twilight of their careers. Sturges had directed, among other fine Westerns, *Bad Day at Black Rock, Gunfight at the O.K. Corral, Last Train From Gun Hill, Hour of the Gun,* and most notably, *The Magnificent Seven.* He was no stranger to the WWII genre either, having brought to the screen *The Great Escape,* which remains one of the best films of its kind. Happily, Warner Bros. was able to unite these talents for *McQ,* a contemporary police drama that can not be placed in the classic category of the aforementioned, but certainly deserves attention as a first-rate detective thriller.

Critics were cynical about Wayne choosing so late in life to begin playing hip street cops. *The New York Times,* in reviewing the film, suggested that there is suspense, but it consisted of wondering whether Wayne was spry enough to get through each scene. This was not only cruel, but untrue. Amazingly, Wayne is very fit and agile in the title role. His age brings dignity and interest to a character that, if played by a younger actor, would have just blended in with the legion of Dirty Harry clones which populated the screen in the early 1970s.

Wayne had originally been offered the part of Dirty Harry, but refused it on the grounds that the script was too violent and repulsive to win over his audiences. Whether Wayne would have stuck with those convictions had he known the blockbuster hit the movie would be, will never be

GETTING A BEAD ON THE DRUG SMUGGLERS

THE SHOOT-OUT ON THE BEACH

known. Is *McQ* Duke's long delayed attempt to capitalize on Clint Eastwood's success? Perhaps, but probably not. Duke would have continued in the Western genre almost exclusively if they had not lost their popularity at the box-office by the mid-Seventies. *McQ* can be seen more as Duke's acknowledgement that the Western was next to dead as opposed to a desperation move to infringe on Eastwood's popularity.

The film opens with the murder of Wayne's partner, Stan Boyle (William Bryant). Duke gets the word, and immediately suspects a drug kingpin played with icy charm by Al Lettieri. After Wayne comforts Boyle's widow Lois (Diana Muldaur), he beats Lettieri to a pulp in a restaurant bathroom. The scene is vintage Wayne, and Duke calmly walks out of the bathroom leaving the roughed up gangster draped over the urinal. Because of actions like this, Wayne is removed from the case by hard-nosed boss Eddie Albert. Wayne suspects Albert is in league with Lettieri and resigns from the department, choosing instead to team with an old friend named Pinky Farrow, a private detective played by David Huddleston.

The trail takes Wayne to a facility in which confiscated drugs are to be burned. He discovers that the secret location for this operation is also known to Lettieri, whose men succeed in stealing the drugs that are scheduled for destruction. Wayne confronts them in a wild shoot-out, but loses them on the freeway. He later learns that even Lettieri has been double-crossed, as the "drugs" have turned out to be sugar. Interestingly, Lettieri protests his innocence in Bryant's death, and tells Wayne that corrupt police officials had obviously stolen the drugs before the criminals could get to them.

This gives Wayne food for thought. He receives encouragement in his investigation from Muldaur and mutual friend and political official Clu Gulager. Muldaur keeps urging Wayne to get out of police work, and even tries to convince him to move away with her. Duke refuses, saying he will not rest until he avenges her husband's death. Several attempts are made on Wayne's life by forces unknown. In an inprobable but highly entertaining scene, Wayne's car, with him at the wheel, is nearly decimated by two garbage trucks which decide to play a deadly game of "bumper cars." Duke later visits an over-age call girl and informant played by Colleen Dewhurst (who was the madam in The *Cowboys*). Her initial resentment of Wayne lends a good, realistic edge to their dialogue and their too brief scenes together are very well acted. As *Variety* suggested, "Someone should write a terrific script for them."

When Dewhurst is murdered, Wayne explodes. He is also outraged when someone tries to frame him by planting dope in his car. Eventually, all the pieces come together, and he realizes that not only was the murdered Bryant "on the take," but also that Muldaur and Gulager are culprits who have designed an elaborate scenario to throw the police off track and use Duke as a fall guy. All of this comes to a head in a terrific car chase along the Olympic Peninsula outside of Seattle, where *McQ* was filmed. To give Wayne an edge against insurmountable odds, he wields an Ingram 9mm. machine gun which he uses to devasting effect on Lettieri, Gulager and his other pursuers. Although one would have imagined that all car chases should have stopped after *Bullitt* and *The French Connection*, Sturges gives this one some originality by having it take place on the beach. Cars crash through sand dunes and Duke uses the spray from waves to slow the bad guys. All of this is given much more credence due to the fact that here, and throughout much of the film, Duke does a great deal of his own driving. The scene ends with an impressive car stunt, as Wayne destroys Lettieri and Gulager and turns Muldaur over to the police.

This writer is an unabashed fan of *McQ*. It is tightly scripted and well directed and boasts an impressive cast in a series of fine performances. This includes Wayne, whose age slows him a bit in the chase sequences, but who proved fans could accept him in this change of pace. *McQ* placed on *Variety*'s list of top film rentals to no one's surprise but the critics.

BRANNIGAN (1975)

Cast: John Wayne, Richard Attenborough, Judy Geeson, Mel Ferrer, John Vernon, Daniel Pilon, James Booth. *Director:* Douglas Hickox. *Screenplay:* Christopher Trumbo, Michael Butler, William P. McGiven and William Norton. *From a screen story by* Christopher Trumbo and Michael Butler. *Music:* Dominic Frontiere. *Released* through United Artists. *Running Time:* 111 Minutes.

At an age when most men have already retired or at least greatly slowed down, Wayne decided to continue to broaden his horizons by starring again in a contemporary police drama, this one titled *Brannigan.* Why the producers decided not to merely call the film *McQ II* is a mystery in itself, as the characters Wayne portrays in both films are pretty much the same. As a film, however, *Brannigan* is much lighter in spirit than *McQ,* and Duke's title character in this one is a bit more tongue-in-cheek. The movie is not generally listed among Wayne's more memorable films, but *Brannigan* deserves far more attention than it initially received. (Along with *The Train Robbers,* it is one of the few Wayne movies of this period not to appear on *Variety*'s all-time box office rental champions list. Its domestic rentals equaled ony half of what *McQ* took in.)

In the title role, Wayne is a tough Chicago detective sent to London to extradite a mob boss, played by John Vernon. When Wayne arrives, he discovers that, having posted bail, Vernon is free, but is under surveillance by Scotland Yard, whose top detective (Richard Attenborough) immediately crosses swords with Duke over proper police methods. The men gradually build respect for each other, as both commit a couple of blunders which allow Vernon to be kidnapped and held for ransom. Wayne suspects Vernon has orchestrated the entire affair to prevent being taken back into custody, but these suspicions are momentarily put aside when the kidnappers send

one of Vernon's fingers through the mail with a demand for a ransom payment.

In fact, Vernon and his attorney (Mel Ferrer) have indeed set up an elaborate scenario in which Vernon is all too happy to lose a finger to lend

149

BRITISH TEASER POSTER

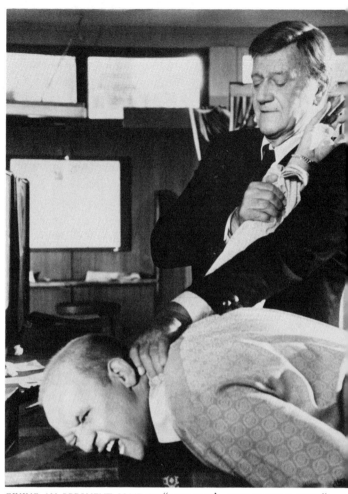
GIVING AN OPPONENT SOME OF "ENGLAND'S FREE DENTAL CARE"

authenticity to the scheme. The plan is to pay the ransom money to Vernon himself who will then abscond to South America. Naturally, Duke and Attenborough foil the plot at the last moment and both Vernon and Ferrer are sent to the slammer.

Several subplots are interwoven with these affairs. One finds Duke matching wits with a young female police inspector, played nicely by Judy Geeson. Unfortunately, Geeson's role is simply there to provide someone for Duke to protect or to relate stories from his past. The script takes pains to have Wayne and Geeson talk openly about their romantic lives with other people. Wayne refers several times to his grown son, while Geeson introduces Duke to her fiancé in a scene which has no relevance other than to appease critics who might scoff at any hint of a romance between Wayne and a much younger woman.

A secondary subplot finds a merciless assassin (Daniel Pilon) stalking Wayne throughout the film. Although we are told he is the best in the business, he chooses to knock off the Duke on a night so rainy and foggy that he mistakes 90 pound Judy Geeson for John Wayne. With tactics like that, Pilon could ill-expect to be accepted into the hitmens' Hall of Fame. One gives him credit for persistence, however, as he rigs a booby trap in Wayne's apartment which is supposed to kill Duke via a shotgun with the trigger wired to a doorknob. Wayne neatly avoids this, and also discovers a bomb in his toilet. Obviously, even the Tidy Bowl man is not safe from international terrorism.

150

BATTLING IN THE PUB

Brannigan would be a standard dirty cop picture, except for the refreshing fact that it isn't dirty. Of all the street-wise detective films made in the Seventies, only *The French Connection* and the *Dirty Harry* films remain memorable. *Brannigan* is almost startling in that it could have been shown almost 20 years earlier, minus a few nods to contemporary moviemaking such as suggestions of nudity or kinky behavior.

The film is actually a good piece of entertainment, primarily due to some elaborate and well-directed action sequences. British director Douglas Hickox staged several scenes which avoid the standard cliches. True, there is the obligatory car chase, but here it is played light-heartedly as Duke commandeers a taxi and proceeds to speed after a villain while a terrified cabbie along for the ride realizes to his horror that Wayne is not exactly well-versed in driving on the "wrong side of the road." The case ends with Wayne driving the car over the open Tower Bridge before crashing it into a construction site.

Likewise, there is the other obligatory sequence—the barroom brawl. This time a London pub is utilized, and again, we find the accent is on laughs. It's a well-choreographed affair, and the 67-year-old Wayne is seen in the same kind of action and stunts that he performed as a young man. It adds realism to the entire scene to see Duke, and not his double, crashing about the place. The film's climax finds Wayne and Geeson on foot and menaced by Pilon in a speeding sportscar. Again, Wayne amazingly close to the action for a man of his age, and his spectacular destruction of his adversary proves a fitting conclusion to the story.

Brannigan may be an unremarkable film, but there is so much to like about it that it can be enjoyed over and over again. Particularly pleasing is Wayne's initial appearance in the movie, framed in a doorway and shot from an angle which makes him look like Paul Bunyan. His quick disposal of a minor crook within the early scenes is also memorable, as is Duke's rapport with his co-star, the inimitable soon-to-be-knighted Richard Attenborough (who acquits himself nicely in fight scenes with Wayne). *Brannigan* deserves another chance; catch it again on video. You won't be sorry.

151

THE SHOOTIST (1976)

Cast: John Wayne, Lauren Bacall, James Stewart, Ron Howard, Richard Boone, Hugh O'Brian, Harry Morgan, Scatman Crothers, John Carradine, Richard Lenz, Sheree North. *Director:* Don Siegel. *Screenplay:* Miles Hood Swarthout and Scott Hale. *From the novel by* Glendon Swarthout. *Music:* Elmer Bernstein. *Released by* Paramount Pictures. *Running Time:* 100 Minutes.

No actor has ever had a more appropriate screen epitaph than the one provided for John Wayne in *The Shootist*. Intimates of Duke's say he never felt this would be his last film, and indeed, he had purchased another property titled *Beau John*. However, Duke was a realist. By the time he received the script for *The Shootist*, his health was deteriorating rapidly, and some people were astonished that he would even consider appearing in another rugged action film when he was approaching his 69th birthday. In a way, it is probably better that Wayne did not accept any film work after *The Shootist*. With his failing health, he might have rushed out an inconsequential "B" movie that would have been all but forgotten in time. Instead, it provided the perfect vehicle to cap what is perhaps the most successful career the movie industry has ever known.

The Shootist paralleled Wayne's own life in so many ways that many fans thought it was expressly written for him. This was not the case. The script was adapted from a novel, and the lead role was originally offered to both Paul Newman and George C. Scott, neither of whom showed interest in it. Wayne was just about one of the last actors on the list to be considered, probably because the producers feared that the tenuous nature of his health would preclude him from completing the film.

Wayne appears as J.B. Books, a one-time notorious gunslinger who is trying to live out the last years of his life in solitude and peace. He comes to Carson City, Nevada, where he seeks advice

He's got to face a gunfight once more to live up to his legend once more TO WIN JUST ONE MORE TIME.

JOHN WAYNE
LAUREN BACALL
IN A SIEGEL FILM
"THE SHOOTIST"

from a doctor friend, played by James Stewart. Stewart reluctantly has to inform Wayne that his recent health problems are caused by terminal cancer and that the aging gunman has only weeks to live. Deeply depressed, Wayne seeks isolation in a boarding house run by widow Lauren Bacall and her wayward son Ron Howard. Although the young man idolizes the boarder, Bacall resents the fact that Duke had tried unsuccessfully to conceal his identity. It is only Wayne's admission of his diagnosis which prevents Bacall from evicting him.

When word leaks out of his presence, an assortment of old foes converge on him trying to get the credit for killing a living legend. Duke manages to get the upper hand, but just barely. He is also distressed by the exploitation of people he once trusted. In desperation for some kind of friendship, he tries—with limited success—to win over Bacall. However, the pain is increasing and Stewart convinces him not to die an agonizing death. Duke gets the hint and decides to go down in a blaze of glory. He arranges to meet with three enemies (Richard Boone, Hugh O'Brian and Bill McKinney) in a saloon, where he knows the ensuing gunfight will claim his life. Ironically, the shootist manages to defeat his adversaries in a blazing battle, only to be killed by a shotgun blast to the back from a cowardly bartender. His final vision is of Ron Howard killing the man, and then throwing his gun away in a rejection of violence.

The Shootist is something like an Irish wake. It is steeped in impending tragedy not only for Wayne's onscreen character, but for the actor himself. Yet, there is something dignified and joyous about the experience. Wayne was able to corral a "Who's Who" of notable co-stars from the past to join with him one last time. We find Bacall from *Blood Alley*, John Carradine from *Stagecoach* and other Wayne films, Hugh O'Brian from *In Harm's Way*, James Stewart from *The Man Who Shot Liberty Valance*, Richard Boone from *The Alamo* and *Big Jake* and Harry Morgan from *How the West Was Won*. All of them give excellent performances, and lend class to the film, the kind that would be hard to achieve with younger actors.

The direction by Don Siegel is first-rate, although he and Wayne had many a battle during production. Wayne was in ill spirits, as he felt the film rapidly sapping his strength. He attempted to "suggest" to Siegel how sequences should be filmed, but found that Siegel was from the school which taught that actors act and directors direct.

ON THE SET WITH JAMES STEWART

Yet, ironically, under more pleasant circumstances, both men had been known to compromise their beliefs. Wayne listened intently to director Mark Rydell on the set of *The Cowboys* and never interfered with his instructions. Likewise, Siegel was known to have accepted suggestions from Clint Eastwood on their many collaborative efforts. Whatever the reason, *The Shootist* proved to be a tense project for all concerned.

To the credit of cast and crew, however, no apparent damage can be seen onscreen. The film is virtually flawless; Wayne's performance is fine work. He allows us to see through this tough killer and view a man who is lonely, stubborn, but also rather gentle. We learn about his past as the credits role through the excellent use of film clips from Wayne's previous films which purport to show events in the life of J.B. Books. It's a classic opening for the movie, and it hooks you from minute one

Among the memorable moments in the film are the all-too-brief scenes between Wayne and Stewart. The quiet intensity of these two men speak volumes about acting skills. Wayne also works well with young Ron Howard, whom he considered to be one of the better performers he

153

CONFRONTED BY AN ILL-FATED ROBBER

had worked with. Wayne insisted that the script be changed so that the resolution found Howard becoming a good guy instead of following a life of crime, as the novel had shown. The movie probably benefits from this change, as Howard is one of the few people in the film who is not despicable or an opportunist.

The Shootist was released in the summer of 1976 to very good reviews. However, Paramount annoyed Wayne by giving the film a less-than-auspicious advertising campaign which failed to capitalize on the glowing testimonials. The film opened strong, even in New York where Wayne was considered box-office poison. I recall seeing the film at the Astor Theatre on Broadway and having to wait in line. Sadly, Dino DeLaurentiis' production company was more interested in spending money on its major release, the ill-fated remake of *King Kong*. While *The Shootist* did not die at the box-office, neither did it gain the word of mouth a stronger ad campaign might have achieved.

With this film, a major chapter in American filmmaking came to a close. Wayne continued to make periodic TV appearances, but his health failed rapidly, and he died on June 11, 1979. At least it can be said that his final contribution to the art of film was a superb one. *Variety*, in its review, called *The Shootist*, "One of the great films of our time."

154

JOHN WAYNE TURKEYS

I can never understand the complete idolization of celebrities. Admiration for a person's work is totally understandable, but to elevate anyone, even the Duke, to the level of a god is inappropriate. Wayne was among the first to admit that he made so many bad movies he could not even recall the leading ladies in them let alone the titles. This section will take a lighthearted examination of those films which were really beneath Dukes talent.

What Wayne boasted in skill, he often lacked in judgment, as reflected on the films in this section. I have intentionally omitted any "B" Western prior to *Stagecoach*, feeling that these were low-budget affairs which could not be faulted for their frequently laughable plots and non-existent production values. Criticizing them is no more sporting than shooting fish in a barrel. It is more appropriate to critique those

instances in which Wayne and/or his advisors should have known better. Not to say that every one of the failures described herein is Duke's fault. Very often the star can be sabotaged by conditions beyond his control, and admittedly this may have happened in some cases to Wayne. But not even a guy like Duke can be absolved of perpetrating *The Conqueror* or *Jet Pilot*.

In answer to all the Wayne fans who will obviously find fault with some of the entries in this section, I will state honestly that some of the films are extremely enjoyable despite their status as "turkeys." I can say unequivocably that I would rather sit through *Hellfighters* many times rather than suffer more than once through many so-called classics, which seem to be so designated as long as someone dresses in a toga and carries a spear.

LADY FOR A NIGHT (1942)

Cast: Joan Blondell, John Wayne, Ray Middleton, Philip Merivale, Blanche Yurka. *Director:* Leigh Jason. *Screenplay:* Isabel Dawn and Boyce De Gaw. *From a Screen Story by* Garrett Fort. *Music:* Ernest Nims. *Released by* Republic Pictures. *Running Time:* 87 Minutes.

Lady for a Night is a film which seems to bear out those anti-Duke Wayne sentiments echoed for so long by so many critics. "It never Waynes, it bores," wrote one cynic of one of Duke's lesser efforts. This also proves to be an accurate description of this dreadful period soap opera. Actually, Wayne comes off relatively unscathed, as this is primarily a Joan Blondell picture. It's sort of a *Rebecca* with cobwebs and, of course, none of the directorial genius that made Hitchcock's thriller so engrossing.

Things move slowly down South, and in the Memphis presented in the film, events almost crawl along. Blondell is cast as a rootin' tootin', showgal who is one of Memphis' more popular belles—for all the wrong reasons. Her dubious morality and the fact that she owns a successful riverboat upon which the local bigwigs gather each evening, endears her to the powers-that-be. However, when she is elected "Queen of the Carnival Ball," she finds to her horror that her "friends" simply can't accept the title of this illustrious position being squandered on the town slut. Blondell is further depressed on learning that she did not actually win the contest. Rather, it was rigged by her flamboyant gambler boyfriend, played by John Wayne.

Determined to get that all-elusive respect, she shuns Duke and takes up with a snobbish aristocrat (Ray Middleton), whose family has fallen on hard times. Blondell offers to pay off the family's debts in return for Middleton marrying her, thereby bringing her the respect she has so long desired. All of this takes forever to unfold, as we are forced to sit through endless production

WITH JOAN BLONDELL IN HAPPIER TIMES (BEFORE THE REVIEWS)

numbers aboard the riverboat, and listen to interminable romantic banter between Blondell and Wayne, who appears to be looking at his watch constantly to see when quitting time is coming around.

The hokey suspense is created once Blondell returns home with her new hubby. Since this is a marriage of convenience, there is no love lost, and before you know it the newlyweds are quarreling like an antique version of George and Martha in *Who's Afraid of Virginia Woolf?* Adding to the pressure, is the determination of Middleton's sister Julia (Blanche Yurka) who is determined to get this hussy out of the family. This she hopes to accomplish by giving Blondell a horse and carriage as a gift. As Joan takes off on a leisurely ride, we learn that the mare is actually blind! (Although no more so than most of the cast who couldn't possibly have had 20/20 vision when they read the script to this turkey and still agreed

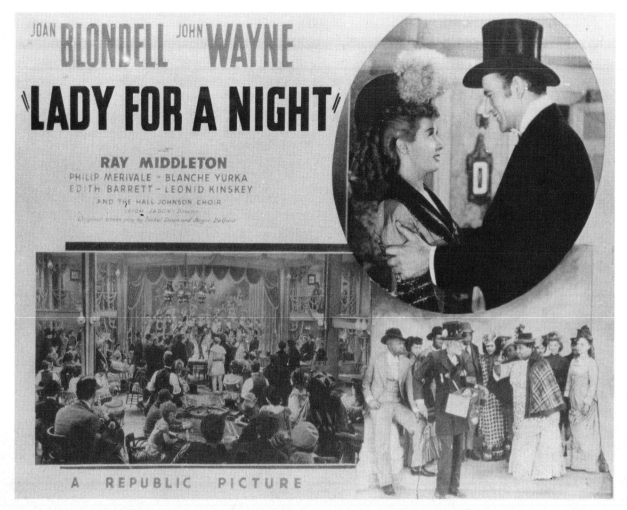

ORIGINAL LOBBY CARD

to act in it.) Naturally, the horse gets startled, leading to the dullest chase sequence in history. Blondell barely survives, and Duke informs her that she has been marked for murder by Yurka.

It goes without saying that this little piece of news doesn't encourage Blondell to move out. Instead, it gives Yurka the opportunity to strike again by lacing a drink with poison. Through an amazing quirk of fate, the fatal drink is consumed by Middleton, leaving Blondell as the prime suspect. What should have been a suspenseful sequence in court is marred by the leaden direction. Blondell appears to be struggling to stay awake as opposed to beating a death sentence. In fact, one suspects that she'd agree to take the poison if given a second opportunity to spare herself the inevitable reviews. Nevertheless, no sooner is she sentenced to death when a con-

scious-stricken relative exonerates Blondell and convicts Yurka of murder and excessive overacting. Blondell returns to Wayne, who offers to marry her as long as she promises to "Sew my buttons, cook my meals and darn my socks." Blondell can't resist the opportunity to live with such a progressive man and the story ends happily with the lovers returning to their lives of relatively modest sin on the riverboat.

This is the kind of "thriller" which uses that highly inventive technique of showing spinning newspaper headlines in order to relate events. However, there is a sordid element to the film that makes it a bit more relevant than just a bad suspense story. Its treatment of minorities is flagrant, and it is almost impossible to believe that this was reflected in a film as late as 1942. Yet, unfortunately, *Lady for a Night* was not unique in that respect. As blacks served their country and died heroically in far off lands, they could not be depicted as anything but mindless simpletons onscreen. The overall Hollywood track record for portraying blacks in films during this period is quite abysmal. However, this one takes the cake when it comes to offensiveness of staggering proportions.

When we see the happy "darkies" they is just-a-whoopin' it up. Fat old mammies tell off their simple-minded husbands constantly, while the slow-shufflin' males grudgingly comply. Every other scene in this costumer depicts dozens of blacks singing and dancing in a manner so appalling it makes Uncle Remus look like *Shaft*. Even Duke is not exempt, telling one servant to shape up "or I'll ship ya back to Africa." One cannot blame the individual actors for such transgressions, as, dreadfully, it was common practice to recite lines as callous as this. Fortunately, as times changed, so too did the Duke. Although his civil rights record and staunch opposition to minority quotas gained both friend and foe, he consistently provided key roles to black actors in later years when he had gotten more artistic control over his films.

WITHOUT RESERVATIONS (1946)

Cast: Claudette Colbert, John Wayne, Don De-Fore, Anne Triola, Phil Brown, Frank Puglia. *Director:* Mervyn LeRoy. *Screenplay:* Andrew Solt. *From the Novel* "Thanks God, I'll Take It From Here" *by* Jane Allen and Mae Livingston. *Music:* Roy Webb. *Released by* RKO Radio Pictures. *Running Time:* 107 Minutes.

If anyone wonders why John Wayne is not primarily remembered for his skills in "screwball comedies," one need only look at *Without Reservations*. This is a good-natured, well-intended farce that squanders the considerable talent that appeared both before and behind the cameras. In fact, it is not really a John Wayne film in the traditional sense, as he takes second billing to Claudette Colbert, who is its real star. Wayne sort of lumbers through the proceedings looking as though he knows he's made a big mistake, and can't wait to collect his paycheck so he can get on with something of consequence.

Without Reservations was obviously intended to be a cute clone of the Oscar-winning *It Happened*

DeFORE, DUKE AND CLAUDETTE DISCUSS WAYS TO GET REVENGE ON THEIR AGENTS FOR INVOLVING THEM IN THE SCRIPT

One Night, which paired Colbert with Clark Gable. The film presents Claudette as Christopher Madden, an author whose most recent book is sending her readers into a frenzy of admiration for her talents. She is enroute to Hollywood to discuss the film version of the book with a heavyweight producer, when she learns that the studio intends to cast an unknown in the lead role. This upsets the author, as she was originally promised that both Cary Grant and Lana Turner would appear in the movie.

In the midst of her brooding, she meets Wayne and buddy Don DeFore, who are Marines traveling on the same train to California. Within seconds, Colbert falls for Duke, and sends a telegram to the studio that she has found the ideal choice for the film's leading man.

Wayne throws a "monkey wrench" into the proceedings, however, by denouncing her book. Colbert keeps her identity a secret in hopes of wooing Wayne into her corner, but the opportunity to tell him the truth never seems to arise. The three companions manage to get thrown off the train and have to fend for themselves, going from town to town by whatever means of transportation they can arrange. This leads to plenty of "madcap" scenes that were obviously intended to draw hoots of laughter from the audience, but barely prompt a smile.

The film limps toward its conclusion by having Wayne reject Colbert after learning of her ruse. She heads to Hollywood where she pretends to be a social butterfly. With DeFore's help, she succeeds in making Wayne jealous enough to swallow his pride and run to Hollywood, where he will presumably star in the film.

The script has more holes than a piece of Swiss cheese. Foremost, the weak link is the idea that an author, no matter how well read, would elicit the type of nationwide hysteria normally reserved for movie stars. It is also rather difficult to believe that an industry known for completely disregarding the feelings of writers, would allow total creative control over the film version of the book to rest in the hands of the author. As for Wayne and DeFore, we are told that they are just typical servicemen. However, they seem to have no timetable in which to report to their base, and except for one brief scene which shows them in an airplane, appear to have no duties other than sitting around discussing the merits of Wayne apologizing to Colbert. It is also never explained just why the studio would be willing to sign

She wrote the book...
But he had the ideas!

When a lady's so easy to look at
. . . can she blame a man if he's
hard to handle? The story of a
writer whose hero comes to life...
and gets plenty lively...with her!

JESSE L. LASKY and WALTER MacEWEN
present
CLAUDETTE COLBERT · JOHN WAYNE
in MERVYN LeROY'S production of
Without Reservations
with DON DeFORE · ANNE TRIOLA and Miss LOUELLA PARSONS
Produced by JESSE L. LASKY
Screen Play by ANDREW SOLT

ORIGINAL PRESSBOOK ADVERTISEMENT

Wayne for the lead in the year's (hopefully) most talked about film without seeing whether he had any acting skills. Likewise, even if he did, one would think the Marine Corps just might have a say in Wayne vanishing for a few months so he can go to Hollywood. These types of inconsistencies show a total disregard for logic, and make the film appear to be even more juvenile than was apparently intended.

The cast tries hard and is reasonably engaging, although Wayne's forte is clearly not broad comedy. However, under Mervyn LeRoy's direction, Duke at least downplays the hamminess that often showed through under in some of his other undistinguished comedies. As for Colbert, she retains her natural charm, but at 41 is a little "over the hill" for portraying a bouncy, virginal

159

type. The supporting cast adds little to the proceedings, and an attempt is made to breath some life into the script by including some superfluous cameos by Jack Benny and Cary Grant, the latter's presence only re-enforcing the fact that his deft ability to carry lightweight comedy may have saved this film had he and Wayne swapped assignments.

Without Reservations was doomed from the start. LeRoy and Colbert did not get along, and their bickering was detrimental to the project. Wayne himself stated for the record that the entire affair was a disappointment. He recalled, "I could have used some help with the comic timing. I was never really at ease up against the likes of Marlene Dietrich and Joan Crawford, and, hell, I knew Claudette could act the pants off me and was by far my superior in comedy. But Mervyn wasn't letting any woman tell him what to do, so her suggestions were largely shunted aside, and that's why we were stuck with such a relatively flat product in the end."

The lack of wit carried over into efforts to promote the film. The studio pressbook suggested the following gimmick to draw in audiences:

Here is a very effective stunt that can be worked several times a day over your radio station. It should feature two voices, one male and one female, along the following lines:

(man's voice): "Good evening, madam. May I help you?"

(girl's voice): "Yes, I want a drawing room to San Francisco!"

(man's voice): "Have you a reservation?"

(girl's voice): Why no, I haven't –"

(man's voice): "No reservation? In that case, I would recommend that you go the Palace Theatre to see *Without Reservations* starring Claudette Colbert and John Wayne!"

Despite plans to use such rib-tickling banter, *Without Reservations* proved that audiences did indeed have reservations—at least when it came to patronizing second-rate comedies. The film died a quiet death at the box-office, and Wayne began to concentrate on action films—not always to better results, as we shall witness with *Tycoon*.

TYCOON (1947)

Cast: John Wayne, Laraine Day, Sir Cedric Hardwicke, Judith Anderson, James Gleason, Anthony Quinn, Grant Withers, Paul Fix. *Director:* Richard Wallace. *Screenplay:* Borden Chase and John Twist. *From the Novel by* C.E. Scoggins. *Music:* Leigh Harline. *Released by* RKO Radio Pictures. *Running Time:* 128 Minutes.

Upon the release of *Tycoon*, critic James Agee wrote a now classic review. It read: "In this movie several tons of dynamite are set off—none of it under the right people." Truer words were never spoken. *Tycoon* proved to be a major mishap for everyone involved. It bears no significant relevance in Duke's career, and is generally only viewed every decade or so by Wayne aficionados simply to remind themselves that even the Duke was not infallible. To be objective, however, I will now list *Tycoon's* negative and positive aspects.

NEGATIVE:
Hammy acting
Boring screenplay

Leaden direction
Overbearing musical score
Ludicrous action sequences
Laughable dialogue
Unbearable length
Waste of a talented cast
Phony sets and backdrops

POSITIVE:
It was shot in color.

Tycoon does have another virtue, however. It is one of those films so completely bad on almost every level, that it actually provides unintended humor. We see Wayne in one of his worst performances, and we have to ask ourselves how an actor could turn in such a lousy performance in 1947, only to rise to such brilliant levels the next

year with *Fort Apache* and *Red River.* In *Tycoon*, Wayne is this rough and tumble bridge builder who prefers to dally with the ladies whenever his hectic schedule gives him some free time. He is assigned to head an effort dedicated to building a tunnel through a mountain in South America, so that a millionaire's mines can eventually be linked by rail.

Wayne agrees to the plan reluctantly, telling his employer (Sir Cedric Hardwicke) that a bridge would be more plausible. Hardwicke won't be swayed and Wayne battles the elements and lack of proper construction materials to get the job done. Trouble erupts when he falls for Hardwicke's beautiful daughter, Laraine Day, who has been suffering in loneliness due to her father's restrictive rules. After eloping with her, he and Hardwicke become embattled in a war of

WAYNE CONSIDERS DYNAMITING HIS AGENT FOR GETTING HIM INVOLVED WITH "TYCOON"

storm. Wayne gets to gaze into Day's beautiful face, only to recite irresistable dialogue like: "You've got the most beautiful eyes in South America...and a cute little nose, too!" Diabetics beware: the sugar content in *Tycoon* could be lethal.

Director Richard Wallace shows a unique talent for bringing out the worst in his cast. Wayne stumbles about like a bull in a China shop, looking as bored with the proceedings as everyone else. With the action scenes few and far between, he has little to do until the end of the film, when, in the "thrilling" climax, he attempts to secure the bridge himself and succeeds in dropping the end of a crane on his head. His double-takes are of the grade-school level, and his romantic scenes with Day evoke more laughter than charm.

As for supporting actors, Wayne does not get much help. Day looks pretty enough, but hardly displays the charisma required to make Wayne risk his career to enjoy. The screenplay was obviously not conducive to showing off Day's good looks and admirable charms as most of the film was shot in a mining camp. Therefore, ludicrous and contrived sequences were written to allow the wardrobe department to garnish Day with some fancy designer clothes. For real laughs, there's plucky Laraine sauntering through the mud and gravel in a floor length evening gown or cocktail dress to tell Duke to return to their hut to eat lunch.

Sir Cedric portrays Day's father in the obligatory "all millionaires are stuffy, so I'll walk around like I'm posing for Mt. Rushmore" style of acting. With his dour, humorless mannerisms, Hardwicke plays the role so stiffly one suspects he has a broom up his...well, never mind. Suffice it to say, Hardwicke would have netted the Oscar for best performance by a Walking Cadaver, if such a category had existed. Anthony Quinn (as Day's Mexican cousin!), Paul Fix and Grant Withers come off best simply because their screen time is limited.

Wayne had made some bad films in his career, but you'd have to look hard to find one that fails as completely as *Tycoon*. It is the cinematic equivalent of watching paint dry.

wills. For reasons never thoroughly explained, Hardwicke attempts to sabotage his own construction project by halting Wayne's supplies. Just why Hardwicke would want to penalize an effort for which he is paying remains a mystery. Also as mysterious is Wayne's dedication to getting the job done despite the shortage of materials.

Wayne eventually tells Hardwicke that he will go with his first instinct and build the bridge within schedule on a tight budget, refusing his father-in-law employer's offer of compromise and truce. Wayne cuts safety measures to get the job done and eventually loses most of longtime associates and crew. When a raging flood threatens to wash away the bridge, his friends unsurprisingly return to his side to help him secure their efforts.

This is one of those ludicrous films in which dramatic dialogue is "subtly" followed by the thunderous noise of a conveniently on-coming

162

BIG JIM McLAIN (1952)

Cast: John Wayne, Nancy Olson, James Arness, Alan Napier, Veda Ann Borg, Hans Conreid, John Hubbard. *Director:* Edward Ludwig. *Screenplay:* James Edward Grant, Richard English and Eric Taylor. *From a Screen Story by* English. *Music:* Emil Newman, Arthur Lange and Paul Dunlap. A Wayne-Fellows Production. *Released by* Warner Bros. *Running Time:* 90 Minutes.

Prominent on anyone's list of bottom of the barrel movies should be *Big Jim McLain.* However, unlike Wayne's fiascos in *Jet Pilot* and *Tycoon,* this movie goes beyond being an incompetently made drama. It is extremely offensive as well. Ironically, the entire project came about through Wayne's involvement with a political group dedicated to rid Hollywood of Communists. The fear at the time was that the left would gain a foothold within the film industry and begin making influential propaganda movies. What is amazing is that *Big Jim McLain* is guilty of precisely the same flaws it was designed to prevent. It is one-dimensional, subjective and completely slanted toward a simplistic political view. Opponents of this view are portrayed as simple-minded thugs or conniving intellectuals who moonlight as Commie spies.

The script presents Wayne and James Arness as roguish agents for the House UnAmerican Activities Committee (HUAC), the pet organization of Senator Joseph McCarthy. The movie portrays the agents of this group as dedicated, understaffed and overworked. What is not mentioned at any point were the justifiable reservations many people had about the purpose and methods of the HUAC group. Under McCarthy's direction, what began as a minor political inquiry organization quickly escalated into a nationwide witchhunt. Hundreds of people in the entertainment business were given a choice: come up with some juicy incriminations of their peers or risk being blacklisted. Many had the

He's a Go-Get-'Em Guy for the U.S.A. on a Treason-Trail that leads Half-a-World Away!

WARNER BROS.

JOHN WAYNE

THE BIG MAN IN HIS BIG ADVENTURE!

'Big Jim McLain'

courage to do the latter, at the expense of their careers.

None of these minor points is ever introduced into the storyline. In the end, Wayne ended up producing and starring in as an offensive a propaganda film as has been made by a major show business figure. As no pro-Communist films were made during this chaotic period, it is unknown whether such an effort would have been as hilariously inept as *Big Jim McLain.* Likewise, there is no way to measure how many

A "DRAMATIC" MOMENT AS JIM McLAIN

I wasn't actually watching Jimmy Olson from the old *Superman* series. Wayne is no slouch in the charisma department either, and at one point murmers in his wife's ear "You're comfy without the French fries." Well, you'd have to see it to understand the context. Other immortal dialogue includes "Seventy six inches??? That's a lot of man!" and "It's a bum job, but it's got to be done." We also learn the shattering news that "(Communism) is a vast conspiracy to enslave the modern man."

For an action film, *Big Jim McLain* drags mercilessly through its endless 90-minute running time. Wayne is shown interviewing various suspects who are guilty of nothing other than bad acting. He is aided in his quest to conquer the Commies in Hawaii by real life Honolulu Police Chief Dan Liu, who delivers his lines as though he was struggling to keep awake. As for the good chief's acting skills, one hopes he did not quit his day job. The operation to which he, Wayne and Arness are assigned has been cleverly titled "Operation Pineapple," a code name so vague that those sly Commies would never associate it with HUAC activities in Hawaii.

There is almost no action in the mundane "adventure" and even Wayne ducks several fights rather than blow his cover. The shocking climax finds Duke inexplicably trying to arrest the entire Hawaiian Communist party by himself, even though the police force is stationed right up the road. Even this opportunity to introduce some excitement is thrown away, as Wayne is merely given the opportunity to throw a couple of punches and get lumped over the head. The "ironic" ending finds the Commie ringleaders getting off the hook by taking the Fifth Amendment as Wayne gnashes his teeth helplessly. The implication is, of course, that America would be so much better if we could just get rid of that damned Constitution!

There is literally nothing to recommend about *Big Jim McLain*. The direction makes for a film that is unintentionally funny. The movie is of minor importance in the Wayne saga, as the maiden effort for John Wayne and hs partner, producer Robert Fellows, and their Wayne-Fellows production company.

loyal Americans may actually have converted to communism out of embarrassment that their country could produce such a ludicrous opus.

There is virually no plot. We see Wayne and Arness wandering door to door aimlessly throughout half the movie. This justifies the movie's second reason for existence: to show the sights of Hawaii, where the duo is sent to check up on Commie activities. Before you can shout "Josef Stalin!" Arness (who had become Duke's protegé) is murdered in one of the confusing action sequences. Big Duke goes into action to avenge his death, but he seems to be constantly sidetracked by wife Nancy Olson, who sits around in halter tops and coos romantic one liners like "Of all the jillions (sic) of people in the world, we two meet." With such terrific sex appeal, I had to double-check the credits to see if

164

BLOOD ALLEY (1955)

Cast: John Wayne, Lauren Bacall, Paul Fix, Joy Kim, Berry Kroger, Mike Mazurki, Anita Ekberg. *Directed by* William Wellman. *Screenplay:* A.S. Fleishman. *Based on his Novel. Music:* Roy Webb. A Batjac Production. *Released by* Warner Bros. *Running Time:* 115 Minutes.

Blood Alley is typical of a "bad" John Wayne film. Even though it fails on almost every level, one can't help being entertained by it, if even for all the wrong reasons. The production had a less-than-auspicious start. As the first film produced by his production company Batjac to star the Duke, it bears some minor significance in the Wayne canon. However, *Blood Alley* was originally designed to star Robert Mitchum, so that Wayne could spend a prolonged vacation with his family. Within a week of the film's start, however, trouble erupted between Mitchum and director William Wellman. Neither man had a reputation for being overly-reasonable during an argument,—Mitchum proceeded, it is reported, to dump Wellman in the drink—and the production had almost ground to halt. Wellman asked Wayne to recast the lead role.

Warner Bros., which was releasing the movie, insisted that if this action was taken, the new star would have to be of the same box-office caliber as Mitchum. The film's leading lady was Lauren Bacall, and Wayne thought that signing Humphrey Bogart might prove to be an inspired piece of casting. Bogart, however, demanded $500,000 for his services—a fee which producer Wayne could ill-afford. To his annoyance (and the studio's delight), Duke had no choice but to cast himself in the lead.

On the surface, *Blood Alley* is a routine action tale about a tough-as-nails sea captain rescued by villagers from a Red Chinese prison. They plead with Wayne to help them in a mass evacuation of their village, with the ultimate destination the free city of Hong Kong. The plan is to steal a

ramshackle ferryboat, which they hope old salt Duke can successfully pilot through rough seas, Communist patrol boats, and an unchartered course down the dangerous Formosa Strait (a.k.a. "Blood Alley"). Naturally, Wayne agrees to do so, especially after he is smitten by the charms of Bacall, seen here as an American expatriate living in Red China.

There are a number of reasons why *Blood Alley*

AT THE HELM ENROUTE TO BLOOD ALLEY WITH BACALL

fails, not the least of them being Wellman's inability to prevent Wayne from hamming it up. Wayne is encouraged to do so by the script's ludicrous dialogue, which has him spouting such naval witticisms as "My achin' fantail!" and "I thought they (the Commies) were pirates...until I saw their stinking tennis shoes!"(?) For some inexplicable reason, Duke is given to talking to an imaginary girlfriend whom he constantly refers to as "Baby." It is with this evasive beauty that he plans his escape route, matches wits and swaps jokes. Presumably, this idiosyncrasy is supposed to make him appear lovable. In fact, he appears to be the victim of an unsuccessful lobotomy operation. One wonders why the Chinese peasants would trust him to boil an egg properly, to say nothing of steering them all to freedom.

The plot has more holes in it than the decrepit ferryboat Wayne captains. His "escape" from the prison cell is accomplished after he finds that someone has smuggled him a Russian army uniform and a pistol. After finding these items, the scene cuts immediately to Wayne simply walking through enemy lines unnoticed. (If you can believe that John Wayne in a Soviet uniform among hundreds of Red Chinese would not draw attention, than you will probably be interested in purchasing the Brooklyn Bridge). In another scene of attempted tension, Bacall must hide Wayne when Communist soldiers search her house. This she accomplishes by having Duke simple hide under her mattress. Naturally, the sight of a 250-pound man hiding under a tiny mattress would never arouse attention, and in this case the Communist soldier who inspects Bacall's boudoir is unable to tell of Duke's whereabouts even after he sits down on the bed!

The casting of Blood Alley is also a bad movie lover's delight. Wayne's old buddy Paul Fix shows up as a Chinese Elder, and buxom Anita Ekberg also appears as a local peasant. The biggest laughs (unintentionally, of course) are served up by Mike Mazurki as possibly the only Chinese peasant on record who is 6'5" tall, built like a line-backer and sports a hairy chest. He delivers his lines of Chinese wit in the dialect fashioned by Joe E. Ross on TV's "Car 54, Where Are You?"

For all of its inadequacies, however, Blood Alley is never dull. The action is always preposterous (Wayne's creaking ferry manages to outrun a Red Chinese destroyer), the chemistry between Wayne and Bacall is about as romantic as that exuded by Huntley and Brinkley, and the acting generally approaches that found in a school play. Yet, you end up liking this nonsense in spite of yourself. The same can be said for Wayne. For anyone to have survived professionally after so many ill-advised epics is a tribute to his charisma and his ability to not take himself seriously. Fortunately, he always had the good sense to counter his weaker screen efforts with something worthwhile. And Wayne would more than compensate for Blood Alley with a string of brilliant film performances in the late Fifties and throughout the remainder of his career—The Conqueror aside.

THE CONQUEROR (1956)

Cast: John Wayne, Susan Hayward, Pedro Armendariz, Agnes Moorehead, Thomas Gomez, John Hoyt, William Conrad. *Presented by* Howard Hughes. *Director:* Dick Powell. *Screenplay:* Oscar Millard. *Music:* Victor Young. Released by RKO Radio Pictures. *Running Time:* 111 Minutes.

There are bad movies, and there are bad movies. And then there is *The Conqueror,* a film held in great esteem by lovers of terrible epics. For those searching for what is arguably a really dreadful movie, *The Conqueror* represents something akin to finding the pot of gold at the end of the rainbow. It is so unspeakably awful that one can only assume that everyone involved with the project must have taken complete leave of their senses for several months.

Just what made John Wayne think he could convincingly play the role of Genghis Khan might never be known. Some say his confidence was inspired by his well-received interpretation of the Swedish sailor in *The Long Voyage Home.* Others speculated that Duke needed the money due to pressing financial concerns and a desire to raise money for his pet project, *The Alamo.* Whatever the rationale, the idea of Wayne as Khan was as ridiculous in its time as Clint Eastwood today announcing he would like to star in a 1990s production of *The Shirley Temple Story*— casting himself in the title role.

Screenwriter Oscar Millard was hired to prepare a script, but this was before Wayne was involved with the project. Ironically, Millard had envisioned Marlon Brando in the role. Brando, however, had the good fortune—or sense—to be unavailable. With the lead role still under consideration, the then-head of RKO, the legendary Howard Hughes, hired actor Dick Powell to produce and direct the film. Sparing little expense, Hughes allocated the then enormous sum of $6 million for the budget. The story goes that

as Wayne was visiting the studio one day, he happened upon a copy of the script. After just glancing at a few pages, Wayne decided this project was for him! Wayne called Powell and bellowed, "Let's do it!" Powell than called Millard to tell him the good news. Millard almost cried. He was somewhat appeased by Duke's

167

promises to take lengthy dialogue lessons so that his portrayal would be convincing.

What is amazing is that no one put an end to the absurdities of this entire affair. Probably any other studio would have laughed Wayne out the front gate, despite his ranking as one of the top box office stars in the industry. Hughes, however, was so rich that he simply made movies for fun. And *The Conqueror* was to be his most elaborate toy ever. As owner of RKO, there was no one to stop him or to talk him into recasting the film

Production got under way in St. George, Utah, where the desert would provide a "realistic" backdrop for the Mongol hordes. It also aided Wayne in his conviction that Genghis should be portrayed as "a gunfighter." In fact, many have observed, *The Conqueror* is merely a Western with a lot of drooping mustaches. Wayne began having second thoughts about the absurd dialogue, which was straight from the "me-Tarzan-you-Jane" school of literati. By then, however, only minor rewrites could be done. Wayne never did get around to taking those silly dialogue lessons, which insured that there was plenty of ammunition for hostile critics who salivated to review the end result.

The production was frought with troubles of every kind. The heat was unbearable, as temperatures neared 120 degrees. There was also plenty of heat off the set as well, when Susan Hayward began making eyes at Duke. At one point, she even challenged Pilar Wayne to fight it out for Duke's attentions. As Ms. Hayward was cast as Duke's Tartar love interest, she apparently went overboard in her desire to bring the same scorching reality to her role as Wayne did. Nevertheless, Pilar gracefully declined the tempting offer to roll around in the mud with Hayward.

So much has been written about the production of *The Conqueror* that nobody seems to get around to the film itself. There is good reason for this. Once you tell anyone that the story involved Genghis Khan and John Wayne, there is no need to say more. We won't attempt to reveal any plot specifics here, either, except to say that *The Conqueror* is a film well worth seeing, as it rivals *It's a Mad, Mad, Mad, Mad World* as one of filmdom's most hilarious, multi-million dollar comedies. The latter has one slight advantage over Duke's epic, in that it was SUPPOSED to be funny.

The Conqueror is perhaps best known for its immortal dialogue. Arguably, the two most famous "knee-slappers" in screen history come from this screwball affair. One occurs when Wayne (with Fu Manchu mustache and Kaiser Wilhelm yak-skin helmet) first glances at Hayward being carried by servants through the desert. He ogles the beauty and mumbles, "This Tartar woman is for me and my blood says take her!" (The publicity department thought so much of this particular line that they used it on the theater posters). Another "gem" comes as Duke sweeps Hayward off her feet and tells her lovingly, "Yer beeeooootiful in yer wrath!" Who said Genghis Khan was all bad? In Wayne's interpretation of the role, we get to know Genghis for what he was—a mad-dog killer with a heart of gold.

Absurdity piles upon absurdity, with other immortal lines like "Death comes not easy to me" spouting from Wayne's lips. When the script ran out of such sterling dialogue, some padding was included in the form of a "native" dance by slave girls. I've seen more authentic ethnic rhythms on New York's 42nd street in "live nude reviews." And the costumes! A fortune was spent on the cheesiest wardrobe this side of Liberace's clothes closet. Half the cast walks around with medallions around their necks large enough to cause whiplash if they were to turn suddenly. One might think "Mr. T" was hired as costume designer. In one scene, a mysterious and deceitful sorcerer is seen wearing a cone-shaped hat that makes him resemble a cross between Billie Burke's Good Witch from *The Wizard of Oz* and the Grand Imperial Wizard of the Ku Klux Klan.

About the only thing to recommend about *The Conqueror* are some large-scale battle scenes featuring impressive stuntwork. Even this is carried to an extreme, as we see so many endless shots of falling horses that the movie begins to resemble an equestrian "sit-in" with more of the beasts on the ground than on the hoof.

The fate of *The Conqueror* is even more bizarre than the film itself. The movie grossed a considerable amount of money, but due to its high costs, never returned a profit. Shortly after its release, Howard Hughes bought back the rights for a staggering $12 million (including his other Wayne clinker, *Jet Pilot*, about which more later). These films were not seen again until after Hughes' death, which may be the only humanitarian act the billionaire ever accomplished.

There is also, ironically, a tragic side to *The Conqueror*. Unbeknownst to the cast and crew, filming took place not far from where the Army had secretly conducted nuclear bomb tests. It is very possible that many of those on the set contracted the fatal cancer which led to their deaths through working on this ill-advised epic. In the years that followed, over 90 members of the production company were diagnosed as hav-ing cancer, and over half of them died, including Duke, Hayward, Moorehead, Powell, and supporting actor (and long time Wayne co-star) Pedro Armendariz. In 1963, Armendariz was told his cancer was terminal. He had just completed the painful task of shooting what was to be his last role—opposite Sean Connery in *From Russia With Love*. Unable to cope with the dim prospects of a slow death, Armendariz shot himself.

Some Wayne intimates feel the rumor linking the location with the tragic deaths of its stars is all wrong. This includes Pilar Wayne, who has stated that the victims all had one other factor in common—they were excessive chain-smokers. Whatever the cause, *The Conqueror* was not a happy experience for anyone. In today's more cynical times, it probably would ruin the career of a leading man. Wayne, fortunately, had something far more impressive up his sleeve for his next picture—a "minor little Western" titled *The Searchers*.

JET PILOT (1957)

Cast: John Wayne, Janet Leigh, Jay C. Flippen, Paul Fix, Richard Rober, Roland Winters, Hans Conreid. A Howard Hughes Presentation. *Directed by:* Josef Von Sternberg. *Screenplay by:* Jules Furthman. *Music by:* Bronislau Kaper. An RKO Radio Picture. *Released by* Universal Pictures. 112 Minutes.

Most film producers dream of making at least one epic that for years to come will stand apart from all other motion pictures of its genre. Howard Hughes fulfilled that fantasy, although in a less-than-enviable way. Following the release of *The Conqueror,* Hughes delivered the second of his "one-two" punch to movie audiences by inflicting on it after a long delay, another pet project starring Wayne: *Jet Pilot.* These two films will forever by responsible for making Hughes' name synonymous with a great achievement in the cinema: producing two of the decade's least regarded movies. (In between these two, Wayne also made the belated flagwaver, *Flying Lathernecks,* for Hughes.)

In actuality, only the absurdity of the casting makes *The Conqueror* a worse film than *Jet Pilot.* The latter is arguably just as silly in virtually every other aspect. However, whereas *The Conqueror* had as its virtue the fact that it was unintentionally hilarious, *Jet Pilot* commits the unpardonable crime for a Wayne film: it is not only bad, it is also inexcusably dull. In fact, the legendary troubles behind the making of this "epic" would have proven far more engrossing a tale than the screenplay which was written by one Jules Furthman.

Hughes legendary ego had him envision a movie thriller in which Wayne would be cast as Hughes's imaginary alter ego: a death-defying playboy Air Force pilot who knows no fear. Hughes was committed to spending any amount to ensure that his lifelong passion for aeronautics would be proudly reflected on film. To this end,

BREAKS THROUGH THE FORBIDDEN BARRIER!

Exploding . . . with all the power of the Jet Age . . . with all the passion of a daring love story!

HOWARD HUGHES'
JET PILOT
JOHN WAYNE · JANET LEIGH
AND THE
U.S. AIR FORCE
JAY C. FLIPPEN · PAUL FIX · HANS CONREID
TECHNICOLOR
Directed by JOSEF von STERNBERG · Written and produced by JULES FURTHMAN

he spent over $4-million on this spectacle, most of which went into what were admittedly high-tech special effects when the movie went into production in late 1949 (after Wayne finished *She Wore a Yellow Ribbon*). Somewhere along the way, however, Hughes lost his rational judgment and became far more interested in the technical aspects of the movie than he was in maintaining audience interest in the story itself. The end result found *Jet Pilot* to be among the most expensive home movies produced.

The main problem with the film is its ridiculous screenplay, coupled with ineffective performances. The story finds Janet Leigh as a

170

sexy Soviet fighter pilot who mysteriously defects to the West. Wayne is a hot-shot U.S. pilot assigned to watch over her and ensure that her defection is legitimate. Along the way, of course, the relationship goes from one of antagonism to a sort-of "Blondie and Dagwood Take to the Skies." Wayne falls in love, marries Leigh, and discovers all too late that she is, in fact, a top Soviet agent. For reasons never quite explained, Wayne feigns his own defection to the U.S.S.R. and returns there with Leigh. After learning that the Soviets intend to drug Duke, and turn him into a human vegetable, she rescues him in a "thrilling" climax and re-defects to the U.S.A., where, presumably they both live happily ever after.

If all of this sounds corny, it's actually worse, played out on the big screen in color. Leigh and her Soviet comrades speak with a wide array of varying American accents, and the lady herself lands her fighter plane at one point and emerges with a new hairdo and exotic lipstick perfectly in place. She is immediately given free rein of the area, and is seen lounging seductively in low-cut, form fitting outfits that would make Marlene Dietrich blush.

As for Duke, he struggles to keep awake, and overacts here with the callowness of a high school thespian. With a goofy grin throughout, Wayne emotes by raising his eyebrows to show pleasure, raising them higher to show surprise, and lowering them dramatically to show concern. With almost no action sequences to meander through, he instead goes through the proceedings trying desperately—and unsuccessfully—to upstage Miss Leigh's ample bosom. (The film demonstrates Hughes' well-known passion for large breasts. Indeed, half of the budget was likely spent on seductive brassieres. Yet for all of the expensive bras, nothing can prevent this story from sagging.)

Dialogue ranges from knee-slapper to knee-slapper. When Wayne first observes buxom Leigh's decolletage, he wittingly observes "We both believe in uplifting the masses!" Although the flying sequences have a certain charm, they are spoiled with sophomoric voice-overs of Wayne and Leigh, who are consistently doing some not-

so-subtle mating rituals with their jets.

The movie was shot at 14 different military bases, and the air sequences alone took 16 months to complete, largely because of Hughes' puzzling insistence that every sequence have enormous clouds in the background. Cinematographer William Clothier was able to accomplish what his four "terminated" predecessors were not: film the jets in action from a plane going just as fast. Problems were many, and at an altitude of 27,000 feet, the cameras froze, necessitating the use of anti-freeze to keep them operable. For all the work, however, the rear-screen projection of Wayne and Leigh (neither of whom were airborne at any time) ruined most of the effect. The air sequences are also marred by the film's bombastic score. (This is one of those movies in which even the slightest revelation is accompanied by the crashing of cymbals and the full blaring of the orchestra.)

Jet Pilot proved to be such a mishap, that it was not released until seven years after its completion. The studio attributed the delay to Hughes' perfectionism, when in fact the movie was simply not releasable. It eventually ran 148 minutes in its original cut, but was edited to 112 minutes for general release. Even at that length, it plods mercilessly until it literally staggers to a climax that is guaranteed to cure insomnia.

The studio tried to push the film by backing it with an expensive ad campaign proclaiming the finished product to be "The Greatest Air Spectacle of the Jet Age." However, by its release date, the planes in *Jet Pilot* were so outdated—like its dialogue—that the movie should have been labeled "The Greatest Air Spectacle of the Stone Age." (It was released by Universal since RKO had shuttered and bolted its doors.)

The pressbook suggested "clever" marketing ploys, such as having a "drill formation" of bathing beauties each wear a placard advertising the film, and a "Miss Jet Pilot" beauty contest in which the winner would get to be photographed in a bikini and fighter pilot helmet. Amazingly, neither of these stunts could help theatre owners pull in reluctant crowds. When *Jet Pilot* received poor reviews, Hughes decided to punish the world by buying back all of the available prints as well as those of *The Conqueror.* They remained unseen again until after the billionaire's death. It was rumored that in his waning days, Hughes, obviously rewarding a masochistic tendency, would stay in his screening room for hours on end watching both flicks.

Amazingly, both of Hughes' fiascos did nothing to harm Wayne's career, and between the release of these two epics, Duke managed to star in both *The Wings of Eagles* and the masterful *The Searchers,* both for John Ford. Both will be remembered long after *Jet Pilot* and *The Conqueror* have long faded from the minds of even "bad movie" buffs.

THE BARBARIAN AND THE GEISHA (1958)

Cast: John Wayne, Eiko Ando, Sam Jaffe, So Yamamura, Norman Thomson. *Director:* John Huston. *Screenplay:* Charles Grayson, Alfred Hayes (uncredited) and Nigel Balchin (uncredited). *From a Screen Story by* Ellis St. Joseph. *Music:* Hugo Friedhofer. *Released by* 20th Century-Fox. *Running Time:* 105 Minutes.

One would think that a teaming between legendary he-man director John Huston and John Wayne would have been a match made in movie heaven. So it was with the highest hopes and the greatest of expectations that 20th Century-Fox proudly announced they had pulled off a coup by having these two giants of the cinema collaborate

for the first time. The occasion was *The Townsend Harris Story*. Harris, a largely forgotten U.S. diplomat, had been given a bad break in the history books, felt Wayne and Huston. As the first foreign consul to Japan, Harris was instrumental in convincing that nation to emerge from centuries of self-imposed isolationism and join the world community. The film would tell of Harris' accomplishments and frustrations from his arrival in Japan in 1856 through his being hailed as a hero by the Japanese people some months later.

Not to diminish Harris' ill-deserved treatment by history, his story is just not very exciting. To liven things up a fictional subplot was added with Duke falling in love with Okichi, a beautiful and subservient geisha girl who is provided to Wayne by a government official. All this served to do was slow down an already snail-paced script and it distracts from the more interesting political aspect of the story. The *really* interesting aspect of *The Barbarian and the Geisha* is the tale of woe which befell the relationship between Wayne and Huston.

Originally, the two men were eager to work with each other. Wayne claimed he did everything possible to endear himself to the director, including joining Huston for hunting and fishing expeditions in order to build rapport. However, as filming began, it became apparent that there would be no meeting of the minds in terms of the movie itself. An enormous sum—$3.5 million—had been allocated by the studio to enable Huston to film on location in Japan. The money is right up there on the screen, along with magnificent views of the Orient. However, the epic envisioned by Huston was far different from that envisioned by Duke and the studio.

The two men came into conflict almost immediately. Wayne took issue with Huston's plan to build a slow, gentle film without any significant action sequences. This disturbed Wayne, who saw the character of Harris as big, brawling and larger than life. Huston demanded Wayne play the role in a quiet, low-key style befitting a diplomat of that era. Wayne contested that his fans always wanted to see him "tall in the saddle." He accused Huston of giving him nothing

to do except walk around dressed like Abraham Lincoln.

Huston did not take the criticism lying down. He slowed the pace of filming even further, an action which infuriated Wayne who criticized the director for being more concerned with sunsets and cinematography than getting a meaningful story onscreen. Huston further fought back by constantly shooting Wayne from angles which the star found unflattering. He overruled Wayne on another occasion and insisted that the film's only fight scene end with Duke being humiliated by a tiny Judo expert.

It is difficult to speculate just who went wrong first, but it is probably safe to say that both Wayne and Huston were responsible for allowing *The Barbarian and the Geisha* to become an undistinguished film. It would be wrong, however, to label this movie a disaster or an embarrassment, á la *The Conqueror*. In fact, everyone performs quite capably both in front of and behind the cameras, and the movie gives us a few sequences that linger in the mind. (Primarily Wayne's attempts to combat a cholera epidemic he is responsible for allowing into Japan.) The problem is, nothing much ever happens. By the end of the film, we feel that the movie has been shot in "real time" and that we actually have lived with Wayne for the many months he impatiently awaits Japan's decision to enter into the world community.

Duke gives a very good performance, but he looks completely uncomfortable. This is mostly due to the fact that for some reason, Huston never allows him to appear in anything but a coat and tails, even when we see Wayne relaxing at home. His character begins to remind you of one of those TV fathers like Hugh Beaumont or Fred MacMurray who "unwound" after a hard day's work by changing into a formal suit and sitting in the living room. It is also somewhat disconcerting seeing Wayne in a top hat. Throughout the film, Duke looks uneasy that the over-sized chapeau might drop from his head.

The weakest element of the film is the relationship between Wayne and the geisha, Okichi (Eiko Ando). We see Wayne curing her of her total subservience to men, and her eventual alienation from the geisha community for becoming too westernized. Yet, a full-blown love story never develops. We see Duke and Ando gawking mawkishly at each other across some tea leaves, but Wayne—ever the gentlemen—gives us no indication that their love has ever been consumated. In fact, pains are taken early in the story to show us that Wayne refuses to bed down with his geisha. This might get him kudos from some ladies at the church social, but it does nothing to add passion to the story. It comes almost as a shock, when late in the plot Wayne is devastated by Ando's sudden departure at the triumphant moment when he succeeds in opening Japan's borders to the world. Just when something interesting starts to happen, the credits suddenly roll leaving the audience unsatisfied.

Interestingly, both Huston and Wayne blamed each other for the film's failure at the box-office.

(One critic remarked cynically, "Oops! There goes $3-million!") Huston was outraged when the title was changed to *The Barbarian and the Geisha*. He also accused of Wayne of using his influence as the star to obtain a work print of the movie prior to release and completely re-editing the storyline. Wayne also was said to have filmed additional sequences on his own without Huston's knowledge. Wayne shot back that Huston was the slowest director he had ever worked with, and had never made a good film without the assistance of his father Walter or Humphrey Bogart. Regardless of who was at fault, the picture was a bomb for both men and neither sought to put it high on his career resume. While it has been treated too harshly by critics, *The Barbarian and the Geisha* does not leave one with the desire to see it again.

DONOVAN'S REEF (1963)

Cast: John Wayne, Lee Marvin, Elizabeth Allen, Jack Warden, Cesar Romero, Dorothy Lamour, Mike Mazurki. *Directed by* John Ford. *Screenplay by* Frank Nugent and James Edward Grant. *From a Screen Story by* Edmund Beloin. *Music by* Cyril Mockridge. *Released by* Paramount Pictures. *Running Time:* 106 Minutes.

It is sad to realize that after the brilliant collaborations of Duke and John Ford, their relationship should end—at least professionally—with the featherweight *Donovan's Reef*. There is nothing intrinsically wrong with the film, if all one expects is low-brow action comedy. But even the most casual vehicle produced by Wayne and Ford always amounted to something memorable, and *Donovan's Reef* lacks anything worth reflecting

upon after the end credits roll. It's sort of like cotton candy: easy to digest, but leaving you hungry for something more substantial.

Donovan's Reef is a slap-dash effort. Ford might have been excused for taking it easy due to his age and failing health, but one wishes that Wayne and Lee Marvin could have persuaded him to at least improve the screenplay by old hands Frank Nugent and the ubiquitous James Edward Grant. One gets the feeling that everyone had been working hard and decided to pay for a joint vacation to Hawaii by pretending to do a film. Paramount probably didn't care, as *Donovan's Reef* produced the desired box-office results.

The almost non-existent plot finds Wayne and Marvin long time friendly enemies who meet annually at Wayne's Hawaiian bar (called "Do-

BIG JOHN WAYNE

IN THE JOHN FORD PRODUCTION

DONOVAN'S REEF

TECHNICOLOR®

Lee MARVIN | Elizabeth ALLEN | Jack WARDEN | Cesar ROMERO | Dick Foran | and | Dorothy LAMOUR

Directed by John Ford / Screenplay by Frank Nugent and James Edward Grant / Story by Edmund Beloin / A Paramount Release

novan's Reef") to rekindle their feuding and fighting of many years. When the movie stays on this course, it at least benefits from some good-natured fun and amusing fight scenes. However, it makes the mistake of introducing Elizabeth Allen as a wealthy snob from Boston who arrives to visit her father, one of Wayne's cronies. Ashamed that he has fathered children with an island woman, he convinces Wayne to pose as the kids' real dad. After a series of prolonged complications and predictable subplots, the truth is revealed, but not until Wayne has "cured" Allen and made her a real woman by spanking her in public. This sequence was repeated almost exactly in Wayne's next film, *McLintock!*, which was scripted by—there's that name again!—James Edward Grant.

By mid-point in *Donovan Reef*, Grant's heavy

hand can be felt bogging down the screenplay. There is a boring religious ceremony set on the island designed to warm the heart of the audience. Wayne is also clearly somewhat "long-in-tooth" to be a love interest for a woman half his age. Although he never looks ridiculous, the story would have benefited from casting an older actress as the female lead.

The movie does have its attributes. The Fordian brawls are frequent and well-staged, and Wayne takes a realistic fall across a barroom table. The stunt looks good, primarily because it was not planned. A "breakaway" table was mistakenly substituted for a real one, and the shocked look on Duke's face as he falls is genuine. Wayne plays well against Marvin, and it is to the story's detriment that the latter virtually disappears as the film drags on. There is beautiful

175

cinematography, and some catchy island songs, as well as having Paramount's old favorite Dorothy Lamour (who else?) thrown in to ensure we all know this is truly a comedy in the style of the old Hope and Crosby "Road" movies.

One could forgive Ford and Wayne if the director was incapable of making another film after *Donovan's Reef.* However, he was able to direct the 1965 epic *Cheyenne Autumn* which was only a moderate success, but would have benefited greatly from Wayne's participation. We must keep in mind, however, that *Donovan's Reef* is only disappointing because of the extraordinary track record of Wayne and Ford. In effect, they made their every teaming an event with great expectations. One cannot fault them for being human and taking the low road once in a while. It is merely a shame that they chose to do so late in Ford's career, when the very fact that they could still make another film was reason for them to try and make such an occurrence something special. In summary, *Donovan's Reef* is a pleasant way to spend some time, but it will remain no more than just another film credit in the careers of two industry giants.

CIRCUS WORLD (1964)

Cast: John Wayne, Claudia Cardinale, Rita Hayworth, Lloyd Nolan, Richard Conte, John Smith, Henri Dantes. *Producer:* Samuel Bronston. *Director:* Henry Hathaway. *Screenplay:* Ben Hecht, Julian Halvey and James Edward Grant. *From a Story by* Philip Yordan and Nicholas Ray. *Music:* Dimitri Tiomkin. *Released by* Paramount Pictures. *Running Time:* 131 Minutes.

One critic said that watching this movie was like sitting with an elephant on your lap for two hours.

Perhaps it is unfair to include *Circus World* among John Wayne's poor films. However, there are enough major errors in evidence to justify its status in this category. *Circus World* was a troubled production from start to finish, and the end result reflects the chaotic problems which almost prevented the film from being made.

Paramount had originally contracted director Frank Capra to helm the mammoth production, which was being filmed in Cinerama. Capra arrived in Madrid, where he wrote the screenplay with collaborator Joe Sistrom. Initially, Capra was enthused about the project, and saw it as a long-awaited opportunity to work with Wayne. Long before Duke arrived on location, however, trouble started brewing when Wayne's long-time friend and screenwriter Jimmy Grant showed up. He informed Capra that his script was not appropriate for Wayne and promised to write a suitable story practically overnight, according to Capra, allegedly stating that "All you gotta have in a John Wayne picture is a hoity-toity dame with big tits that Duke can throw over his knee and spank, and a collection of jerks he can smash in the face every five minutes." Capra, needless to say, was less than enthused about this prescription to fix a screenplay which he considered a vehicle that would allow Wayne to give the performance of his life.

As these grievances flared, Wayne was cruising off the coast of Spain on his yacht, a converted minesweeper named "The Wild Goose." Some industry insiders speculated that he was actually fanning the troubles on the set in order

Hathaway to take over for him, stating cynically to his fellow director that all he needed to direct Wayne was "a hoity-toity dame with big tits, etc." (Capra retired from filmmaking altogether.) Hathaway accepted the challenge, having himself just walked out on the remake of *Of Human Bondage* due to conceptual disputes with star Kim Novak. Apparently, Hathaway was equally unimpressed with Grant, and summarily fired him. For once Wayne did not go to his old friend's aid, and veteran screenwriter Ben Hecht began working on the script.

The end result of this battle royale is a rambling, often unconvincing screenplay. For the record, Wayne insisted for years that the failure of *Circus World* was the fault of Capra, whom he referred to as a "son-of-a-bitch." He accused Capra of lying about the problems he claimed Wayne and Grant caused, and theorized that the director was merely trying to find a scapegoat for having been fired by Paramount. Capra's opinion of Wayne was not much better, and in his autobiography, *The Name Above the Title*, he refers to the Duke as "tired, bloated and aged."

As for the film itself, *Circus World* is a talky soap opera masquerading as a big-screen spectacle. Sort of an "As the World Turns" episode with elephants. The story lumbers from one unconvincing scene to the next, and the occasional shots of actual circus performances are never as thrilling as intended. This is partly due to the use of rear-screen projection in order to show the stars appearing to be in the midst of the action. Unfortunately, for all the money spent on the film, the projection techniques are poor.

In the movie, Wayne plays Matt Masters, the head of a troubled Wild West-themed circus. He is plagued by the loss of most of his props and equipment during the capsizing of his ship during a European tour. He is further haunted by the fact that his former lover Lili Alfredo (Rita Hayworth) is now a reclusive derelict, having deserted her daughter Toni (Claudia Cardinale) after Lili's husband/partner was killed during their trapeze act. According to the contrived plot, Hayworth feels he intentionally killed himself after suspecting she had been in love with Wayne.

to panic Paramount into paying him a higher salary as nearly the entire project depended upon his participation. Duke never officially commented on the Capra/Grant war, but even his non-involvement was seen by some as devious. Critics said that Wayne hesitated to support Grant in full, yet hoped that by his refusal to fire him from the project, Paramount might be intimidated to go with Grant's version of the script in order to avoid angering Wayne.

Whatever the case, Capra walked away from the project, and asked his old friend Henry

Duke gets his circus back on the road, and searches Europe for Hayworth. He eventually finds her, of course, and shames her into rejoining the circus and taking responsibility of being a mother to Cardinale, whom he has raised since infancy.

The script is full of stilted dialogue, leading one to assume that since Grant is at least partly credited for the screenplay, these clumsy exchanges could well be his doing. As for the performances, Wayne is hammy here, overplaying his role of the tough but tender circus man. His reaction shots are often childishly enacted, and it is difficult to believe this was all under the guidance of the man who would later direct *True Grit*.

Both Hayworth and Cardinale are equally unimpressive, the latter playing a tomboy sort of "The Flying Nun" in spangles and spurs. John Smith, a nonentity who appeared with Wayne in *"The High and the Mighty,"* makes a cardboard love interest for Cardinale, and veteran Lloyd Nolan is saddled with what could be called the obligatory "Old Geezer" role.

Circus World is not without its merits, however, and probably turned out to be better than the course of production indicated. There are two impressive action sequences which prove to be fairly exciting. In the first, the circus ship capsizes, leaving Wayne to lead an intricate rescue effort. In the second, and best scene, a fire virtually destroys the circus on the eve of its premiere. During the actual filming of this scene, Wayne was nearly killed. He had not noticed that the director and crew had fled when the flames got out of hand, and he narrowly escaped death. Although Wayne was said to be furious about this near-tragedy, it definitely provides the movie with its most successful and exciting scene.

Circus World also contains a haunting score by Dimitri Tiomkin. Yet, these factors were not enough to make the movie a memorable entry in the Wayne canon. Duke appears stiff and uncomfortable throughout most of the film, indicating that he, too, was less than enthused about the project.

As a footnote, it should be mentioned that this movie proved to be Wayne's last collaboration with buddy James Edward Grant, who died two years later.

THE GREATEST STORY EVER TOLD (1965)

Cast: Max Von Sydow, Charlton Heston, Sal Mineo, Donald Pleasance, David McCallum, Telly Savalas, Van Heflin, Sidney Poitier, Roddy McDowall, Dorothy McGuire, Jose Ferrer, Carrol Baker, Angela Lansbury, Pat Boone, Michael Anderson, Jr, Shelley Winters, John Wayne, Ed Wynn. *Director:* George Stevens. *Screenplay:* James Lee Barrett and George Stevens. *From The Bible*, other ancient writings, and the book by Fulton Oursler and writings by Henry Denker in Creative Association with Carl Sandburg. *Music:* Alfred Newman. *Released by* United Artists. *Running Time:* 196 Minutes.

Director George Stevens had long dreamed of filming an intelligent Biblical epic, which would

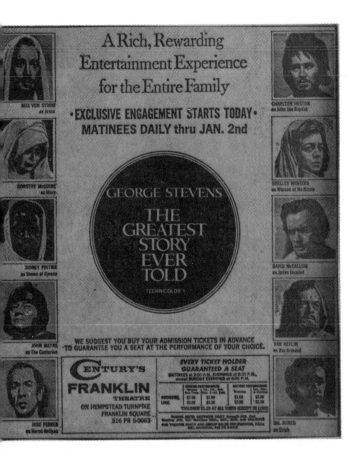

steer clear of the special effects and "tits-and toga" mentality of most movies of this type. He envisioned a thinking man's spectacle which would concentrate more on the the characters than action sequences. For five years, he labored to get financing for this project. 20th Century-Fox had originally invested close to $3-million in development monies, but since Stevens had not even begun to film, the studio cut its losses and retired from participation.

Undaunted, Stevens began to raise money from private investors. Impressed by his stamina, as well as his reputation as one of the screen's great directors, United Artists threw the financial weight of the studio behind him.

Stevens eventually accumulated an impressive cast and crew and headed off into the deserts of the American West to begin filming. This bizarre choice of locations caused two problems. The first was the additional costs to the budget, as animals had to be transported from Africa to one of the sets in Waheap, Arizona. The second

problem is the most obvious—one is always aware that Jesus is walking through scenery in which we are more accustomed to seeing stage-coaches and shoot-outs. One half expects the Prince of Peace and his Disciples to be confronted at any given point by the Lone Ranger and Tonto.

Nonetheless, Stevens spent more than $1-million re-creating the city of Jerusalem. He employed hundreds of extras and technicians for whom prefabricated cottages had to be constructed. Costume designers worked around the clock to clothe the cast, and there are more sheets on display in this film than a combination January white sale and Ku Klux Klan meeting. Almost immediately, the movie fell behind schedule. The cast complained of Stevens' painstakingly slow style of reshooting scene after scene until perfection was achieved. Months passed, and so did the good weather. The actors began to suffer from frostbite. One morning, a blizzard struck, leaving Stevens unable to shoot sequences in "Jerusalem." Everyone pitched in and shoveled the snow away, only to have a second storm paralyze the cast and crew once more. Stevens packed everything up and headed to the studio, where some enormously expensive sets were constructed to compensate for the inability to shoot on location. During this time, Stevens also had to cope with the death of his cinematographer, as well as the demise of actor Joseph Schildkraut. Both blows served only to aggrevate Steven's ulcer, and yet he persisted.

Eventually, the movie was completed, but not without considerable pressure from the studio. The end result was heavily promoted, and it must be said, was hailed by most as being quite "tasteful." Steven's movie is reverent to the point of boredom. Cecil B. DeMille arguably could not direct traffic, let alone a major film, but his epics were never dull. In watching *Story*, how one hungers for the unintentional hilarity of DeMille's *The Ten Commandments*, with its ludicrous dialogue and casting choices (remember Edward G. Robinson as Dathan and Vincent Price as an ancient Egyptian). Alas, *Story* does not even have the benefit of being funny.

As Jesus, Max Von Sydow looks fine and plays

the role in an understated and intelligent manner. However, he is so understated that his charisma is non-existent. One wonders why the apostles would follow him across the room, let alone all the way across the desert. Other casting choices range from the sublime to the ridiculous. Charlton Heston makes a brief appearance as the ill-fated John the Baptist, and his scenes ring with conviction and some dramatic tension. But Heston goes and gets his head chopped off near the beginning of the film, and it's all downhill from there.

In order to increase box-office appeal, Stevens made the mistake of casting in cameo roles any available "name" actors he could find. If an actor expressed an interest in appearing, George would just use the Divine shoehorn to squeeze him in somewhere along the line. This device proves distracting, as we are constantly peeking under veils and helmets to see if we can spot a familiar face. As Jesus is seen dragging his crucifix up to Cavalry, all dramatic tension is lost as we say gleefully to ourselves, "Isn't that Sidney Poitier in the crowd? And next to him, isn't that Pat Boone?" The scene becomes sort of a "Jesus on the Love Boat" with all the celebrities trying to crowd out the Saviour.

It is during the crucifixion scene that Duke Wayne makes his mercilessly brief appearance as a Roman Centurion. Not having learned from his prior experience in playing Genghis Khan, Wayne all too readily accepted Stevens' invitation to strap on the wardrobe of a Roman soldier. The sight of Davy Crockett shoving the Prince of Peace toward His fate is more than a bit startling. Yet, to show that he is actually a sadist with a heart of gold, we are eventually shown Wayne gazing admiringly up at Christ while speaking his only line in the film, "Truly, the man was the son of God." Yes, it comes across every bit as badly as one would expect. Years later, critic John Simon was still citing Wayne's inept recitation of this single line as evidence that the man could not act.

Wayne's dialogue in this film was the basis of one of Hollywood's apocryphal anecdotes. Supposedly, director Stevens had instructed Duke to repeat his line with a little more awe. Wayne supposedly then said, "Awe, truly this man was the son of God!" There was no truth to the story whatsoever, but even Wayne enjoyed repeating it on occasion.

One must give Stevens some credit, however. No matter how dull his film proved to be, it did avoid the types of biblical cliches he wanted to avoid. There are a few other notable performances, specifically that of David McCallum as a haunted and tormented Judas.

One aspect of the epic that should not go unmentioned is the fact that you have to wonder where the film's $10 million budget went. Except for the Jerusalem set and a few impressive crowd scenes, most of the scenes are set indoors. Here, the set decoration is infinitely inferior to the backdrops found in almost any Sunday school production of the life of Christ. In one scene, Jesus confronts Satan (Donald Pleasance) under a night sky with a moon so large, that one expects Jackie Gleason's face to appear on it, along with opening credits of "The Honeymooners "

The Greatest Story Ever Told proved to be one of the major box-office duds of the Sixties. Originally, the film ran more than four hours, and had been cut and recut for general release. It can now be seen in a 196 minute version on videocassette. While not the original "roadshow" version, the video does restore many scenes that had been edited over the years. The movie sadly closed the curtain on the career of George Stevens, who would make only one more movie. He need not be ashamed, as the memorable films which he gave us more than compensate for this failure. As with all biblical efforts, *Story* was well intentioned. However, if one views the film expecting something exciting to happen—well, let's just say it's the equivalent of leaving the porch light on for Jimmy Hoffa.

THE GREEN BERETS (1968)

Cast: John Wayne, David Janssen, Jim Hutton, Aldo Ray, Raymond St. Jacques, Jack Soo, Bruce Cabot, George Takei, Patrick Wayne, Luke Askew, Irene Tsu, Edward Faulkner. *Directors:* John Wayne, Ray Kellogg. *Screenplay:* James Lee Barrett, *Based Upon the Novel by* Robin Moore. *Music:* Miklos Rozsa. *Released by* Warner Bros.–Seven Arts. *Running Time:* 141 Minutes.

Some years ago during the Vietnam conflict, I saw *The Green Berets* and thought it—as did many critics—a poor film. I watched it again recently in relation to writing about it for this book. I was prepared to find it even more dreadful at this point in time, but I was somewhat pleasantly surprised. *The Green Berets*, like Wayne himself, is a paradox. There are so many negatives about this film that I have decided to run it in the section detailing the worst movies of Wayne's career. However, to my amazement, I found almost as many elements that I admired. Time has not been unkind to *The Green Berets*, and if I must label it a "turkey," I do so reluctantly and not without examining the controversial film's many merits.

One of the great joys of writing a book like this is that you can be totally subjective, and say "to hell with popular opinion." I might stand alone in admitting that *The Green Berets* has any merits at all, but my conscience tells me I cannot go with the flow on this one. First, however, a bit of background on the making of the film.

John Wayne had toured Vietnam in 1966, and was deeply moved by the experience. Ironically, he initially was personally reluctant to get the U.S. involved in the conflict at all. However, he subscribed to the belief that, once committed, we should strike the North Vietnamese quickly and with full force in order to win. When Barry Goldwater ran for President in his ill-fated 1964 campaign, Wayne found that the Senator had echoed these exact sentiments and he supported

So you don't believe in glory. And heroes are out of style. And they don't blow bugles anymore. So take another look—at the special forces in a special kind of hell—

THE GREEN BERETS

JOHN WAYNE **DAVID JANSSEN** **JIM HUTTON**

A BATJAC Production co-starring ALDO RAY RAYMOND ST JACQUES · BRUCE CABOT · PATRICK WAYNE · LUKE ASKEW Screenplay by JAMES LEE BARRETT Produced by MICHAEL WAYNE Directed by JOHN WAYNE and RAY KELLOGG TECHNICOLOR® PANAVISION® FROM WARNER BROS.–SEVEN ARTS

him fully. Wayne always blamed Lyndon Johnson for what he felt was his deception of the American people. He believed L.B.J. painted Goldwater as a "hawk" while adopting a dovish attitude himself in order to win the election. After this was accomplished, it was Johnson who engaged the U.S. in a "no-win" policy in Vietnam. Wayne found this despicable, and following his tour in Southeast Asia, returned home committed to tell the silent majority's side of the war.

Through his production company, Batjac,

Duke purchased the rights to Robin Moore's best-selling novel, *The Green Berets*, which had also recently been immortalized through Sgt. Barry Sadler's popular recording. He approached Paramount with the chance to finance and release the film, and was promptly turned down, despite the string of hits he had given the studio over the years. "Too controversial," they told him. Wayne succeeded in getting Universal to agree to release the film, but at the last minute, that studio backed down presumably because it didn't like the script. Wayne saw it as caving in to the "East Coast liberals." He finally convinced Warners to go with the project, and allow him to star and direct as well. Warners reluctantly agreed, largely because of the film's patriotic message. However, the studio had a keen sense for turning a profit as well. Alarmed at Duke's spending habits on *The Alamo*, Warners insured that no such cost over-runs would foul up *The Green Berets*. Veteran director Mervyn LeRoy was sent to the set as an "advisor" to Duke. This did not hide the obvious fact that he was there as studio watchdog, and to take the directorial reins if needed.

Filming began at Fort Benning, Georgia, and required large-scale military assistance. Depending on whether you listen to Wayne or his liberal critics, the Army was either stingy in its cooperation, or extremely generous. In any event, the film was completed only after an arduous shooting schedule lasting three months. This was an enormous strain on Wayne, who was working up to 14 hours a day not only directing but playing in key action sequences.

Upon release, the film was ravaged by critics who not only faulted its merits as a movie, but assailed its unabashed support for a war that was rapidly losing popularity throughout the citizenry. Wayne expected controversy, but nothing like the storm of criticisms which almost buried him in scorn. Chief among his opponents was *The New York Times* critic Renata Adler, who published one of the most scathing indictments of a motion picture to date. Publicly, Duke dismissed the critics, but intimates say he was deeply wounded by the severity of their attacks.

As a film, *The Green Berets* often literally jumps up and begs to be mocked. It is filled with stock characters in stock situations we have seen many times before. More than one critic commented on the fact that Wayne was out of touch with Vietnam, and simply remade *Sands of Iwo Jima* with some modern technology thrown in. This opinion is reinforced by the characters in the story. Every cliche imaginable seems to be used, including characters named Muldoon (gruff Sergeant with a heart of gold) and Kowalski (down to earth ethnic type, heroic to the end). We also see Jim Hutton as the inevitably charming "scrounger" who is able to con his way into getting whatever Wayne needs. Then there is the Vietnamese orphan boy who has only Hutton and his pet dog to help him through the brutal nightly attacks by the Viet Cong. And of course there's the liberal reporter, played by David Janssen, whose opposition to the war is both knee-jerked and devoid of any rationale (just like the East Coast press, right?)

The film begins with a simplistic device to get across Wayne's political views. Aldo Ray as Muldoon is giving the press and public a tour of a Green Beret training center. He deflects those liberals at every turn and manages to turn the skeptical crowd into dedicated supporters. Janssen decides to go to 'Nam to get the goods on the U.S. forces there once and for all. Naturally, in doing so he comes into conflict with Wayne, who is also sent there to command a base which is under construction. It doesn't take long for Janssen to agree with Wayne in his opinion that in Vietnam, "Due process is a bullet."

Duke and his soldiers expose Janssen to numerous Viet Cong atrocities, some of which are based on fact, according to Wayne. Not even a hint of impropriety by U.S. forces is suggested, although we are told that Uncle Sam also employs razor sharp bamboo sticks as booby traps. (Unlike the Cong, however, our bamboo sticks are civilized in that they simply impale a man, but do not contain the poison used by the enemy.) The U.S. is shown as being consistently kind to the local populace, but Wayne stumbles here trying to make a compassionate statement which comes across as patronizing. (A doctor tending an elderly Vietnamese man with wounds comments, "He's dyin', poor old thing. Can't even keep his rice down," as though referring to a favorite old hound.)

There are a lot of doomed people in *The Green Berets*. Unfortunately, none of these tragedies comes as a surprise due to the cliches spoken by the ill-fated characters earlier in the story. One sergeant comments that he is one day away from going home. The orphan child is constantly seen hugging his dog, as well as telling Hutton that the mutt and Hutton are the only friends he has in the world. The only way to insure more certain death onscreen is to befriend Charles Bronson in one of the *Death Wish* films or to be a minor character assigned to assist James Bond. Both the sergeant and Hutton die horrible deaths, the latter being impaled on the (presumably poisoned) bamboo sticks. Even the dog is killed in a sequence shamelessly designed to rouse our anger against the Cong.

Few of the performances are anything to rave about, although Wayne dispelled doubts that he was too old to carry the lead. He does a fine job throughout, as does David Janssen. Most of the other characters are cliches on the hoof, and are enacted accordingly. Interestingly, Vera Miles shot a sequence as Wayne's wife, but it was deleted before the film's release due to length. This might have given additional insight into Wayne's character, whom we never really get to know on a personal level.

With that all said, what, you may ask, did I find to recommend about *The Green Berets*? The answer is, taken purely as a war film, it works very well. The battle scenes were realistic enough to merit special effects supervisor Ray Kellogg co-directing credit with Wayne. The Viet Cong assault on the base is extremely exciting and captures the confusion, uncertainty and madness of a night battle. Overwhelmed, Wayne and men uncharacteristically retreat, adding a touch of realism to the action.

There are many other scenes that are effective in spite of the script deficiencies. A sub-plot about a pro-South Vietnamese seductress aiding Wayne in capturing a Cong general is fairly engrossing and suspensefully directed. (Even though he is seen wearing pants in the middle of what was designed to be an erotic moment. This is, after all, a John Wayne film.) Other effective scenes include Hutton's death, which, although expected, nonetheless comes as shock by virtue of the sudden and hideous way in which he dies. Despite his grief, Wayne is forced to hurry on as though he hasn't a second thought about the incident, even though it pains him terribly.

The movie concludes with a sentimental scene in which Duke tells the orphan about Hutton's death and promises to work to keep Vietnam free. Despite the platitudes, the scene works, and it is actually somewhat touching (distracted only by the fact that the sunset over the ocean is geographically wrong.)

Wayne may have borne the brunt of the scoffing critics who claimed the movie would flop terribly. However, he had the last laugh. *The Green Berets* proved to be one of the biggest box-office draws of the year, and returned a nice profit to all concerned. This undoubtedly gave Wayne a great deal of satisfaction. Some of the points which are so poorly made in the film bore the sting of truth in later years. When Aldo Ray warns that if Vietnam fell, the Communists would massacre all intellectuals and their families, liberals scoffed. Yet, only a few years later Pol Pot and the Khmer Rouge would reduce Cambodia to a wasteland through the massacres foretold in *The Green Berets*. Right or wrong, John Wayne stuck with his convictions until the day he died. During the rape of Cambodia, his most vocal critics were silent. He was never silent in his opposition of what he felt was a genocidal regime. Ironically, the same cannot be said of many of his normally outspoken opponents.

HELLFIGHTERS (1968)

Cast: John Wayne, Katharine Ross, Jim Hutton, Vera Miles, Jay C. Flippen, Bruce Cabot, Edward Faulkner, Barbara Stuart. *Director:* Andrew V. McLaglen. *Screenplay:* Clair Huffaker. *Music:* Leonard Rosenman. *Released by* Universal Pictures. *Running Time:* 121 Minutes.

There is some sort of irony that almost 20 years to the day that Wayne filmed *Tycoon*, bad judgement would come back to haunt him in the form of *Hellfighters*. With this film, Wayne seemed to prove wrong those people who always say "They don't make 'em like they used to." *Hellfighters* is every bit as bad as its predecessor. It's hard to begin listing everything wrong with this "epic," as this book must be confined to less than 300 pages.

Let's start with the screenplay which casts Big Duke as a veteran oil well firefighter. When we first meet him, he's happily winging his way around the world with his fellow daredevils, defying all odds by putting out the impossible infernos. Lest the script get too interesting, however, within minutes, Duke is at death's door due to an accident, and we are forced to hear the obligatory cliches about how he's a tough guy with a heart of gold.

Enter estranged daughter Katharine Ross,

JOHN WAYNE
KATHARINE ROSS
THAT "GRADUATE" GIRL
JIM HUTTON

"HELLFIGHTERS"

[G] Suggested for GENERAL audiences.

JAY C. FLIPPEN · BRUCE CABOT and
VERA MILES

When in Southern California visit Universal Studios

who struts through the proceedings with the movies most unattractive hair-do. (All right, maybe the SECOND worst in movie history, if you count Wayne's rug in *The Conqueror.* In any event, Ross resembles a cross between a young Mary Tyler Moore and George Washington.) She hasn't seen daddy Wayne since childhood, due to the fact that he's estranged from wife Vera Miles. Miles could no longer bear the tension and worry of having her big guy out fighting fires while she is left at home wearing a collection of incredibly ugly designer clothes.

Ross goes to visit Duke on his deathbed and—PRESTO!—he recuperates immediately, only to learn that his daughter has fallen in love with his right hand man, Jim Hutton, whom she marries on the spur of the moment. This alarms Wayne, as Hutton is the town playboy. (We know he's a playboy because he calls all the chicks "baby" and wears polyester turtlenecks.) Through a long, boring series of uninteresting events, Wayne learns to respect wife and daughter, Jim learns to respect Duke and Vera, and no one learns to respect scriptwriter Clair Huffaker.

The screenplay of *Hellfighters* reads like an encyclopedia of cliches. The men and women spend a lot of time fighting about the gals' fearless desire to join the guys up there on the front line of the fire. Much is made of this issue to no avail. When the women do get within the scene of the action, they seem to spend all their time in cabins playing poker or cleaning coffee urns. Like Laraine Day in *Tycoon,* both Vera Miles and Katharine Ross just drive up undetered to the site of a blazing inferno and hang out in evening wear. Suddenly, Wayne decides to retire in order to please Vera, and leaves the company in Hutton's hands. Naturally, we know Wayne can't be kept out of the saddle. As if the point needs to be illustrated, we see him sitting uncomfortably on the board of another company in which all the high level executives are having a heated discussion over restroom decor. Before you can say "A man's got to do what a man's got to do," the Duke is back in a hard hat and up to his neck in more oil than can be found in Jerry Lewis' hair.

This is the kind of movie that feels it can get across some uninteresting facts about fire fighting in the guise of having a nerdy TV reporter cover the sight of a blaze. In what has to be the longest "live" report in the history of broadcasting, the newsman asks all the questions we are supposedly anxious to know. The acting is uniformly awful, and even Wayne comes across badly as he is forced to play second fiddle to Ross and Hutton, both of whom are supposed to represent the average young American and pull in the younger audience. As *Hellfighters* was made at a time when most young people were wearing their hair long and protesting, one might ask which century's youth Ross and Hutton are supposed to represent. The camera does them one favor: in a nightclub scene, we see both actors about to start indulging in a "hip" modern dance. Fortunately, the cameraman has the sense to cut away before the audience sees that Bruce Cabot has more rhythm in the film's bar fight than either Hutton or Ross can display on the dance floor.

The script contains some howlers of dialogue:

Female admirer to Wayne: "When Ahmal phoned you were coming, my heart went a-glowing!"

Wayne to Miles: "Well, I'll be damned" Miles to Wayne: "That's the most romantic greeting a woman's ever heard!"

Other cliches abound, and all the bickering principal players begin to resemble Ralph and Alice Kramden in asbestos suits. Director Andrew V. McLaglen was so obviously inspired by the mediocrity of TV movies, that one can literally see breaks for commercials built into the editing process. Everything about *Hellfighters* seems fake, including some of the flimsiest sets since *Plan 9 From Outer Space.* On next viewing, pay special attention to the "highway" which can be viewed from Wayne's office. It appears to be a treadmill upon which all traffic moves at exactly the same pace. This prompted critic Rex Reed to write that he had counted the same red station wagon go by 17 times in one scene. (I only counted 15 but I might have blinked or nodded off.)

There is also some terribly inept rear-screen projection. In one "dramatic" sequence, Vera

WAYNE AND HUTTON SPORT THE
LATEST IN IVANHOE HAIR-DOS

Miles abruptly slams on the brakes and begins to go backwards before even putting the car in reverse. In another scene, Bruce Cabot is shown sleeping. We know he's really dozing, because we hear the loud snoring. In fact, I kept waiting for some cartoon "Z's" to appear in a balloon above his head.

The film's one virtue is in the actual scenes of the oil well fires, and if McLaglen had concentrated on this area, he may have fashioned a fairly tense film. The movie's script is loosely based on the exploits of oil well firefighter Red Adair, who

also acted as technical advisor for the film. Undoubtedly due to his participation, the action sequences ring true and approach some level of believability. Whenever the action threatens to take precedence over the "Brady Bunch"–level melodramatics, Katharine Ross and Vera Miles drive up and put things in reverse. After seeing the completed film, it's a wonder even a lifelong fighter of fires like Adair wasn't tempted to ignite the negative.

Hellfighters is just *Tycoon* with a few weenie roasts thrown in. There's a lot of smoke and fire everywhere, but in the end the entire project is more like a false alarm.

JOHN WAYNE GOES ON THE RECORD

In this section, we will look at the many influences of music on John Wayne's films. A composer's contribution to a film is often overlooked. Wayne movies benefited from some of the most beautiful and memorable scores created for motion pictures. Try to envision the Ford films bereft of their haunting themes, or the battle of the Alamo without Tiomkin's marvelously exciting sountrack. The major studios always valued the best scores from their films and tried to capitalize on them via soundtrack albums and/or 45 RPM singles from various movies.

Wayne himself made contributions to the record industries. In 1972, he narrated an album titled *America—Why I Love Her* in which he read patriotic verses to the accompaniment of an orchestra and choir. It was corny, all right, but Duke had the last laugh. Not only was he nominated for a Grammy Award, but the record sold well enough to inspire a paperback version of the poems he read. While Wayne had the good sense to realize he was not musically inclined, his

films featured the contributions of many others who were. A number of the best scores from his films were available on albums, although today, these collector's items can be quite expensive to obtain. Some soundtracks, such as those from *The Alamo, Cast a Giant Shadow* and *How the West Was Won*, are still readily available, having been re-issued throughout the years. However, try to obtain a copy of the music soundtrack for *McLintock!* or *Island in the Sky* and be prepared to spend at least $50 per title.

It has always been frustrating to Wayne fans that many fine scores from his films were never released commercially on albums. Despite having very good scores, no soundtrack albums exist for *The High and the Mighty, Rio Bravo, The War Wagon, Chisum* and *McQ*. Fortunately, some smaller record companies have put out original soundtracks for *The Cowboys* (which includes one of John Williams' best scores), *Sands of Iwo Jima* and *Rio Grande*. Of these, the latter two are fairly easy to find in major record stores, while the

187

RECORD AND SHEET MUSIC PROMOTION
FOR "HOW THE WEST WAS WON"

THE RADIO VERSION OF
"STAGECOACH" WAS ISSUED ON AN L.P.

album for *The Cowboys* is quite obscure.

Additionally, two relatively recent albums compile original soundtrack music which had been unavailable until now. These are titled "The John Wayne Films" and "The John Wayne Films, Vol. 2." The first features soundtrack music by Elmer Bernstein from his classic scores for *The Comancheros* and *True Grit* (the latter is a series of selections which differ from that on the previously released *Grit* soundtrack). Ironically, despite having one of Bernsteins most memorable scores, the only record tie-in for *The Comancheros* was a 45 RPM with a ballad sung by Claude King. Such a song was never featured in the film, but is doubtless treasured as a collector's item. Volume 2 features music from *The Shootist, Cahill: U.S. Marshal,* and *Big Jake.* All of the music was written by Elmer Bernstein.

THE EVER-CHANGING JOHN WAYNE

Several of John Wayne's films were destined to have title changes before their release. Some of these changes occurred before the start of production, while others were changed immediately before the premiere date. In fact there are some rare stills available which have the pre-production or original title listed on the credits line.

Also, although one would expect that many of these titles would be significantly altered for the European market, it is interesting to note that some of Wayne's films underwent title changes even for their release in the United Kingdom. All such differences are designated in the list which follows.

FILM	ORIGINAL TITLE	U.K. TITLE
Maker of Men	Yellow	
Lady and Gent	The Challenger	
The Three Musketeers (Serial)	Desert Command	
Paradise Canyon	Paradise Ranch	
The Night Riders	Lone Star Bullets	
Seven Sinners		Released in U.K. Under this title. However, reissued in 1947 as "Cafe of the Seven Sinners"
Three Faces West	Doctors Don't Tell	
Allegheny Uprising	Allegheny Frontier	The First Rebel
Three Texas Steers		Danger Rides the Range
College Coach		Football Coach
Ride Him, Cowboy		The Hawk
The Drop Kick		Glitter
A Man Betrayed	Citadel of Crime	Citadel of Crime
Lady from Louisiana	Lady from New Orleans	
Reunion in France	Reunion	Mademoiselle France
A Lady Takes a Chance	The Cowboy & The Girl	
In Old Oklahoma	War of the Wildcats (also reissue title)	
Back to Bataan	The Invisible Army	
Without Reservations	Thanks God, I'll Take it from Here	
Angel and The Badman	The Angel & The Outlaw	
Fort Apache	War Party	
The Fighting Kentuckian	A Strange Caravan	
Rio Grande	Rio Bravo	
Big Jim McLain	Jim McLain	
Trouble Along the Way	Alma Mater	
Legend of the Lost	Legend of Timbuktu	
The Barbarian and The Geisha	The Townsend Harris Story/ also: The Barbarian	
North To Alaska	Go North	
Circus World		The Magnificent Showman
Rio Lobo	San Timoteo	
Big Jake	The Million Dollar Kidnapping	
Cahill: U.S. Marshal	Wednesday Morning	Cahill
Brannigan	Joe Battle	

"WAR OF THE WILDCATS" ORIGINAL
TITLE: "IN OLD OKLAHOMA"

"THE BARBARIAN AND THE GEISHA"
NOTE THE FILM'S ORIGINAL TITLE
"THE BARBARIAN" ON THE BOTTOM CREDIT

A Scene from the 20th Century-Fox Production
"THE BARBARIAN"
In CinemaScope

"THE FIGHTING KENTUCKIAN"
ORIGINAL TITLE: "STRANGE CARAVAN"

"LEGEND OF THE LOST" ORIGINAL
TITLE: "LEGEND OF TIMBUKTU"

Note: It is also reported in some places, but unsubstantiated, that the original title for "McQ" was to be "McQueen"

191

THE JOHN WAYNE SURVEY

In December 1985, the John Wayne journal *The Big Trail* published the results of a readers poll in which fans were questioned about their preferences regarding Duke's films. The results are as follows.

John Wayne's Three Finest Westerns
#1. The SEARCHERS (50%) #2. Red River (39%) #3. True Grit (27%)
Runners-Up: The Shootist (22%); Rio Bravo, She Wore A Yellow Ribbon and Stagecoach (19% each) Hondo (11%), The Man Who Shot Liberty Valance (10%)

John Wayne's Three Finest Non-Westerns
#1. The Quiet Man (59%) #2. Sands Of Iwo Jima (42%) #3. The High And The Mighty (20%)
Runners-Up: In Harm's Way (19%); The Green Berets (17%); Donovan's Reef (16%); Wings Of Eagles (14%); Flying Tigers (10%); They Were Expendable (9%)

ONE OF THE FAVORITE LEADING LADIES...KATE HEPBURN IN "ROOSTER COGBURN"

Favorite Pre-"Stagecoach" Film
#1. The Big Trail (12%)
Runners-Up: The Star Packer (8%); Pals Of The Saddle (8%)

The Film Would You Most Recommend to a Friend Who Had Never Heard of John Wayne
#1. The Searchers (19%)
Runners-Up: True Grit (14%); The Quiet Man (12%)

The Film Most Recommended to Change the Opinion of a Friend Who Thinks John Wayne Always Played the Same Role
#1. The Quiet Man (24%)
Runners-Up: Trouble Along The Way (8%); The Long Voyage Home (7%)

Which Is the Worst John Wayne Movie?
#1. The Conqueror (24%)
Runners Up: The Barbarian And The Geisha (14%); "There's No Such Thing!" (10%)

Besides "True Grit," the Film for which Duke Should Have Won The Oscar
#1. The Searchers (27%)
Runners Up: The Shootist (26%); Red River (14%)

The Three Favorite Female Co-Stars in a Wayne Film
#1. Maureen O'Hara (88%) #2. Katharine Hepburn (22%); #3. Patricia Neal (21%)

The Three Favorite Male Co-Stars of a Wayne Film
#1. James Stewart (33%); #2. Ward Bond (28%); #3. Robert Mitchum (26%)
Runners-Up: Dean Martin (23%); Lee Marvin (19%)

Favorite Supporting Players in a Wayne Film
#1. Ward Bond (39%); #2. Walter Brennan (31%); George Hayes (33%)
Runners-Up: Ben Johnson (20%); Hank Worden (18%)

The Film That Shows Duke At His Most Heroic
#1. The Alamo (26%)
Runners-Up: Sands Of Iwo Jima (21%); The Fighting Seabees (7%)

The Film That Shows Duke At His Most Humorous
#1. McLintock! (31%)
Runners-Up: North To Alaska (20%); True Grit (17%)

The Favorite Scene from a Wayne Movie
#1. True Grit: Rooster Charges the Outlaws (19%)
Runners-Up: McLintock!: The Mud Fight. (13%) The Quiet Man: The Donnybrook (11%) The Searchers: Ethan Sweeps Debbie Into His Arms (11%).

DUKE ON TELEVISION

John Wayne was consistently wooed by television to partake in the medium in any capacity. Over the years, Wayne rejected most offers. He didn't mind watching TV but had no real interest in participating in any shows. As TV grew as a medium, practicality set in and Duke, reluctantly at first, began to make periodic appearances, sometimes to promote a film. In his later years, Wayne learned to love television, and began appearing as a guest on many shows. He often did it for only hundreds of dollars in pay, so money was definitely not a factor.

Duke was originally approached to take the role of Matt Dillon when CBS began to formulate plans in 1953 to convert the radio hit "Gunsmoke" to TV. The Dillon role was played on radio by portly but sonorous actor William Conrad, and his presence in the (all-too-much) flesh would never have convinced audiences that he was an agile lawman. (Ironically, unlikely leading man Conrad had a smash hit in the 1970s as an action star with the series "Cannon" and in

the 1980s in "Jake and the Fatman".) Duke was not interested in acting on TV, but suggested young friend and protegé James Arness to the producers. Arness, who had appeared with Duke in a few films, was dubious, claiming TV would ruin his career. Wayne called him a "dumb S.O.B." for failing to realize that stalwart Arness' large build precluded anyone other than Wayne from working with him. He convinced Arness to take the role, and the rest was history. In 1989, Arness still thought so highly of Wayne that the normally reclusive actor hosted a special titled "John Wayne: Standing Tall." (By the way, for trivia buffs, Duke did consent to film the introduction for the first episode of "Gunsmoke.")

Wayne was a frequent guest on "Rowan and Martin's Laugh-In" (appearing once as the Easter Bunny), as well as on "I Love Lucy" and "The Dean Martin Show" and a number of Bob Hope specials. He seemed to enjoy sitcoms and variety shows, and made some classic appearances on talk-fests with Johnny Carson, Merv Griffin and

Joey Bishop. He made only a couple dramatic appearances on TV, usually for John Ford. He remained a mainstay on awards programs, whether presenting tributes to other artists or accepting them himself. His reversal toward the medium was interesting enough to capture the cover of *TV Guide* with an article titled "How John Wayne Came to Love TV."

Audiences loved Wayne, and even a brief appearance by him would send ratings sky-rocketing. For a complete listing of all of Duke's TV appearances, I suggest you check *The Official John Wayne Reference Book* (Citadel), which offers the most comprehensive record of all such work by the Duke to be found anywhere.

WITH "PAPPY": ON THE SET OF
"THE AMERICAN WEST OF JOHN FORD"

RATINGS OF JOHN WAYNE FILMS ON TV

Traditionally, telecasts of John Wayne films promised guaranteed high ratings for the networks over the years. Although cable TV and video cassette rentals have greatly diminished the value of telecasting theatrical films in recent years, syndicated stations virtually thrive on showing popular feature films, and in this all-important area, Wayne's are still very much a valuable commodity. This is proven by the continuing investment the syndicated stations make in advertising his films (examples of such advertisements appear elsewhere in this section).

TV broadcasts of Wayne's movies are valuable in that they continue to introduce his work to new generations. If there has been a drawback at all, it can be in the way in which stations have often butchered these telecasts. Wayne films are not unique in having this problem, of course, but one cringes when one sees classic footage cut from his better films merely to make way for more commercials, or to compromise "pro-censorship" bluenoses.

When ABC first telecast *True Grit* in 1972, the film predictably drew a huge audience. Unfor-

PUBLICITY PHOTO FOR ABC'S "OSCAR PRESENTS THE WAR MOVIES OF JOHN WAYNE"

198

tunately, technical mishaps resulted in much of the movie being broadcast in an almost unwatchable state. Additionally, Wayne purists were horrified when his famous "Fill your hand, you son-of-a-bitch!" line was shortened so that this expletive would not offend the audience. (Several weeks later, however, the same network left most of the expletives in its broadcast of *Patton*.)

Even Wayne himself expressed annoyance at ABC for its telecast of *The Cowboys*. Specifically, he protested that a sequence in which he intentionally chastises a stuttering young man as part of a plan to cure his speech impediment was edited so that the entire meaning of the scene was lost, making his character appear to be cruel. Other sequences massacred by censors included most of Wayne's classic fistfight with Bruce Dern, as well as the final sequence in the film in which Dern is dragged to death by his horse. In the network version, it is never clear exactly what Dern's fate is.

Nevertheless, Wayne films have been extremely popular with home viewers, and when *The Cowboys* was rerun almost intact by CBS as a "filler" item on its weeknight primetime schedule in 1986, newspapers reacted with amazement that despite its many previous showings, the movie was one of the top-rated programs of the week.

What follows is a *Variety* compilation of movies which can be called ratings blockbusters. The list includes all such films for telecasts since September 1961. Some notes to keep in mind: a ratings point shows the number of viewers watching at any given time. Since these telecasts cover several years, the exact number of viewers is not listed here as the number of households represented by each point has changed drastically over the years. Currently, each ratings point indicated approximately 900,000 viewers. This figure is not appropriate for earlier broadcasts, however, as far less sets were in use at the time. Also, the "share" statistic indicates the percentage of all sets in use which are tuned into a specific telecast.

Filmed in black and white, the show is nevertheless fascinating at this late date. A few copies are floating around on the black market video

circuit, and a viewing of the special is considered quite a coup by Wayne buffs. Duke is seen strolling around the set of *The Alamo* in Brackettville, Texas, interviewing co-stars and local officials. The show is fine when it sticks with promoting *The Alamo* movie. Where it goes astray is in its pretentious attempts to make a patriotic statement. There's a lot of soggy soliloquies about the meaning of freedom, but one can't help but get the feeling that despite the well known patriotism of those involved, the raison d'être of the show was simply to make sure a lot of people paid their money at the box-office to recoup the costs of the epic into which Duke had sunk his fortune.

A great deal of time is spent with people like Frankie Avalon singing a couple of love songs, or engaging in some "spontaneous" buffoonery. There are some unintentionally hilarious sequences in which local officials and other "nobodies" are interviewed for no apparent reason. Obviously, Duke had been coerced into letting

these people appear on-camera in some rather thin guises. The joke, however, was on the hammy locals, for onscreen they come across absolutely petrified and make fools of themselves. There is one genuinely funny moment in which Duke attempts to talk with four-year-old daughter Aissa about her cameo role in the film. He cannot get the girl to do so, and must abruptly bail out the child by simply carrying her off camera. It's one of the few moments that comes across as natural, and proved to the world that even Duke Wayne was subject to the frustrations of parenthood.

The special concluded with clips from *The Alamo*, which are not done justice by being shown in black and white. Interestingly, most major cast members agreed to participate in the show, with the exception of key player Richard Widmark. Widmark lends his voice to a brief narrative segment, and is seen in clips, but his conspicuous absence was probably the result of his battles on the set with Duke.

THESE MONTAGES ILLUSTRATE THE VARIOUS WAYS NETWORKS HAVE PUBLICIZED SHOWINGS OF DUKE'S FILMS

ORIGINAL ABC TELOP SLIDE FOR THE
BROADCAST OF "THE ALAMO"

The following are the highest rated Wayne films broadcast by the three major networks. They are listed in order of rank among only the Wayne films, and their overall rank from the *Variety* chart appears in parenthesis. This is followed by the network, day and date of the showing, rating and share.

#1 (#9)	TRUE GRIT	ABC	SUNDAY	11/12/72	38.9	63%
#2 (#62)	McLINTOCK!	CBS	FRIDAY	11/3/67	31.2	54%
#3 (#86)	THE WAR WAGON	NBC	SATURDAY	10/31/70	30.0	53%
#4 (#111)	THE GREEN BERETS	NBC	SATURDAY	11/18/72	28.9	45%
#5 (#126)	IN HARM'S WAY (Pt.2)	ABC	MONDAY	1/25/71	28.6	42%
#6 (#152)	THE COWBOYS	ABC	TUESDAY	11/13/73	27.8	42%
#7 (#157)	THE SONS OF KATIE ELDER	ABC	SUNDAY	11/17/68	27.7	46%
#8 (#189)	McLINTOCK! (R)	NBC	SATURDAY	2/27/71	27.1	44%
#9 (#195)	IN HARM'S WAY (Pt.1)	ABC	SUNDAY	1/24/71	27.1	41%
#10 (#267)	HOW THE WEST WAS WON	ABC	SUNDAY	10/24/71	26.0	46%
#11 (#278)	CHISUM	NBC	SATURDAY	10/27/73	25.9	43%
#12 (#291)	THE MAN WHO SHOT LIBERTY VALANCE	CBS	FRIDAY	9/22/67	25.7	46%
#13 (#330)	THE SONS OF KATIE ELDER (R)	ABC	SUNDAY	3/1/70	25.4	42%
#14 (#420)	THE MAN WHO SHOT LIBERTY VALANCE (R)	CBS	THURSDAY	2/3/68	24.6	40%
#15 (#457)	HATARI (Pt.2) (R)	CBS	FRIDAY	2/13/70	24.3	41%
#16 (#493)	EL DORADO	ABC	SUNDAY	9/19/71	24.1	40%
#17 (#499)	TRUE GRIT (R)	ABC	SUNDAY	1/13/74	24.1	36%
#18 (#514)	HATARI (Pt.1) (R)	CBS	THURSDAY	2/12/70	24.0	38%

NOTE: (R) DENOTES RERUN. ALSO, OVER THE YEARS, SOME OF WAYNE'S FILMS HAD BEEN TELECAST IN TWO PARTS TO INSURE HIGH RATINGS ON TWO SEPARATE EVENINGS. THUS, SOME OF THE ABOVE DENOTES WHICH PARTS GAINED SPECIFIC RATINGS.

LEARN TO DRAW FROM THE MASTERS.

CLINT EASTWOOD

JOHN WAYNE

A FISTFUL OF DOLLARS
MONDAY 8PM

FOR A FEW DOLLARS MORE
TUESDAY 8PM

TRUE GRIT
WEDNESDAY 8PM

TRIBUTE TO A BAD MAN
THURSDAY 8PM

FOX WNYW 5

WAYNE AND CLINT ARE ALWAYS RATINGS-GETTERS

THE JOHN WAYNE TV SPECIALS

Despite his initial disdain for the medium of television, Wayne knew that one TV appearance would reach more people than the total audience for any ten of his films. Therefore, he sought to exploit TV if he felt the subject matter was important enough. Over the years, Wayne was the creative force behind two television specials. The first was based on his enthusiasm for his film version of *The Alamo*. As noted previously, Duke had "bet the ranch" —literally— on the box-office success of this film, and did everything within his power to promote it.

Wayne came up with what was then a unique concept. That is, to tie the promotion of a film into a television entertainment special. The re-sult of this idea was "The Spirit of the Alamo," a one-hour program broadcast by ABC on November 14, 1960. Duke served as the host and narra-tor for the show, which turned out to be a rather awkward and unstructured attempt to blend history, singing, dancing and comedy with film clips from *The Alamo*. In essence, the program, which was sponsored by Pontiac, was a long and expensive version of a publicity featurette—a short like those which are thrown on to promote films if the ballgame ends early.

Ten years later, Wayne would appear as the host of another TV special for which he was the creative force. Titled "Swing Out, Sweet Land," the show was the most expensive variety special

TV GUIDE PROMOTION FOR "THE SPIRIT OF THE ALAMO," 1960

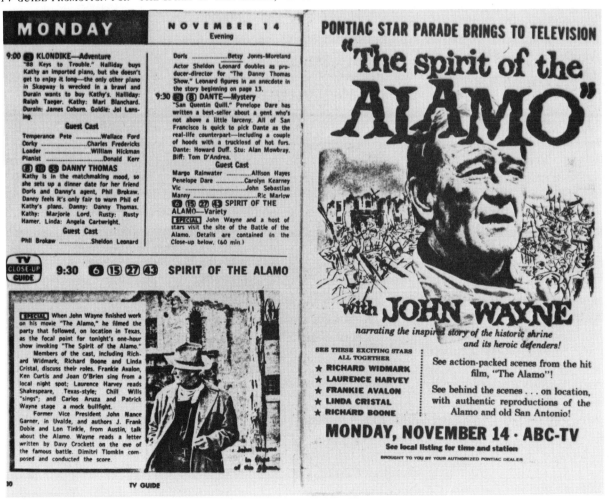

203

*TV GUIDE GAVE ITS
COVER TO DUKE'S 1970 SPECIAL, "SWING OUT, SWEET LAND"*

televised up to that time. Sponsored by Bud-
weiser, the show cast Wayne in sort of an *Our
Town* scenario, in which he would freely wander
into different settings at different times. The
nature of the program was to show the develop-
ment of America in its first century, with a host
of superstars playing cameo roles as famous
Americans. Among those participating were Bob
Hope, Jack Benny, Bing Crosby, Johnny Cash,
Dean Martin, Lucille Ball, Ed McMahon, Ann-
Margret, Red Skelton, Lorne Greene and many
others. The special featured a gigantic state-of-
the-art set which depicted a map of the U.S.
upon which the actors stood. The total cost of
the production topped $2-million, with Duke's
salary the most ever offered to a performer to
date for hosting a TV show. All other participants worked for "scale." The show was a combination of variety and comedy acts performed
before a live audience, intermingled with historical re-enactments shot on location throughout
southern California. Producer Paul Keyes, of
"Rowan and Martin's Laugh-In," reported that
scheduling all the actors' sequences was a mind-
boggling task. In some cases, previous committ-
ments limited the actors to ensuring that their
scenes be done right the first time, as there was
no room in their schedules for another take.

There was reluctance on the part of some
participants to join the show. These individuals,
like Tommy Smothers, feared that the program
would be a glorification of Wayne's conservative
viewpoints at the expense of the liberals. This
did not prove to be the case, as the program
ended up presenting all sides, with the central
agreement being that America is stronger because of people's inherent right to dissent. From
an entertainment point of view, the show is less
successful. Variety programs were waning by
1970, and the flashy production numbers were
no more impressive than those which audiences
long since had tired of on "The Ed Sullivan
Show." The comedy was also corny and predictable, with only a few acts mustering an occasional laugh. The patriotic dramatic sequences
such as the one featuring Bing Crosby as Mark
Twain and Roscoe Lee Brown as Frederick Doug-
lass were embarrassingly overstated.

Yet, despite the special's faults, Wayne could
take great satisfaction that the show continues to
rank among TV's highest-rated entertainment
events of all time. Although the rights reverted to
Wayne after the special's second telecast, it has
not been seen in most areas of the country again.
Hopefully, the Wayne family will authorize its
release on video so that an important event in
Duke's career can be enjoyed by his fans once
more.

JOHN WAYNE AND THE OSCARS

"Nobody seems to like my acting but the public," John Wayne once said. He was referring to critical indifference for most of his films, along with his basically being ignored by the Academy of Motion Picture Arts and Sciences at Oscar time. Wayne had been nominated twice in his career. The first time was in 1950 for Best Actor for *Sands of Iwo Jima*. The second two decades later for *True Grit*. It was no coincidence that the 1970 Oscar telecast was the highest rated to date. This was simply due to the fact that the fans were tuning in by the millions to root for Wayne. Unlike many actors today who find it fashionable to use the Oscar ceremony as a podium for political causes, or to shun the event altogether, Duke was not too proud to tell the world how much this long-delayed honor meant to him.

The night of the ceremony, Duke was quite nervous and feeling like a defeatist, according to Pilar Wayne in her book *Duke: My Life With John Wayne*. The competition was tough: Dustin Hoffman and Jon Voight, both superb in *Mid-night Cowboy*, Richard Burton for *Anne of the Thousand Days* and Peter O'Toole for *Goodbye, Mr. Chips*. Most observers felt Wayne was a favorite, but it was true that Burton and O'Toole had been unjustifiably overlooked so many times that perhaps the Academy might want to correct its failure to reward them. Yet, when Barbra Streisand strode to the podium, she announced as expected "...and the winner is......John Wayne!"

Duke received a thunderous ovation, kissed Streisand, brushed away a tear and gave the following speech:

WOW! If I'd have known that, I'd have put that [eye] patch on 35 years earlier! Ladies and gentlemen, I'm no stranger to this podium. I've come up here and picked up these beautiful golden men before, but always for friends. One night, I picked up two: one for Admiral John Ford and one for our beloved Gary Cooper. I was very clever and witty that night—the envy of even Bob Hope. But, tonight, I don't feel very

THE NOMINEES FOR BEST ACTOR OF 1969: DUKE, HOFFMAN, VOIGHT, O'TOOLE AND BURTON

206

clever; very witty. I feel very grateful, very humble, and I owe thanks to many, many people. I want to thank the members of the Academy. To all you people who are watching on television, thank you for taking such a warm interest in our glorious industry. Good night.

Duke returned the next day to location work on Howard Hawks' *Rio Lobo* and was greeted by the entire cast and crew—including his horse—wearing eyepatches.

Over the years, Wayne had appeared as a presenter at the Oscars on numerous occasions. Only one moment topped his triumphant win, however. This occurred at the 1979 ceremonies. Duke had recently come through major surgery for removal of his stomach due to cancer. Newspapers had virtually written him off as not being able to survive the operation, as his health had been not the best since he underwent open heart surgery some months earlier. Wayne knew he was not long for this world, but was determined to show that he was a fighter. The Academy announced that Duke would be asked to present the prestigious award for Best Picture. He accepted, and the world held its breath: would Wayne be able to go on live television in his present state without collapsing. Many fans of the Duke wanted to spare him any chance of embarrassment and hoped he would not attend. Duke would have none of it. After an agonizing day preparing for the show, the big moment came. He appeared to a standing ovation, and although he looked weak and thin, the total courage it took him to appear at all made most viewers just relish the fact that despite all the premature obituaries, John Wayne was still with us. His announcement of *The Deer Hunter* as Best Picture was probably the only time in Oscar history that the most important award of the evening had been overshadowed by the presenter himself.

207

"THE ALAMO" AND THE OSCARS

No producer ever tried harder to garner Oscar nominations for a film than John Wayne did for *The Alamo*. Duke spent a fortune on full page ads in the trade papers like *Daily Variety* and *The Hollywood Reporter*. Such practices are discouraged by the Academy as trying to buy votes. Nevertheless, the tradition is still going strong today. No one faulted Wayne for pushing his film, but he came under intense criticism for the tasteless way in which the promotion was handled. Academy voters were turned off to the movie before it was even released on the basis of a $150,000 three-page advertisement Wayne had taken out in *Life* Magazine. Titled, "There Were No Ghost Writers at the Alamo," the ad lam-

basted contemporary politicians for being robots and not writing their own campaign speeches. No one was surprised by Wayne espousing his political views, but the Duke was deluged with criticism for tying those views into the exploitation of *The Alamo*.

To Wayne's great relief, Academy members let bygones be bygones and rewarded the film with eight Oscar nominations, although Duke was conspicuously ignored in the directing category. This left *The Alamo* at a distinct disadvantage, as a film is seldom likely to take home the Best Picture Oscar if the person who brought it to the screen is not nominated. Wayne began an intensive campaign to ensure the movie could at least

THE ALAMO REPLICA BUILT IN BRACKETTVILLE, TEXAS

clean up in the lesser catagories. Batjac Productions spent a great deal of money in an all-too-obvious attempt to woo votes. He threw parties with "Alamo" themes, and sent the press publicity kits which weighed two pounds!

The "kiss of death" came when actor Chill Wills decided to put a little fire into his campaign to win the award for Best Supporting Actor, buying trade paper ads extolling his "cousins" in the Academy to vote for him. Wills "bottomed out" in the taste catagory when he ran a full page ad of the cast and crew standing in front of the Alamo set. The text read:

We of *The Alamo* are praying harder than the real Texans prayed for their lives in the real Alamo for Chill Wills to win the Oscar. Cousin Chill's acting was great! Signed Your Alamo Cousins

A previous ad had informed the Academy members that whether Wills won or lost, they, too, were all his cousins. This prompted Groucho Marx to respond through a now classic ad of his own: "Dear Mr. Wills, I'm delighted to be your cousin, but I'm voting for Sal Mineo." Groucho and Wills himself had helped make a mockery of *The Alamo*'s chances to win major awards.

Wayne put out a series of ads denouncing

Wills' campaign, saying he felt the actor's intentions were not as bad as his taste. However, it was too little too late. On Oscar night, *The Apartment* won for Best Picture, and *The Alamo* won only an award for Sound. Through the mishandling of the campaign, Wayne and company had unintentionally snatched defeat from the jaws of victory.

209

THERE WERE NO GHOST WRITERS AT THE ALAMO

by RUSSELL BIRDWELL

Very soon the two great political parties of the United States will nominate their candidates for President. One of these men, by a vote of the people, will be assigned the awesome duties of the White House: civilian leader of the nation, commander-in-chief of all its armed forces and keeper and director of its nuclear weaponry.

Who are these men who seek the most formidable job on earth? But more important: who is the one man who, after the political merry-go-round has stopped, will hold in his hand the gold ring of victory?

Do we know him? Have we ever known him? Will we ever know him?

Who has written his speeches? Who—or what board of ghostwriting strategists—has fashioned the phrases, molded the thoughts, designed the delivery, authored the image, staged the presentation, put the political show on the road to win the larger number of votes?

Who is the actor reading the script?

Or, in this moment when eternity could be closer than ever before, is there a statesman who for the sake of a vote is not all things to all men; a man who will put America back on the high road of security and accomplishment, without fear or favor or compromise; a man who wants to do the job that must be done and to hell with friend or foe who would have it otherwise; a man who knows that the American soft-ness must be hardened; a man who knows that when our house is in order no man will ever dare to trespass.

In shor' a Man!

There is a growing anxiety among the people to have straight answers. They don't want the handiwork of the opinion molder. They have had a bellyful of payola, influence peddling, quiz show rigging, the ghost-writing of political speeches—symptoms of a pallid public morality.

They are finished with the great deceptions.

They wait impatiently, as the free world becomes smaller and small-er, for a return to the honest, courageous, clear-cut standards of fron-tier days—the days of America's birth and greatness; the days when the noblest utterances of man came unrehearsed.

There were no ghost writers at the Alamo. Only men. Among them Colonel David Crockett, who was 50 years old; Colonel James Bowie, 40; Colonel William Barret Travis, 26.

These men left a legacy for all who prize freedom above tyranny, in-dividualism above conformity. They had gone to Texas to carve out new lives. Their ranks included men from 18 states and 6 foreign nations. Their foe was a Mexican dictator, General Santa Anna, at the head of an army of 7,000 well-equipped, well-trained troops, who in 1836 sought to crush the growing state of that faraway land now known as Texas. Santa Anna crossed the Rio Grande River, invaded San Antonio. His first target was the Alamo, a mission built in 1718 by Franciscan Friars and manned in the year 1836 by 185 volunteer citizen-soldiers. Presum-ably an easy target: 185 against 7,000.

The dictator did not realize that his enemy were not a common breed. He faced hard-living, hard-loving, hard-fighting believers in freedom.

Let us look now at the words of a few of them. Their own words.

Defeated for his fourth term in the United States Congress, Crockett announced: "You all can go to hell—I'm going to Texas."

And then he rode 1500 miles on horseback to Texas, not yet a part of the United States, and in his diary he wrote:

"I promised to give the Texans a helping hand in their high road to freedom. If there is anything in the world worth living for it is freedom. Early this morning the enemy came in sight, marching in regular or-der and displaying strength to the greatest advantage in order to strike us with terror. That was no go. They'll find they have to do with men who will never lay down their arms as long as they can stand on their legs."

In 1834, two years before Colonel David Crockett rode into the Alamo with his followers "to hit a lick against what's wrong and say a word for what's right," he toured the New England states as a United States Con-gressman and while visiting in Boston he wrote:

"We then went up to the old battleground on Bunker's hill, where they were erecting a monument to those who fell in that daybreak battle of our rising glory. I felt as if I wanted to call them up, and ask them to tell me how to help protect the liberty they brought for us with their blood; but as I could not do so, I resolved on that holy ground, as I had done elsewhere, to go for my country, always and everywhere.

After entering the Alamo Colonel Crockett wrote to his children in Tennessee: "I hope you will do the best you can and I will do the same. Do not be uneasy about me—I am with my friends . . . Your affection-ate father, Farewell. David Crockett."

As the Santa Anna hordes pounded against the mission that had be-come a fortress Colonel Crockett wrote in his diary: We are all in high spirits though rather short of provisions for men who have appetites that could digest anything—but oppression."

Land was cheap in Texas in those days—it was selling for 12 1/2 cents an acre. But the price of free-dom and liberty came high. Before the Alamo fell Crockett wrote: "We will go ahead and sell our lives at a high price."

Colonel James Bowie, in words remembered by Mrs. Susanna Dickinson (she and her 3-year-old daugh-ter with a little Negro boy were the only survivors of the glorious disaster). said: "I prefer to die in its ditches rather than give up an inch of Texas soil to a dictator."

When word of Jim Bowie's death reached his mother she said: "So Jim is dead. I bet they found no bul-lets in his back."

Colonel William Barret Travis, the young South Carolina lawyer entrusted with command of the Alamo by General Sam Houston, in a letter to Texas' Governor Henry Smith:

"We are ill-prepared for attack. yet we are determined to sustain it as long as there is a man left. Death is preferable to disgrace. Should Bexar (San Antonio) fall, your friend will be buried beneath its ruins. I shall not surrender or retreat."

The situation hopeless, Colonel Travis gave his men a way out just before the final onslaught: "Any of you who wish may leave with honor. Here on these ramparts you have bought a priceless ten days of time for General Houston. You are brave and noble soldiers. God bless you."

No man gave up his post. All gave their lives, after killing 1700 and holding the enemy for 13 days. The precious time bought enabled General Houston 46 days later at San Jacinto to win Texas' liberation.

There were no ghost writers at the Alamo. Only men.

A STATEMENT OF PRINCIPLE
JOHN WAYNE, BATJAC PRODUCTIONS
JAMES EDWARD GRANT, AUTHOR OF "THE ALAMO."

The gatefold advertisement on the following pages appeared in the July 4th issue of LIFE—one week be-fore the political conventions, four months before the premiere of "The Alamo."

Never before in the motion picture in-dustry had three consecutive pages of advertising said so few words about a film—and yet said so much about its uniqueness.

When he wanted to say something of the film's meaning, suggest something of the film's magnitude, Wayne came to just one magazine—confident that a Statement of Principle on its pages could capture a nation's attention... would recapture a nation's spirit.

That such confidence was justified is confirmed by the national and world-wide reaction to this advertisement.

DUKE'S CONTROVERSIAL AD IN LIFE MAGAZINE

ADVERTISING BLOOPERS AND ODDITIES

No one is perfect—not even John Wayne! In this section, we will examine some unusual advertising campaigns, most of which feature some form of error or "blooper." While some of the mistakes are subtle, many are quite blatant. Other posters are included simply because they have an unusual number of changes to the artwork (i.e. *The Alamo*).

ARTIST'S ORIGINAL SKETCH OF THE POSTER FOR "THE ALAMO"

IN THIS VERSION, DUKE HAS A NEW HEAD. ALSO BODIES OF DEAD MEXICANS ARE MISSING

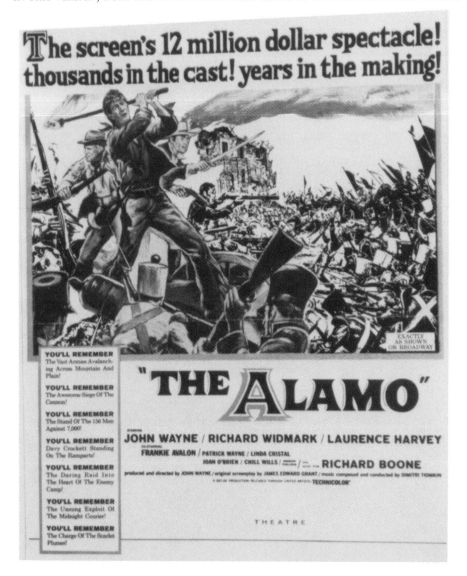

212

THE FINISHED PRODUCT...OR IS IT? SEE NEXT PHOTO
FOR THIS 1967 REISSUE, DUKE HAS
YET ANOTHER HEAD—THIS ONE TOO LARGE FOR HIS BODY

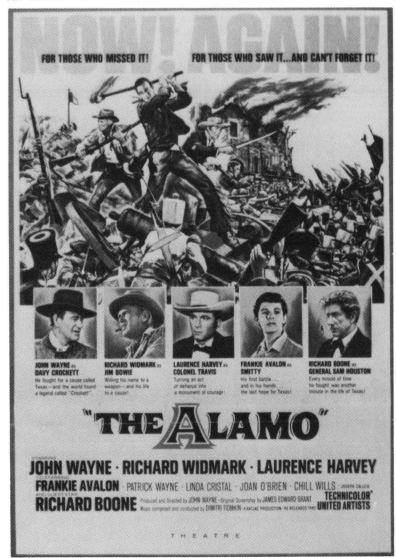

*THIS LOBBY CARD DEPICTS WAYNE CLEAN SHAVEN. YET, IN THE FILM
HE SPORTS A MUSTACHE AND GOATEE.*

ALTHOUGH JAMES STEWART RECEIVED TOP BILLING IN MOST ADVERTISING, THIS BILLBOARD PUTS DUKE'S NAME FIRST

IF FANS DON'T RECALL SEEING DUKE IN THIS OUTFIT IN "CAHILL," IT'S
BECAUSE THE PHOTO USED IS FROM "CHISUM"!

NOW YOU CAN SEE THE INTERNATIONALLY ACCLAIMED HIT JUST AS IT WAS SHOWN IN THE MAJOR CAPITALS OF THE WORLD!

DARRYL F. ZANUCK'S

THE LONGEST DAY

WITH 42 INTERNATIONAL STARS!

NEVER SO TIMELY! NEVER SO GRE

SEE IT DURING THE 25TH ANNIVERSARY YEAR OF D-DAY

"Stupendous! There are no more worlds to conquer."
— New York Times

DARRYL F. ZANUCK'S

THE LONGEST DAY

Based on the Book by CORNELIUS RYAN
Released by 20th Century-Fox

WITH 42 INTERNATIONAL STARS!

S I G   G SUGGESTED FOR GENERAL AUDIENCES

"THE ALAMO"   JOHN WAYNE / RICHARD WIDMARK / LAURENCE HARVEY

ROBERT WAGNER, FABIAN, PAUL ANKA AND TOMMY SANDS WERE FEATURED IN THIS AD FOR THE ORIGINAL 1962 RELEASE...

...BUT FOR THE 1969 REISSUE, THE HEADS OF BIGGER BOX-OFFICE STARS RICHARD BURTON, ROBERT MITCHUM, WAYNE AND HENRY FONDA WERE SUPERIMPOSED OVER THE OTHER ACTORS' BODIES

THIS LOBBY CARD DEPICTS A SCENE ACTUALLY SHOWN ONLY IN THE TV SPECIAL "THE SPIRIT OF THE ALAMO"

JOHN WAYNE—FAMILY MAN

If there was one thing John Wayne valued as much as love of country, it was love of family. Duke had gained a reputation as the consummate family man, despite the fact that he endured two stormy divorces and a separation from his last wife. Duke's well-known penchant for Latin women was responsible for his "love at first sight" attitude toward Josephine Saenz, whom he first met while attending college. Duke had been dating Josie's sister, but once introduced to his future wife, he knew immediately that this gorgeous woman would be a part of his life.

Josie was the daughter of a prominent doctor, and was accustomed to a lifestyle far beyond Wayne's means. They courted for seven years before marrying. Trouble eventually began, however, due to Josie's strict religious beliefs which contrasted with Duke's casual attitude about religion and church-going. She was Catholic, he was a semi-practicing Protestant, and neither person could compromise to the satisfaction of the other. Josie also sported a possessive

nature that irritated Duke. Furthermore, she committed the unpardonable sin of not accepting Wayne's circle of friends. Her abhorrence of Duke's drinking bouts with John Ford and his stock company was the final straw.

From Duke's marriage to Josie came four children: Michael in 1934, Antonia Maria ("Toni") in 1936, Patrick in 1938 and Melinda in 1940. Shortly after Melinda's birth, the couple separated, and Wayne sought a divorce. Due to her religious beliefs, Josie refused for several years before relenting. Although their relationship was tempestuous immediately following the divorce, they learned to treat each other amicably. Patrick Wayne recalled later that neither of his parents ever tried to use the children as pawns in the divorce, and the kids visited both their mother and father frequently.

Duke's marriage to Josie seemed like wedded bliss compared to what romance had in store for him: a sultry vixen named Esperanza Diaz Ceballos Morrison. "Chata," as she was known to

WITH FIRST WIFE JOSIE

*WAYNE AND SECOND WIFE CHATA
AT A PARTY FOR TENNESSEE WILLIAMS IN 1950*

her intimates, was an aspiring actress when Duke first met her on a trip to Mexico City in 1941 (several years before the breakup of his first marriage). In order to force Josie into granting him a quick divorce, he had Chata flown in to Hollywood, where the couple set up house for two years. Eventually they married, only weeks after Duke's divorce from Josie.

By all accounts, Wayne's friends warned him not to marry Chata. Their pleas fell on deaf ears and Duke and his latest lady tied the knot in January 1946. Although Chata and Duke seemingly were compatible in terms of enjoying the good times on the Hollywood party circuit, the couple battled frequently and fiercely. Chata resented Duke's long absences for location work and the fact that her domineering mother had moved in with the Waynes scarcely helped matters. Both women drank heavily and took out their frustrations on Duke. Wayne, at the time a good drinker himself, displayed his temper just as frequently. Newspaper headlines were made when Chata accused Duke of having an affair with actress Gail Russell, his co-star in *Angel and the Badman* and *Wake of the Red Witch*. Wayne denied the charge, although his story sounded a bit shaky. Eventually, all of this culminated in one of Hollywood's more publicized divorce trials. Accusations were flung on both sides, some bordering on the absurd. Wayne tried to link Chata with hotel heir Nick Hilton, and the mess got even messier. Chata failed in her attempt to sue Wayne for a preposterous share of his assets. The modest sum the court allocated seemed hardly worth her efforts. She returned to Mexico to live with her mother, who later died of alcoholism. Tragically, Chata died a short time later, presumably of a heart attack at age 32. Following her death, Wayne was a gentleman and prefered to recall the many good times the couple shared early in their marriage.

While still married to Chata, Wayne fell in love yet again. This happened when he visited the set of a movie being filmed in Peru. Duke fell head-over-heels for the film's leading lady, Pilar Palette. He was intrigued by the fact that the actress was basically unfamiliar with his work. This did not stop her from sensing the chemistry

DUKE WITH AISSA AT HOME, 1964   *WAYNE AND SON JOHN ETHAN, 1964*

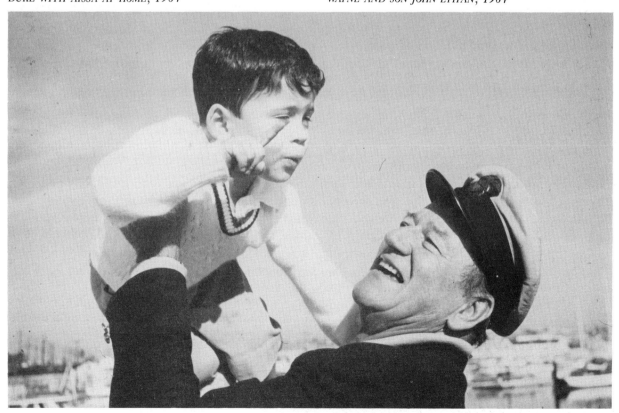

WAYNE WITH AISSA, MELISSA, PILAR AND ETHAN, 1970

they had created together. Pilar eventually followed Duke's request that she remain in Hollywood, where she had come to dub her film. Ironically, this left Wayne with the necessity of hiding his new relationship from his second wife, just as he had done the first time around with Josie.

The couple kept a low profile until Wayne was granted his second divorce. He then married Pilar in 1954. She never acted again onscreen, and was quite content to raise the children she had with Duke: Aissa in 1956, John Ethan in 1962 and Marissa in 1966. Pilar was a quiet and dignified woman who seemed to embody the best qualities of Wayne's two former wives, without the temperamental Latin streak they also showed. It appeared Duke had at last found

happiness. Pilar encouraged him throughout the most productive years of his career. She was not a wild party-goer, but good naturedly tolerated Wayne's drinking buddies.

It was Pilar who helped Wayne in his almost miraculous recovery from cancer in 1965, and she did her best to see to it that the family stayed as close as possible throughout the years. The relationship with Duke's oldest three children was not close at first, and Michael never accepted her as Duke's wife, according to Pilar's memoirs. Michael shared his natural mother's strong religious convictions, and was reluctant to acknowledge the breakup of the marriage between Josie and Duke. Nevertheless, for all intents and purposes, the family enjoyed many wonderful times.

Wayne was a doting father, particularly with the children he had late in life. Until the day he died, he delighted in sharing his time with them and doing his best to ensure they wanted for nothing. The loyalty was returned, and unlike many of the children of famous actors, Wayne's kids never made headlines with embarrassing behavior. Over the years, they have maintained a low profile and a good deal of dignity.

To the astonishment of many in Hollywood, Duke and Pilar separated in 1973. It's difficult to say just why, but a good account can be read in Pilar's book, *Duke: My Life With John Wayne*. There never was a single instance which precipitated their split, but rather they just "grew apart." The two remained close friends throughout Wayne's remaining years, and talked about reuniting, despite Duke's well-publicized latter-day romance with his secretary Pat Stacy.

Pilar does not hear very often from Wayne's older children, and the strain between her and Michael remains. She does stay extremely close to the children she bore with Duke, and they are frequent visitors to her home. Over the last few years, I have become acquainted with Pilar and have had the pleasure of talking with her in her home about her life with Duke. The thing that strikes me the most is her strong love for the man she still refers to as "my husband." It is no wonder that she still proudly proclaims herself to be Mrs. John Wayne.

JOHN WAYNE COLLECTIBLES

Throughout his career, and especially since his death, there have been thousands of items produced bearing Wayne's likeness. Some have been well-crafted artifacts which did justice to the man, while others were so tacky they motivated his son Michael to try stopping distribution of those products which he felt demeaned Duke's image.

In this section, we will illustrate a few representative samples of unusual memorabilia. You be the judge as to whether they represent the good, the bad or the ugly.

PAPERBACK TIE-INS FOR WAYNE FILMS

UPON DUKE'S DEATH, MAGAZINE
TRIBUTES WERE PLENTIFUL

222

JOHN WAYNE COMMEMORATIVE PISTOL

CASTLE FILMS 8mm COLLECTOR'S
PRINT OF "HELLFIGHTERS." THIS
WAS MARKETED IN BLACK AND WHITE

DUKE WAYNE BELT BUCKLE

...WHILE THE CONDENSED VERSION
APPEARED IN COLOR

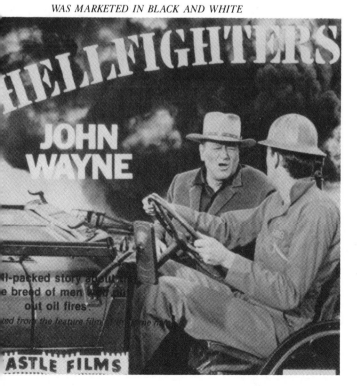

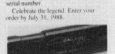

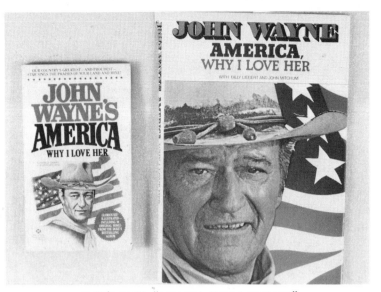

DUKE'S BOOK: "AMERICA: WHY I LOVE HER"

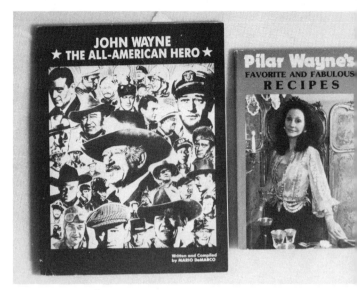

MARIO DeMARCO'S SELF-PUBLISHED
TRIBUTE   RIGHT: PILAR WAYNE'S
COOKBOOK INCLUDES PHOTOS OF DUKE

JOHN WAYNE DOLLS

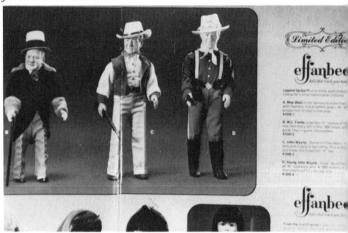

THE DUKE ON VIDEO: THE "LOST" INTERVIEWS

Two videos have been released in recent years which have proven to be of interest to John Wayne fans. (In the interest of full disclosure, the author served as a coproducer on both projects.) *The Duke and the General* offers a treasure trove of rare interview footage with Wayne and James Stewart. This fascinating documentary was originally shot in 1971 and aired only once, on a midwestern TV station. The show covered Duke on location with director Mark Rydell on the set of *The Cowboys*, as well as Jimmy Stewart filming his last starring role in Andrew V. McGlaglen's *Fool's Parade*. Entertainment correspondent Bill Carlson adeptly handled the interviews with both legendary actors, and the show was intercut with comments from the directors and fellow cast and crew members. Both Wayne and Stewart spoke unapologetically about their views on patriotism, the current political climate, and their many years in show business. Best of all, the show gives us a precious glimpse of a sequence from *The Cowboys* which did not make the final cut: Duke's Wil Andersen meeting with a group of Indians.

After the show was telecast, it was quickly forgotten and presumed lost over the years. However, in 1996, Jack Jones, the cameraman on the shoot, found a remaining print of the film along with some never-before-seen outtakes. It has since been released on video in a special collector's edition which includes seldom seen TV spots, trailers, and promotional shorts featuring both Duke and Jimmy Stewart.

Another video of Wayne rarities is *John Wayne: Behind the Scenes With the Duke*, which features rare, original production shorts about the making of some of Wayne's most popular films. These were originally shot in 16mm and were commonly referred to as "featurettes." They would air at odd times on TV networks when a time filler was needed if another show—usually a live event—ended a bit early. Considered largely disposable after the film's theatrical release had ended, these featurettes are today regarded as priceless bits of movie history. This video contains such gems as original behind-the-scenes shorts on the making of *Chisum, In Harm's Way, The Cowboys, Brannigan, McQ, The War Wagon, The Train Robbers, El Dorado,* and others. There is also a very rarely seen production short about *McLintock!* hosted by Maureen O'Hara.

Both of these titles are available for $24 each (postage included) through:

Spy Guise Video
POB 7013
Jersey City, NJ 07307
Phone/fax: 201-653-7395

They can also be ordered via the company's Web site at www.spyguise.com, which features a number of rare John Wayne poster reproductions.

THE JOHN WAYNE BIRTHPLACE

The house in which Duke was born on May 26, 1907, still stands in the picturesque town of Winterset, Iowa. The home is now preserved under the auspices of The Birthplace of John Wayne, a society dedicated to maintaining the modest four-room structure as it appeared when Duke first entered the world. Wayne spent his formative years in Winterset and always regarded his time there with great affection.

Countless numbers of Wayne fans have visited the site over the years, and enjoyed the many photographs of Duke throughout his career, along with some original props from his films. Even those who can't make the trek to Iowa can help support this worthy cause by joining the John Wayne Birthplace Society. As of this writing, there are two levels of membership:

Supporting Role members will receive a John Wayne Congressional Medal of Honor coin, an 8″ x 10″ print of John Wayne, a Certificate of Membership, and a John Wayne Birthplace Society membership card. Current contribution: $35–$99.

Starring Role members will receive a 12″ x 16″ color print of John Wayne, a John Wayne Congressional Medal of Honor coin, an 8″ x 10″ print of John Wayne, a Certificate of Membership, and a John Wayne Birthplace Society membership card. Current contribution: $100 and above.

For more information, call or write to the Birthplace at:

Birthplace of John Wayne
216 South Second Street
Winterset, Iowa 50273

(515) 462-1044

There is also a Web site at www.johnwaynebirthplace.org. The web page provides links to many other Wayne-related Internet sites.

"THE ALAMO VILLAGE" MOVIE SET BRACKETTVILLE, TEXAS

When John Wayne wanted to accurately recreate the original Alamo for his epic 1960 film, he obviously could not consider filming anywhere near San Antonio. The city was a mere dot on the map at the time of the real battle, but had since evolved into a booming metropolis completely impractical for filming a historical movie of this magnitude. Indeed, the real Alamo is embarrassingly surrounded by commercial establishments and office buildings. Wayne settled on the remote town of Brackettville, Texas, 120 miles west of San Antonio, near the Mexican border. Here, the lavish and historically accurate recreation of the famed adobe mission was created in the midst of an expansive and remote area.

The land Wayne leased for the film was the property of local businessman and entrepreneur J. T. "Happy" Shahan. The Brackettville ranch on which the movie was shot comprised 30,000 acres. Shahan had the foresight to see that the set could be a popular tourist attraction and a condition of his deal with Wayne was that he be allowed to operate it as

such after filming was completed. Shahan and his family called the location "Alamo Village," and word quickly spread that this was where Wayne fans and history buffs could visit to get a feel for what life was like at the real Alamo. Indeed, the main structure of Wayne's fortress makes a magnificent impression, rising in the sands amidst the splendor of the open plain. Shahan also preserved the town of San Antonio which was recreated in the film. Over the years, many other films and TV series have utilized the Alamo Village location for principal photography. Countless thousands of film lovers and Wayne aficionados have made a pilgrimage to this wonderful, understated place which retains an old-world atmosphere.

The village consists of a number of real buildings, not the typical "storefront sets" found in many films. The Shahan family converted many of these into practical tourist attractions such as blacksmith shops and jails. Additionally, the small cantina where much of *The Alamo* was filmed is now a charming restaurant where you can indulge in a light meal, and perhaps be serenaded with some genuine cowboy songs. There are also several gift shops featuring a plethora of Alamo and Wayne-related collectibles, as well as a small museum featuring a wealth of original props and production photos from the film. For any true Wayne fan, this is like a visit to Mecca.

Alamo Village also offers a number of special events throughout the year including trail rides, family days, and cowboy competitions. Don't be surprised if you're "held up" by a gunslinger or two while visiting the set—or perhaps coerced into a "gunfight" more one-sided than the one poor Jimmy Stewart had to contend with in his confrontation with Liberty Valance.

For more information about the Alamo Village, call (830) 563-2580 or write to:

Alamo Village
POB 528
Brackettville, TX 78832

You can also visit the village's Web site at www.alamovillage.com

FILMS AND TV SERIES SHOT AT "ALAMO VILLAGE"

1951 *Arrowhead*—Charlton Heston
1955 *The Last Command*—Ernest Borgnine
1958 *Five Bold Women*—Irish McCalla
1959 John Wayne's *The Alamo*
1960 *The Spirit of the Alamo* (TV)—NBC
1960 *Roy Rogers Show* (TV)
1960 John Ford's *Two Rode Together*—Jimmy Stewart
1966 *Top Hand* (TV)
1967 *Aye, That Pancho Villa* (TV)
1967 *Bandolero*—Dean Martin
1968 *Children's West* (Lon Chaney Jr.) (TV)
1973 *A Death in Tombstone*
1974 *The Texas Ballad* (KLRN-TV)
1978 *Adventures of Jody Shanan*
1978 *Centennial*, "The Longhorns" (TV)—Dennis Weaver
1979 *Code of Josey Wales*—Michael Parks
1980 *Barbarosa*—Gary Busey
1980 *Seguin* (American Playhouse)—Edward James Olmos
1981 "*Kathleen*" Kestrel Films
1982 *Tennessee to Texas—a Musical Affair* (TV)—Tanya Tucker
1984 *Up Hill All The Way*—Burt Reynolds

1986 *Houston—Legend of Texas* (TV)—Sam Elliott
1986 *The Alamo—Thirteen Days To Glory* (TV)— Alec Baldwin
1986 *No Safe Haven*—Wings Hauser
1987 *Alamo: Price of Freedom*—Caser Biggs
1988 *Lonesome Dove* (TV)—Robert Duvall
1989 *Gunsmoke—The Last Apache* (TV)—James Arness
1991 JCV Japanese Quiz Show (TV)
1991 American Movie Classics (TV)—Bob Dorian
1992 *Travis Smith* (direct to video)
1993 *Bad Girls*—Madeleine Stowe
1994 *Gambler V* (TV)—Kenny Rogers
1994 James A. Michener's *Texas* (TV)—John Schneider
1994 *Gold Old Boys* (TV)—Sam Shephard
1995 *Streets of Laredo* (TV)—James Garner
1995 A&E History Channel's *The Alamo* (TV)
1995 Discovery Channel's—*The Battles of the Alamo* (TV)
1995 PBS—Ken Burns's *The West* (TV)
1995 A&E Biography—*Davy Crockett: American Frontier Legend* (TV)
1995 The Learning Channel's—*Famous Battles—Alamo Segment* (TV)

1995 Discovery Channel's—*Buffalo Soldiers* (TV)
1996 *Once Upon a Time in China and America*—Sammo Hung
1999 *Alamo . . . The New Defenders* (direct to video)

1999 *The Bullfighter*—Domineca Scorcese
1999 The History Channel's—*Haunted San Antonio* (TV)
2000 *Jericho*—Mark Valley—Leon Coffee—Buck Taylor

MUSIC VIDEOS

1980 Willie Nelson—"Tougher Than Leather"
1995 Brooks & Dunn—"You're Gonna Miss Me When I'm Gone"
1996 Gary Hobbs—"Corazon de la Ardiente"

1996 La Tropa F—"The Sheriff"
1996 "Los Palominos"
1999 Shade of Red—"Revolution"

THE JOHN WAYNE FAN CLUB

With so many Wayne enthusiasts around the world, it seems hard to believe that it would take until 1984 for an organized fan club to appear. There had been various attempts by professional businesses to market fan clubs in Wayne's name as well as that of many other actors. However, the first—and only— "grassroots" attempt to honor Duke on a regular basis came as the brainchild of Tim Lilley of Akron, Ohio. Tim founded and publishes "The Big Trail," a bi-monthly "home grown" effort to analyze Wayne and his career.

The first issue of "The Big Trail" appeared in June of 1984. It has appeared consistently since then. Lilley, a Wayne afficionado since the age of 12, is committed to reviewing at least two films in each issue. Cast and credit information are provided, along with reprints of notable critical reviews and interesting anecdotes about the making of the films. Refreshingly, Tim is one of the few sources to treat the early "B" westerns on the same level as the more notable Wayne films. Although there is no rhyme or reason to the order

in which the films are covered, Tim promises not to cease publication of "The Big Trail" until every Wayne film appearance has been reviewed.

The publication is also useful in that it reflects upon many little-seen Wayne TV appearances such as his guest-starring stints on "Wagon Train" and in the drama "Rookie of the Year." Other regular columns spotlight the actors who have co-starred with Wayne, and a section titled "The Collectible Mr. Wayne" is devoted to various merchandising pertaining to the Duke. Each issue also features ample advertisements from Wayne collectors who are looking to buy or sell memorabilia, as well as correspond with fellow aficionados. A valuable listing of many prominent Wayne collectors has also been featured, along with a separate section detailing where many items can be purchased.

Among the more notable issues of "The Big Trail" is one in which the full story behind the filming of *The Alamo* appeared. There have been book reviews, trivia contests and a "bloopers" column. Input has been given from those who knew Wayne, or from relatives of his co-stars.

Tim's magazine is not fancy, but it does contain information that is highly informative. It is also primarily a non-profit publication that boasts a very modest subscription fee. More information can be obtained by writing to:

Tim Lilley, Editor
"The Big Trail"
540 Stanton Avenue
Akron, Ohio 44301

E-mail: bigtrailak@aol.com

DUKE IN "THE UNDEFEATED"

ENDORSED BY THE DUKE

Throughout his career, John Wayne was never shy about lending his name to the endorsement of products. As we shall see in the following pages, Duke pitched for products as diversified as mobile homes and tuna fish. His endorsements were not limited to print advertisements, and he frequently made TV commercials. Sponsors loved Duke's participation as a spokesperson, and attributed the inevitable increase in sales to his popularity. Duke also believed in publicizing charities, and did several spots for the television public service benefit of cancer research, orphanages and retarded people. There is a certain sadness about some of these endorsements, however, I refer to Wayne's enthusiastic TV and print ads on behalf of cigarettes. In viewing a videotape which included several of these commercials, one feels a great sense of irony that the product Wayne naïvely recommended in the 1950s would one day contribute to his death.

233

DUKE AND PILAR IN A 1957 RAZOR PROMOTION

DUKE SPEAKS OUT FOR THE GOOD TASTE OF COFFEE

DUKE IN A CAMELS AD

PICNIC PROMOTION FOR "THE HIGH AND THE MIGHTY"

CHARLIE THE TUNA
WASN'T THE ONLY
CELEBRITY TO HAWK STAR-
KIST

WORCESTERSHIRE SAUCE
PROMO

235

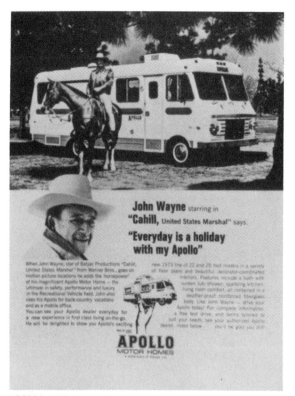

APOLLO MOTOR HOMES PROMO TIED
IN WITH THE RELEASE OF "CAHILL"

ANOTHER ENDORSEMENT OF APOLLO
FOR RELEASE OF "McQ"

THIS AD FOR STETSON PROMOTES
"TRUE GRIT," BUT THE PHOTOS ARE
ACTUALLY FROM "THE UNDEFEATED"

STAR ENDORSEMENTS FOR
"STAGECOACH"

JOHN WAYNE'S TOP BOX-OFFICE HITS

Throughout his career, John Wayne remained consistently in the top ranks of those actors whose films could be counted upon to return a profit. While no individual Wayne film ever approached being an absolute blockbuster by today's mega-hit standards, most of his movies managed to return a handsome profit to their respective studios. Collectively, Wayne's films had grossed over $700 million by 1975. If one adds residual rights for TV broadcasts, video cassettes, etc, the sum would be even more staggering today.

The section which follows is based upon *Variety*'s All-Time Film Rental Champs, a listing which appears and is updated annually in the trade newspaper. To qualify for inclusion, a film must have returned a minimum of $4-million in rentals to its studio. (The list consists of rental totals only.) The actual gross for each film is always much higher. Also, several factors should be remembered when reading the list. First, the rental amounts pertain only to the U.S.-Cana-

dian market. Worldwide rental amounts could equal or surpass these totals. Also, although $4-million in rentals is not overwhelming by today's standards, it was indeed an impressive sum throughout the Forties and Fifties.

Readers will probably find a surprise or two, not only in the ranking of some of the films, but also in the inclusion of some efforts in the list, while many presumably less popular Wayne titles do not appear (i.e., *The Horse Soldiers* appeared on the listing until some years ago when United Artists discovered it had not returned enough rental revenue to justify its inclusion). One should also keep in mind that a film is not successful simply by virtue of appearing among the rental champs. *The Alamo* figures prominently in Wayne's higher rental films, yet because of its huge budget, its sizable box-office dollars were not enough to make it profitable in its initial release. *Sands of Iwo Jima*, however, which was made on a far tighter budget, is considered a major success with rentals of $5-million.

"HOW THE WEST WAS WON" $20,932,883

"THE LONGEST DAY" $17,600,000   "TRUE GRIT" $14,250,000

"THE GREEN BERETS" $9,750,000   "THE ALAMO" $7,910,000
"ROOSTER COGBURN" $7,731,447   "THE COWBOYS" $7,500,000

"HATARI!" $7,000,000

"THE GREATEST STORY EVER TOLD" $6,930,0

"THE SEA CHASE" $6,000,000

"THE SONS OF KATIE ELDER" $6,000,000

"CHISUM" $6,000,000

"THE SHOOTIST" $5,987,000

"EL DORADO" $6,000,000

"RIO BRAVO" $5,750,000

"NORTH TO ALASKA" $5,000,000

"McLINTOCK!" $4,525,000

JOHN WAYNE'S BOX-OFFICE RANKING

	1949	*1950*	*1951*	*1952*	*1953*
1.	Bob Hope	*John Wayne*	*John Wayne*	Martin & Lewis	Gary Cooper
2.	Bing Crosby	Bob Hope	Martin & Lewis	Gary Cooper	Martin & Lewis
3.	Abbott & Costello	Bing Crosby	Betty Grable	*John Wayne*	*John Wayne*
4.	*John Wayne*	Betty Grable	Abbott & Costello	Bing Crosby	Alan Ladd
5.	Gary Cooper	James Stewart	Bing Crosby	Bob Hope	Bing Crosby
6.	Cary Grant	Abbott & Costello	Bob Hope	James Stewart	Marilyn Monroe
7.	Betty Grable	Clifton Webb	Randolph Scott	Doris Day	James Stewart
8.	Esther Williams	Esther Williams	Gary Cooper	Gregory Peck	Bob Hope
9.	Humphrey Bogart	Spencer Tracy	Doris Day	Susan Hayward	Susan Hayward
10.	Clark Gable	Randolph Scott	Spencer Tracy	Randolph Scott	Randolph Scott

	1954	*1955*	*1956*	*1957*	*1958*
1.	*John Wayne*	James Stewart	William Holden	Rock Hudson	Glenn Ford
2.	Martin & Lewis	Grace Kelly	*John Wayne*	*John Wayne*	Elizabeth Taylor
3.	Gary Cooper	*John Wayne*	James Stewart	Pat Boone	Jerry Lewis
4.	James Stewart	William Holden	Burt Lancaster	Elvis Presley	Marlon Brando
5.	Marilyn Monroe	Gary Cooper	Glenn Ford	Frank Sinatra	Rock Hudson
6.	Alan Ladd	Marlon Brando	Martin & Lewis	Gary Cooper	William Holden
7.	William Holden	Martin & Lewis	Gary Cooper	William Holden	Brigitte Bardot
8.	Bing Crosby	Humphrey Bogart	Marilyn Monroe	James Stewart	Yul Brynner
9.	Jane Wyman	June Allyson	Kim Novak	Jerry Lewis	James Stewart
10.	Marlon Brando	Clark Gable	Frank Sinatra	Yul Brynner	Frank Sinatra

	1959	*1960*	*1961*	*1962*	*1963*
1.	Rock Hudson	Doris Day	Elizabeth Taylor	Doris Day	Doris Day
2.	Cary Grant	Rock Hudson	Rock Hudson	Rock Hudson	*John Wayne*
3.	James Stewart	Cary Grant	Doris Day	Cary Grant	Rock Hudson
4.	Doris Day	Elizabeth Taylor	*John Wayne*	*John Wayne*	Jack Lemmon
5.	Debbie Reynolds	Debbie Reynolds	Cary Grant	Elvis Presley	Cary Grant
6.	Glenn Ford	Tony Curtis	Sandra Dee	Elizabeth Taylor	Elizabeth Taylor
7.	Frank Sinatra	Sandra Dee	Jerry Lewis	Jerry Lewis	Elvis Presley
8.	*John Wayne*	Frank Sinatra	William Holden	Frank Sinatra	Sandra Dee
9.	Jerry Lewis	Jack Lemmon	Tony Curtis	Sandra Dee	Paul Newman
10.	Susan Hayward	*John Wayne*	Elvis Presley	Burt Lancaster	Jerry Lewis

	1964	*1965*	*1966*	*1967*	*1968*
1.	Doris Day	Sean Connery	Julie Andrews	Julie Andrews	Sidney Poitier
2.	Jack Lemmon	*John Wayne*	Sean Connery	Lee Marvin	Paul Newman
3.	Rock Hudson	Doris Day	Elizabeth Taylor	Paul Newman	Julie Andrews
4.	*John Wayne*	Julie Andrews	Jack Lemmon	Dean Martin	*John Wayne*
5.	Cary Grant	Jack Lemmon	Richard Burton	Sean Connery	Clint Eastwood
6.	Elvis Presley	Elvis Presley	Cary Grant	Elizabeth Taylor	Dean Martin
7.	Shirley MacLaine	Cary Grant	*John Wayne*	Sidney Poitier	Steve McQueen
8.	Ann-Margret	James Stewart	Doris Day	*John Wayne*	Jack Lemmon
9.	Paul Newman	Elizabeth Taylor	Paul Newman	Richard Burton	Lee Marvin
10.	Richard Burton	Richard Burton	Elvis Presley	Steve McQueen	Elizabeth Taylor

	1969	*1970*	*1971*	*1972*	*1973*
1.	Paul Newman	Paul Newman	*John Wayne*	Clint Eastwood	Clint Eastwood
2.	*John Wayne*	Clint Eastwood	Clint Eastwood	George C. Scott	Ryan O'Neal
3.	Steve McQueen	Steve McQueen	Paul Newman	Gene Hackman	Steve McQueen
4.	Dustin Hoffman	*John Wayne*	Steve McQueen	*John Wayne*	Burt Reynolds
5.	Clint Eastwood	Elliott Gould	George C. Scott	Barbra Streisand	Robert Redford
6.	Sidney Poitier	Dustin Hoffman	Dustin Hoffman	Marlon Brando	Barbra Streisand
7.	Lee Marvin	Lee Marvin	Walter Matthau	Paul Newman	Paul Newman
8.	Jack Lemmon	Jack Lemmon	Ali MacGraw	Steve McQueen	Charles Bronson
9.	Katherine Hepburn	Barbra Streisand	Sean Connery	Dustin Hoffman	*John Wayne*
10.	Barbra Streisand	Walter Matthau	Lee Marvin	Goldie Hawn	Marlon Brando

JOHN WAYNE'S BOX-OFFICE RANKING

No other star has achieved the box-office success of John Wayne. It is true that by today's standards, individual actor's films may have collectively outgrossed Wayne's due to inflationary factors. However, for pure consistency in remaining among the Top Ten box-office attractions year after year, no one comes close. This is the real test of Duke's enduring popularity. On the accompanying listing (opposite page), compiled annually by the *Motion Picture Herald*, Wayne appears every year among the top box-office attractions, with the exception of 1958. This is an incredible run of 24 years. As of this date, only one star is close to giving Duke a run for his money: Clint Eastwood. Wayne could do worse than to eventually give up his crown to the man he himself called "my natural successor."

PUBLICITY GIMMICKS AND CAMPAIGNS

Movie studios never lacked imagination when it came to promoting films, although in recent years there has been little creativity in this area. In the past, however, lavish budgets were spent to publicize every major film. In addition to the standard 27″ x 41″ one-sheet posters which still grace theaters today, standard publicity tools included 11″ x 14″ lobby cards, pressbooks (which informed theater owners of all material available for a film), and paperback novel tie-ins. Additionally, stars of the film often toured the country promoting their films. The various ways in which Wayne films were promoted are shown in the following pages.

Most Waited-For Pictures

RADIO PROMO CONTEST FOR
CHICAGO PREMIERE OF "THE COWBOYS"

PRESSBOOK PROMO IDEAS FOR "THE SEARCHERS"

SET OF THEATER DOOR PANELS FOR "THE BARBARIAN AND THE GEISHA"

"ROOSTER COGBURN" RECEIVED EXTENSIVE TV COVERAGE

THEATER ACCESSORIES FOR "STAGECOACH." TODAY,
THESE ITEMS ARE WORTH THOUSANDS OF DOLLARS

THE ORIGINAL PRESSBOOK FOR
"STAGECOACH," NOW A PRICELESS COLLECTOR'S ITEM

A SERIES OF CHILDREN'S TRADING
CARDS WERE GIVEN AWAY TO PUBLICIZE "HATARI!"

THE GREEN BERETS JOINS THE SALUTE TO AMERICA PARADE

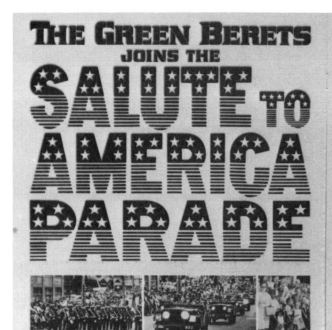

STARS OF FILM PARTICIPATE

The Atlanta July Jubilee is the South's—and one of America's— giant annual sports and entertainment explosions. It runs about ten days, from the end of June through the first part of July, and it is one long array of people and events of the kind that bring the crowds pouring out. The peak of the jubilee is the Salute to America Parade, sponsored by station WSB-TV. Since its inception in 1961, it has become the biggest Fourth of July celebration in the country. The city is turned into a flapping sea of red, white and blue. More than 350,000 spectators swarm into downtown Atlanta, another 250,000 watch the festivities on WSB's live and repeat telecasts. The floats, the marching bands, the military units, the clusters of famous personalities stretch for miles. It is American patriotism at its finest, its most spectacular. This year, 1968, 'THE GREEN BERETS' had a dominant role.

Accompanied by a large contingent of world-wide press, and through the cooperation of Lockheed Aircraft Corporation, seven stars from 'THE GREEN BERETS' took part. John Wayne on July 3 dedicated a memorial to Green Berets everywhere at Lockheed's installation just outside Atlanta, and led press and his fellow stars on an inspection tour of the new C5A airplane. On July 4, John Wayne and David Janssen headed the Salute to America Parade as Grand Marshal and Honorary Grand Marshal respectively. Jim Hutton, Irene Tsu, Raymond St, John, Pat Wayne and Bruce Cabot were also Honorary Grand Marshals. At the electrifying debut of 'BERETS' in the Fox Theatre, on the night of July 4, Wayne received the Salute to America Award from the mayor of Atlanta. All major events were telecast by Station WSB-TV. The opening-night events were fed to the NBC Network by the station. Millions of Americans saw Atlanta in action, and saw 'THE GREEN BERETS' in Atlanta in the picture's big kick-off.

WAYNE WAS AMONG STARS TO JOIN A PARADE TO PROMOTE "THE GREEN BERETS"

PUBLICITY GIMMICKS FOR "CAHILL: U.S. MARSHAL"

ACCESSORIES FOR "THE ALAMO"

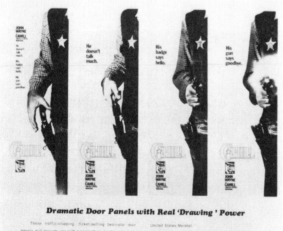

Dramatic Door Panels with Real 'Drawing' Power

Special Giant 27 x 41 Souvenir Poster of John Wayne

Exploitation Campaign

GIANT STANDEE FOR LOBBY!

$14.00

'ALAMO' ATMOSPHERE

SATIN ACCESSORIES

JOHN WAYNE IN THE COMICS

Like many other Western heroes, John Wayne was honored with a series of comic books bearing his name which were published by Toby Press between late 1949 and May 1955. A total of 31 issues were printed over that time, indicating a generally good acceptance by the comic book buying public. Even in the comic-crazed 1950s, many titles never lasted beyond their initial issues. The fact that *John Wayne Adventure Comics* were published bi-monthly indicated that there was not sufficient enthusiasm to sustain a monthly publication. However, the series did generate enough revenue to merit a run considerably longer than many skeptics might have felt possible.

The Wayne comics were rather bizarre in nature in that Wayne plays himself. Within the context of each issue, Wayne would generally become embroiled in two different stories which inevitably would plunge him into international intrigue. According to the context of the stories, Wayne is depicted as a two-fisted drifter who never really has anything else on his agenda but seeking damsels in distress. The plots were usually ludicrous, but almost always a great deal of fun. The editors and writers could never seem to make up their minds whether Wayne should be seen in a Western or contemporary environment. They came up with an awkward compromise in which (like some of Roy Rogers' later movies and on his TV series) the Duke roams around the modern West in airplanes and jeeps. However, for all intents and purposes, this modern West is in every other aspect much like the Wild West of days past.

Wayne's enemies are usually the type of villain who populated his "B" Westerns. In later issues, however, the Duke was called upon to do battle for the U.S. government against Nazis and Communists. Wayne is not usually referred to as a screen actor, but, rather, as a living embodiment of the characters whom he portrayed on screen. He is seen as an expert horsemen, an unsurpassed prize-fighter and a proficient marksman.

248

He also seems to have no problem with the law when it comes to strapping on some six-guns in order to resolve a few problems.

The comic books were usually attractively packaged, with covers employing color movie stills from an actual Wayne film. Occasionally comic art was used on the covers instead. Inside, the artwork of Wayne usually bore a fairly decent resemblance to the Duke and such noted comic artists as Frank Frazetta and Al Williamson, kings of the genre in the 1950s, were employed to lend their talents to the line. Although all of the *John Wayne Adventure Comics* initially sold for ten cents each, they command prices today of anywhere from $50 to $200.

An entirely different line of Wayne comic book appearances concerns movie tie-ins designed to promote a Wayne film whose release was imminent. These adaptations of the screenplays usually followed the basic storyline with consistency, although for considerations of time and space, many plot devices were abbreviated or eliminated. Throughout the Fifties and Sixties, quite a few comic book adaptations of Wayne's films appeared under a variety of different publishing houses. Most, however, were printed by Dell. It is safe to say that all of the comic adaptations were very well designed and generally featured an excellent selection of stills on the color covers. Occasionally, stills appeared on one or both of the inside covers in the form of a plot synopsis. Some comics, such as the one published to publicize *McLintock!*, had a back cover photo labeled as a "pin-up." Many of these issues were free of all commercial advertisements.

Artwork in the movie tie-ins varied wildly. Most stories featured uncredited artists who managed to provide at least a passing resemblance to Wayne in their work. *El Dorado*, for instance, has some of the best artwork of the Duke, while *The Horse Soldiers* features likenesses of Wayne so poor that one might mistake him for Dale Evans. Nevertheless, these comic books remain quite valuable and much sought-after. Throughout the early days of comic collecting, the movie tie-ins were generally disregarded by serious collectors, who prefered to concentrate more on the superheroes such as Superman and Spider-man. During these years, the Wayne tie-ins could be had for a few dollars. Today, however, the average title can run over $50.

There were several other unique adaptations of Wayne films which appeared on a one-shot basis. *Stagecoach*, *Reap the Wild Wind*, *Lady for a Night* and *Red River*, all were adapted as part of various publishers' series of film tie-ins. The middle two titles were limited to four page give-aways designed to gain some quick publicity for the movies. These are among the rarest of Wayne collectibles, and can command very high prices, if they can be located at all. The other notable Wayne tie-in which ranks as unique is Dell's adaptation of *The Longest Day*, a thick, advertisement-free issue which featured movie stills in place of artwork. Published on slick, glossy paper, this was an impressive issue, although the format did not set any precedents for movie tie-ins to follow. Wayne is featured prominently in many of the black-and-white photos reproduced within the comic.

Following is a complete listing of all John Wayne comic book appearances. The information was compiled for "The Duke in Print," a bibliography written by Tim Lilley, founder and publisher of "The Big Trail." Helping Tim compile the listing were Wayne buffs Michael "Duke" Jensen and Dan Stodhill.

JOHN WAYNE ADVENTURE COMICS
Published by Toby Press
Issues 1-31 published between 1949–1955.

FOUR PAGE MOVIE COMIC GIVE-AWAYS
REAP THE WILD WIND
LADY FOR A NIGHT
(Both issues published in 1942)

TIM McCOY WESTERN MOVIE STORIES
Issue #16 (January 1948) featured an adaptation of
Red River

OXYDOL/DREFT PUBLICATIONS
Issue #4 published in 1950 was one of six pocket-size give-away comics. This issue featured John Wayne.

TOBY PRESS RARITIES
Two issues in 1953 featured Wayne appearances in stories entitled "Big Tex" and "With the Marines on the Battlefronts of the World."

MOVIE COMICS
Published by National Periodical Publications (D.C. Comics)
Issue #2, (dated) May 1939, featured an adaptation of *Stagecoach*.

GOLD KEY MOVIE COMICS
Published by Gold Key/Whitman publishers.
Titles: *How the West Was Won*
and *McLintock!*

DELL MOVIE CLASSICS
Published by Dell
Titles:
The Longest Day (1962)
Hatari!—Issue # 12-340-301 (1963)
Circus World—Issue # 12-115-411 (1964)
The Sons of Katie Elder—Issue # 12-748-511 (1965)
The War Wagon—Issue # 12-533-709 (1967)
El Dorado—Issue # 12-240-710 (1967)

250

DELL FOUR-COLOR MOVIE COMICS
Published by Dell
Titles:
The Conqueror—Issue #690
The Searchers—Issue #709
Wings of Eagles—Issue #790
Rio Bravo—Issue #1018
The Horse Soldiers—Issue #1048
North to Alaska—Issue #1155
The Comancheros—Issue #1300

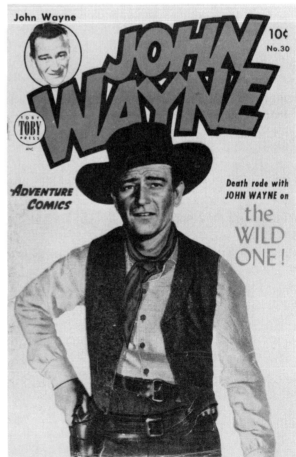

THE FRENCH ALAMO COMIC BOOKS

The comic books pictured here represent two of the most sought after items of Wayne memorabilia. Printed in France in 1960, the comics contain no actual artwork. Rather, they show the entire story of the film through black and white "frame blow-ups" taken from the actual negative of the movie. One issue is devoted exclusively to *The Alamo*, while the other comic also contains other film adaptations, including the classic Western *The Magnificent Seven*. What makes these comics even more desirable is the fact that they contain footage from the 192 minute version of *The Alamo*, including a page devoted to Laurence Harvey giving the "Jeffersonian speech" as well as the Parson's death scene. There is also a sequence illustrated in which Jim Bowie is berated for his drunkenness by Col. William Travis. Both *The Alamo* and Wayne enthusiasts have searched high and low for these collector's items to no avail. The photos which appear herein are courtesy of Wayne collector and *The Alamo* buff Mike Boldt, whose impressive collection of memorabilia boasts the only known copies of these books to have surfaced in recent years.

THIS PAGE FEATURES "THE JEFFERSONIAN SPEECH" WHICH WAS DELETED FROM THE FILM

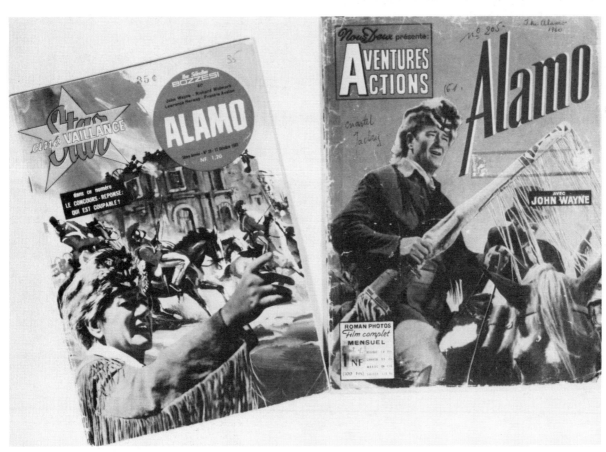

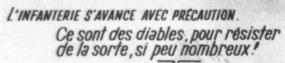

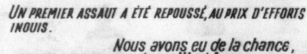

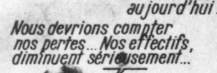

ANOTHER DELETED SCENE—THE DEATH OF THE PARSON

INTERNATIONAL ADVERTISING POSTERS

John Wayne's appeal crossed over many national borders, and people around the world loved his films. There is perhaps no more appropriate way to bid a fond farewell to this tribute to the Duke than by giving an indication of how widespread his popularity remains today. On the following pages are examples of some extremely rare theatre posters and lobby cards from the U.S. and overseas. They are indicative of the broad appeal John Wayne enjoyed throughout his career, and the ability he had to transcend all languages.

253

"EL DORADO," BELGIUM

"IN HARM'S WAY," BELGIUM

"CONFLICT," U.S.A.

"OVERLAND STAGE RAIDERS," U.S.A.

TOP: ITALIAN REISSUE FOR "STAGECOACH."

BOTTOM: "SHE WORE A YELLOW RIBBON," BELGIUM

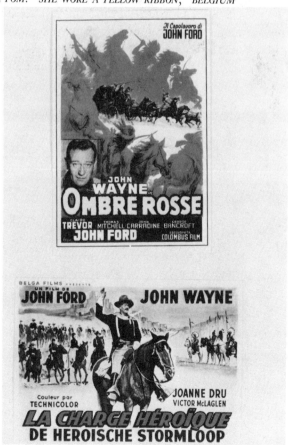

ABOUT THE AUTHOR

LEE PFEIFFER has extensive experience in the publishing world. He has authored or co-authored over a dozen highly successful books pertaining to the cinema, including *The Essential Bond: An Authorized Celebration of 007* (with Dave Worrall), an official reference guide to the series which has reached best-seller status in England with almost 250,000 copies; *The Incredible World of 007* (with Philip Lisa), the official history of the films written at the express request of legendary producer Cubby Broccoli; *The Films of Sean Connery* (with Philip Lisa), *The Films of Harrison Ford* (with Michael Lewis), *The Official Andy Griffith Show Scrapbook* (one of the top-selling entertainment books of 1993), and *The Films of Tom Hanks* (with Michael Lewis). Pfeiffer has also written about and dis- cussed the career of Clint Eastwood in numerous media outlets. He co-authored *The Films of Clint Eastwood* (with Boris Zmijewsky), an in-depth analysis of the actor's individual films, and pro- vided extensive research into Eastwood's career for Starwave's CD ROM tribute to the actor / director. Pfeiffer's company T.W.I.N.E. Entertainment pro- duces documentaries about the making of classic films, including *The Making of Goldfinger* and *The Making of Thunderball* for MGM Home Entertain- ment, and Inside Dr. Strangelove, released by Columbia Pictures Video. He is currently working with co-author Dave Worrall on a book about the collaborative films of Clint Eastwood and Sergio Leone. He resides in New Jersey with his wife Janet and daughter Nicole.